Crossed Over

Crossed Over

A
Murder

A
Memoir

Beverly Lowry

Alfred A. Knopf   New York   1992

For Karla: long life

THIS IS A BORZOI BOOK
PUBLISHED BY ALFRED A. KNOPF, INC.

ISBN 0-679-41184-4
LC 91-58558

Manufactured in the United States of America
Published August 10, 1992
Second Printing, August 1992

I know I've done this, but I don't know what I've done.

—KARLA FAYE TUCKER, 1984

ACKNOWLEDGMENTS

A lot of people helped on this one. Special thanks go to Jackie Oncken, Henry Oncken, Mack Arnold, Joe Magliolo, Rusty Hardin, Mac Secrest, and my good friend Jim Pape; also, to Warden Catherine Craig and her staff, Charles Brown, and David Nunnelee, J.C. Mosier, Jimmy Ladd, Ted Thomas, Myra Lopez, Kathleen Powers, Debi Bullard, Glenn Lowry, Glenn Cambor, Amanda Vaill, Amanda Urban, and Gary Fisketjon. A special nod to Kim Ogg for her tireless help, not to mention the title of the book.

To insure the privacy of people who had only a marginal connection to the incidents reported and described here, the following names are fictional: Sideburns, Mohawk, Adele, Laura Sue, and Scott.

The story of Karla Faye's childhood and young womanhood has been set down in this book mostly as it was told to me and to others by Karla herself. With her help and permission, I have mixed letters with interviews and material from transcripts of both trials. Kari Burrell Garrett and Shawn Jackson Dean were given an opportunity to tell their version of these stories; they declined. I did not attempt to make contact with Karla's father or her grandmothers. Karla and I agreed that they deserved to be left alone.

Deepest gratitude, of course, goes to Karla Faye, who participated in the creation of this book mainly because she thought it would help me. In time, I think—despite Plexiglas and all the other barriers meant to come between us—we both crossed over.

Crossed Over

Snapshots

I have always worked facing a blank white wall. With nothing to look at, no green view, no enticing piece of artwork to offer up distraction, the mind travels inside itself, into the imagination where—for writing fiction, making stuff up, or so I have always thought—the mind belongs.

Now when I look up, all I see is Karla Faye: snapshots, Polaroids, studio shots, blurry black-and-white prints made from copy negatives; pictures of Karla with Kari, Kari with their father, Karla and Danny, Kari and Douglas, Karla with her dogs, Karla with Kari and a leering john, all three wearing funny hats at a New Year's Eve party. Baby pictures, beach pictures. Karla in the air doing the Russian splits. Pictures of Karla Faye and her virtual ongoing *tribe,* from babyhood to the present, on Death Row in prison whites with her new clan.

In the center of the snapshots is the *Houston Chronicle* story that first captured my attention and hooked my heart, the color shot of Karla Faye, head tilted, hand cupping her chin, that look. People come into my office, they see the snapshots, they want to know who the girl is. Once they've read the newspaper headline, they want to know what in the world I am doing with pictures of a convicted, for God's sake, murderer on my wall.

If they are from Houston, they may remember the trial. "The thing about the pickax and climaxing," one friend recalled with a shudder. "It's not something you forget."

Karla Faye sent the pictures, of course. She is clearly a girl who likes having her picture made—a ham, she freely admits, laughing, tossing her dark, lovely head. Also, she has an enviable gift, the ability, when the camera's on her, to invite the lens closer, then sit there and plain smile. As a result, snapshots look like a real *her* and not some stiff, stuffed facsimile.

Sitting here working, from time to time I look up and get lost. Studying hairdos, earrings, facial expressions, before long I am off in my head and then . . . gone. Other places, forgotten times. I have arranged the snapshots by chronology and character, as if they were a novel I was writing: Mama Carolyn at seventeen, eighteen, thirty-eight; Karla happy at six months, a fireball at five, surly at four-teen. . . . As carried away as if I were the source instead of something like a clerk doing grunt work—the listening, the studying, the shuf-fling and assembling—I envision the context, set up the narration, try to imagine what was going on before the shutter clicked, what happened after, who set up the picture, who insisted on running a quick comb through her hair beforehand, who it was who said, "Okay now, everybody smile."

I am trying to make connections; to link the story the pictures tell with the ones I hear and read so that the captured images come to illuminate or at least make a case for a plausible narrative. I am trying to get the whole of it to come into focus until, maybe, some of it adds up and even, possibly, makes some sense.

Not just Karla's life and why she did what she did; my own as well. Why I got so carried away, what I'm doing writing these constant letters to Death Row, mailing off these books and pictures, sending these magazine subscriptions, making these trips to the penitentiary; why I have given my heart to a girl who not only has admitted having killed two people, but who then went home and boasted to her rowdy friends of having done it.

Used to be, when you bought a watermelon they cut out a chunk to show you how red the meat inside was. "Plugged," they called it. There were a few years there, it seemed all I did was choose caskets and throw funerals. My mother died; my son was killed; my father had both legs amputated, lived two years, then died. The death of parents is never easy, but your child's death, pure and simple, puts you under. Sometimes, it seems, for good.

When Peter died, I felt as if somebody had plugged me like a watermelon, right about at my middle, where the reddest, tenderest

meat is. "Try this," life seemed to be saying. "See how you like it." I knew the plug was permanent. I could heal enough to fit the chunk back in, but the lines, the cut, the excised piece, would always be there.

It has been seven years. I am hoping by now to have earned a good seat in this drama; to have gained perspective enough to be able to start figuring out what is what and which empty place this loving girl-woman, Karla Faye Tucker, this convicted murderer, has at this exact point in my life come to fill and who exactly she has become to me, off on Death Row over her schoolbooks, making her dolls, taking her speed walks, doing her aerobics.

Reasons are slippery. A good fiction writer makes use of reasons but doesn't dwell on them, much less write them out. Reasons are not the point; still, we modern decoders of our own experience chase them. We hound-dog the whys.

Here's a connection I'm sure of: *If Peter hadn't been killed, I would not have made the first trip up to see Karla Faye.*

I didn't figure this out at the time, didn't think things through, made no attempt to make going to Death Row make sense.

I had no idea what I was getting into when I went. I just went.

That was three years ago. And now?

It's Karla Faye's life at stake. I am the other one, her friend, her biographer, listening, attending, trying to figure out—for her, for me, for the record history and time will make of all this—what it is Karla actually *has* done.

As for the future, *Keep on* is all I can come up with. See her through. Live out what I have freely chosen to get myself into, until, I don't know . . . whatever happens happens.

February 1992

I / Getting There

We were very wired and we was looking for something to do. . . . We went there to case the place and something said go.

—KARLA FAYE TUCKER, 1983

We . . . was . . . overamped. I was to the point of yeah, okay.

—JIMMY LEIBRANT, 1984

I wasn't raised up to be a killer.

—DANIEL GARRETT, 1989

Mountain View

From your car, Mountain View is not a terrible-looking place. Nothing at all like the Alcatraz/Sing Sing notion of prison—that cold, gray, isolated *rock*—we all mostly carry around in our movie-glutted imaginations. Set against rolling hills, the Mountain View unit of the Texas Department of Corrections (TDC) comprises low red-brick one-story buildings, sidewalks, trees, flower beds; the grass is tended. Texas and American flags fly side by side.

Not that you want to move in. Double chain-link-and-barbed-wire fences mark the unit maximum security; armed-guard towers steal the breath and—even though you know in advance they're bound to be there—chill the heart. Driving down Texas State Highway 36 that day, mainly I was thinking how grateful I was not to be locked up in there. What trees there are are small: scrub oaks, mesquite, scrawny cottonwoods. Prisons aren't built in lush landscapes. As one correctional officer told me, "I don't know whether TDC chooses the worst places in the world to build on or if they just get that way."

East across Highway 36 from Mountain View—from which raw, craggy hills but no mountain can be seen—is the less restrictive Gatesville Unit. Only one row of chain link and barbed wire over there.

Guards on horseback carrying rifles at the ready rode down through the hills to my right, watching over the single file of a work squad, all men, marching in. The inmates wore stark white. The guards were in gray. Lunchtime; in prison parlance, chow.

On the way to Gatesville from my home, a drive of some two and a half hours, I had been alternating tapes of Maria Callas and Aaron Neville. In the shadow of the penitentiary, I switched the music off.

Although the morning had been cool, as the day wore on the

temperature climbed fast, the way it can in Texas in early March. In this part of the state, the sun, once it gets its strength up, gives no mercy. I had my windows up, the air conditioning on. In the course of driving to Gatesville, I had stripped off my jacket, then my sweater, and was down to wide-legged pants and a cotton blouse.

What am I doing here? I kept asking myself this question. *I am fifty years old, a fiction writer; I could be home in my nest of an office, making stuff up. What am I doing here?*

Answers flitted by; cheap, glib notions, nothing I trusted. *Don't ask* made more sense. *Don't figure it. Just go.*

In my rearview mirror, as guards on horseback watched for traffic, the work squad filed across the highway. On the phone the warden had been cordial, her directions explicit, and so I had no problem finding Mountain View. I had an hour to spare. At the intersection of new Highway 36 with the old business route, I turned right. The entrance to Mountain View was right there. Men repairing the road in front of it looked up, waved. I waved back, turned my car around, and took Business Route 36 to downtown Gatesville.

When I mentioned to friends that I was considering making this trip, they all disapproved. I tried to explain, I was not out to spring Karla Faye Tucker or even to save her life. Karla's imprisonment was not a railroad job; on the witness stand she had admitted having participated in two unspeakably hideous murders. She did what they said she did.

"But look at her," I said to my skeptical friends. And I showed them the newspaper picture.

Friends only glanced at the photograph. I knew what they were thinking: if I needed a cause, there were plenty of far more deserving people out there to feel sorry for. Without exactly saying so, friends encouraged me to drop this new idea. They meant well. Having seen me through bad times, now that I seemed to be on my feet again they didn't want me to slide back into the dark. Eventually I solved the problem. I didn't show the picture anymore. My feelings, however, did not change. I was captivated by her, that's all. Her looks, her story, the extremes to which passion, circumstance, and drugs had taken her.

Almost three years had passed between the time I first saw the newspaper story and March 9, 1989, when I put the Callas and Neville tapes in my car and finally went.

You can find a town like Gatesville anywhere in Texas—county seat, built on a square, courthouse in the middle, around it stores, a pool hall, title company, cafe serving a steam-table all-you-can-eat noon meal. The Coryell County Courthouse is as fancied up as a wedding cake, but the stores and businesses surrounding it are plain and flat-fronted, with a strained grit-free look, as if having been scrubbed within an inch of their life by wind, sun, and the Protestant—mostly Baptist—work ethic. In a rock building which used to be a lumberyard there is a county museum, closed except on weekends. The museum is run by a historical society, mostly made up of ladies with time, energy, and intelligence to spare.

I stopped at a grocery store for lunch—diet Coke and Fritos— then took Business Route 36 back out to the prison. A couple of miles out are the No Hitchhiking and Do Not Pick Up Hitchhikers signs that mark the boundaries of state prison property. To my right was the Gatesville Unit. Ahead was Mountain View.

I slowed down.

Everyone who visits a prison says the same thing. "I knew how it was going to be. I'd seen the movies. I'd psyched myself up. Still . . ."

It must have to do with dream recall, the nightmare reality of being locked up, the terrifying notion of how easy it might be to trip over the line into lawlessness and, then, the place beyond the fences. Or with not wanting to see—prisons, prisoners—and not wanting, once they're locked up, to have to think about those people anymore.

Along the road to my right, chain-link fence topped by six-strand barbed wire stretched ahead to the intersection. Guard towers interrupted the fencing every fifty yards or so. A guard in one tower sat with his feet propped on a desk and a portable telephone in his hand. In the next one, the guard stood gazing out at the prison yard and down across the road.

I wondered if they were calling ahead tower to tower to report the location of my car. There was no reason to think they had; I was driving slowly, keeping to my lane, obeying every rule. It just seemed such a lonely job up there. Punch in, punch out. No radio, no newspaper, no pal to chat with. Only the wind, the sun, the endless parade of inmates, the telephone, that gun. Lacking reason, mightn't a guard eventually make up some excuse to fire it—for something to do?

The picture of Karla Faye in the *Houston Chronicle* had been a page-one close-up color head shot, remarkably clear for a newspaper photograph, Karla Faye at twenty-six. Mostly what you saw at first were her dark eyes, that tumbling mane of hair. Unfold the newspaper and out came the rest of her, a pretty young woman in prison whites, head slightly tilted, left hand cupping her chin. I didn't know who she was then, of course, although I vaguely remembered the trial, one of those daily horror stories you hate to read and can't get enough of. Mostly, like everyone else, I remembered the weapon and some splashy comments she'd made about sex.

Long face, high cheekbones, black hair (an escaped curl created a single parenthesis around her left eye), soft smile, a chipped tooth. At the very center of her dark brown eyes the camera flash had left its mark, a pinpoint white dot. Like a doorway to her thoughts, the dot made her look vulnerable.

Next to the photograph was the headline ON DEATH ROW, PICKAX MURDERER FINDS A "NEW LIFE."

In the spring of 1986, I read the *Chronicle* story, read the sidebar, turned back to the picture, studied it, reread the story: a young woman on Death Row, the rock-and-roll life that had got her there; the gruesome crime with its nightmare weapon, thing of grade-B horror films; her hot sexual comments and subsequent jailhouse rehabilitation.

Karla Faye Tucker made page one some two years after her death sentence for a number of reasons. For one thing, the fact that, however our thinking has shifted, when a woman kills it's still news.

A lot more women commit crimes now. More women sell drugs, rob, steal, burgle, sell their children, go to prison. But men are the ones who commit the violent crimes, at a rate of almost nine to one, therefore it is men who receive death sentences, men who sit out their lives warehoused on various Death Rows, waiting to die or not. In

Texas in the spring of 1990, there were four women on Death Row in Gatesville, 287 men in Ellis I Unit in Huntsville. In the country, there were a total of 2,185 Death Row inmates, only 25 of whom were women. Between 1976 and 1992, 166 men had been executed but only one woman, Velma Barfield in North Carolina.

Karla Faye makes for good copy also because she's a paradox. She's attractive, she's photogenic, she knows how to pose; her crime is unthinkable yet she has confessed to it, and now she has this look of sweetness, this spontaneity, this look of being altogether *present* for the camera, no secrets. You read Karla's life story, you look at her picture, you think, if things had been different. . . . It makes you want to believe that people change, that confession helps, that there is hope.

She looks so serene. The state I was in at the time, I envied her. I wondered if you had to go to jail to get calm again.

For the *Chronicle* photograph, Karla had cupped her chin in her hand and tilted her head—not *into* the hand but slightly away from it. Her chin rests in the meat of her palm, her ring and little finger cover a part of her lower face, her slim fingers extend from her jawline to her earlobe. Her nails are long and carefully tended, she is wearing a gold watch and a ring, and she is looking into the camera without—it seems—a twitch of restraint or unease. In the caption she is quoted as saying she is happy. She looks happy. She looks—we don't speak this way anymore, but the word that came to mind the first time I saw the photograph was "good." And yet this same person had confessed to having committed acts that might well be called—if we talked that way anymore—evil.

The sidebar to the main story was entitled "The Embodiment of Evil?" Down in the story, one of the men who prosecuted Karla's case is quoted as saying that when he first saw Karla in 1983, just after she was arrested, he didn't want to turn his back on her. "Her attitude and the way she looked and everything about her was the personification of evil."

Trying to imagine this attractive young woman as evil incarnate, I read the story again and again. I thought I might like to write about a girl whose life had made such swings, from darkness to hope. More than write about her, I wanted to meet her. Just lay eyes on her.

That was in 1986. Friends said, "Don't do it," and I didn't. I trusted them. And that was proper. It was right to wait.

After reading the story one last time—the murders of course were unthinkable; women don't get the death penalty for fathomable crimes—I put the paper on the floor by my office chair, where I file things I'm not finished with. A few days later I read the story again. The same prosecutor who in 1983 thought Karla Faye Tucker was the personification of evil was now saying she was a brand-new, caring person, intelligent, helpful, getting her high school diploma, taking college correspondence courses, reading everything in sight and almost gushy, "like a puppy." Prosecutors, prison officials, policemen—people who routinely refuse to go behind a jury when it recommends the death penalty—were making a case for lifting the sentence in her case. "The person who is Karla Tucker today," said one, "is not the same person who was Karla Tucker at that time."

Did I believe that? I did not. People don't become other people.

"I like her," said another. "And I hope she doesn't die."

J.C. Mosier, a homicide detective who had worked on the case, was not sure what to think. "I don't want to see her die," he states, then he catches himself. "I believe in the death penalty," he explains, "and she's not the only person that I've ever sent to Death Row. But in most cases, they're bad people, period. She never had a chance from the start. There was no way for her to go but bad. . . . When it comes down to seeing someone die, I don't think I would like that."

Okay, I told myself, *so let it go. You don't want to get involved with another young person who will die.*

Peter had been dead since September 1984, the victim of an unsolved hit-and-run. There was a time, not that long prior to the appearance of Karla's page-one picture, when I had lain on the couch for days, not changing clothes, hardly lifting my head, just lying there, a person who felt she no longer had edges to define her, who felt more like a cracked and spilled raw egg than a person, a person gone from the world as she knew it. Adrift from time itself, I considered madness a reasonable option in those days: one more snapped thread and I'd be there.

By the spring of 1986 I knew I was better. With the help of time, friends, family, a psychiatrist, a bereaved-parents support group, books, poems, Mozart, a palm reader, and a psychic, I had made my way to a bearable state of mild depression and chronic disappointment. And so I meant to listen to the voice of reason, to pay attention to my friends. I meant to be cautious, to take care.

I set the story about Karla Tucker aside. I did not, however, throw it away; I simply folded it and laid it on a desk I use for storage. Other papers were piled on top. Occasionally I cleaned them off. When I got to the bottom, there Karla Faye was again, chipped tooth, chin cupped, that look. I would stand in my office alone and just look at her.

Two and a half years later, in December 1988, another newspaper story about Karla Faye appeared, on page one of the B section, where the less noteworthy crime and court stories run. At the state level, the petition appealing Karla Faye's sentence had been denied, the death sentence affirmed eight to one by the Texas Court of Criminal Appeals. (DEATH PENALTY UPHELD, the headline read, FOR PICKAX MURDERESS.) The dissenting judge had not chosen to write a minority opinion. I was going through a flat time then, with no particular project to work on and little or no enthusiasm for finding any. I was worn out with making stuff up—in addition to which, I was feeling seasonally cranky and very much out of the mood for being sensible. And so I dug out the 1986 newspaper story, picked out some names, looked up some numbers.

Eventually I found Jackie Oncken, wife of Henry Oncken, one of the two court-appointed lawyers who had represented Karla in her trial. In 1988, Henry Oncken no longer worked as a defense attorney. As a U.S. attorney—one of only four in the state—he was the top law-enforcement official in the southern judicial district of Texas.

Jackie Oncken was appropriately suspicious. Who was I, and why did I want to know about Karla Faye? I told her I didn't know why I was calling, I wasn't even sure I should be, but there I was.

We talked for the better part of an hour. Jackie Oncken is terribly caught up in Karla Faye Tucker's life, and so is her husband, Henry Oncken, a strict law-and-order Republican who firmly supports the death penalty. They go to see Karla several times a year; Karla knits them sweaters and afghans for Christmas and birthdays.

Jackie warned me, Karla was not giving interviews. One of the people she had helped murder had a son. Karla's position was, she had done enough to the boy without making him live through his mother's death once again, every time a story appeared. I said fine, I wasn't doing an interview; the next day, I wrote to Karla Faye. The day I heard back from her—it took two months—I called the prison and set up a date and time.

"Come anytime," Karla Faye had written. "My schedule is flexible. (Ha!)"

At the entrance to Mountain View, I passed the road workers again, then some plain brick two-story apartment buildings. There was a sign reading Slow—Children, another one warning visitors in Spanish and English that entry into prison territory was tantamount to consent to a search. In the field to my left, a female hoe squad overseen by a male guard on horseback chopped unenthusiastically at the grass, *plick . . . plock*. The guard held the reins in one hand; the other one was casually draped over the saddle horn. He had a rifle. His horse grazed.

There was no indication of what I was supposed to do or where I should go. Spotting a small hand-lettered Visitors sign, I drove in the direction the arrow pointed, down a narrow asphalt road to a parking lot facing a ranch-style brick house with a churchy pointed roof. No one in sight, no other cars in the parking lot. As I stepped from my car—going I had no idea where—a guard emerged from the brick tower across the road. The towers are square, topped by a glass-enclosed room with a walkway, maybe thirty feet up. The guard came out on the walkway. He was clutching his portable telephone.

"Ma'am?" I shaded my eyes from the sun. "Can I help you?" I gave him my name and told him whom I had come to visit. "Please sit in your vehicle and wait," he said, and ducked back into the tower. I got back in my car and sat as ordered, face forward.

Beyond the brick house with the churchy roof there were open

fields and then plain hot nothing: landscape going on and on. The
trees were scrawny, none big enough to provide much shade, or cover
for escape.

I waited ten, fifteen minutes, opened the car door for air, eventually
heard the tower guard's voice—"Ma'am?"—and got out. The guard
told me to go back to the parking lot I had previously passed, to the
front gatehouse. Someone, he said, would help me there. I thanked
him—I made it my business that day to thank everyone profusely—
and drove back. The lot was full—it always is. I parked in an
unmarked space and went toward a small square brick building so
elaborately fenced it looks like a fancily wrapped birthday present.
No sign. As I approached the gate—the usual chain link plus barbed
wire—two female guards were coming out. The lock was buzzing.
The women held the gate open and I went in.

Having seen the same newspaper story and picture I had—re-
printed in a tabloid—Melissa Malkovitch of the CBS television news
program "West 57th" had been to Mountain View to try to convince
Karla to be on her program. David Frost had written to ask for an
interview. Karla was happy to see Melissa Malkovitch and to hear,
through her lawyer, from David Frost. But, she insisted, no interviews.

In a letter to Henry Oncken, Melissa Malkovitch had written, "I
can't believe it. Oral Roberts said yes and Karla said no."

The front gatehouse is the hub of Mountain View, through which
all who enter, including employees, must pass. Inside a plain gray
room, behind a thick mesh enclosure, a guard processes visitors and
buzzes people in and out of gates. On the walls, notices on bulletin
boards announce jobs, cars for sale, houses for rent; official documents
give notice of the Mountain View employee of the month and new
Texas Department of Corrections (TDC) rules and regulations.
There's a soft-drink machine, a snack machine offering crackers,
cookies, chips. For a while a handwritten note was taped on the wall
above a water fountain: "Do not spit snuff or tobacco in the water
fountain. Due to it stops it up."

The gatehouse guard asked for a picture ID. I took my driver's
license from my wallet and handed it over.

The Mountain View unit of the TDC was originally built to house wayward boys in trouble with the law. Back then it was called simply Gatesville. A friend of mine who grew up there says, "Gatesville was better than a spanking to keep boys in line. 'You keep that up,' parents used to tell their sons, 'you're going to end up a state boy.'" My friend's mother has lived too long a life in a nursing home. Sometimes out of her mother's senseless babble comes a sharp memory. "The state boys are in the yard," she will say, and she shivers in fear.

Under the windows overlooking the prison yard is a display of inmate-arranged artificial-flower arrangements for sale. The bouquets are tagged with prices and names—"Blue Hawaii," "Spring Madness," "Arrangement in Pink." ("Inmate," I quickly learned, is officially correct terminology. In my many visits to Gatesville, I have never heard one TDC employee use the word "convict" or "prisoner." They also say "officer" or the more formal "correction officer" instead of "guard.")

Beside the soft-drink machine is an architect's rendering of Mountain View, dated 1960. Underneath the drawing is the caption "Home for Boys." Someone has scratched out "Home" and written in "School."

When Peter was alive, I used to think about Gatesville a lot. I thought Peter might end up a state boy. Then he got too old for Gatesville and my fears graduated.

I don't dream about Peter as much as I used to, but when I do, it's not like looking at a picture of him, then letting myself go back and float awhile in the waters of memory; it's not like memory at all. In dreams he's really there; he *visits*. Sometimes he's a baby; more often than not he's as he was the year or so before he died. Seventeen, eighteen.

There are a couple of dreams that keep coming back. In one, I'm back seven, eight years ago; Peter's alive and he's in trouble—sometimes with the law, other times at school. Whatever the territory—the specific area of authority and its rules—it's the kind of trouble that clots and thatches and grows more complex but never comes to any point of resolution, much less understanding.

In the dream, I walk up to Peter. Trouble is all over him, an aura of dire unease and hushed, dark expectation. It is a feeling I know well, being every second on the rim of no-telling, wondering what will happen next and how far the trouble will take him and how I can stop it and what in God's name the end of it will ever be.

He's not a bad boy, I kept saying to myself at the time. Then I'd flip-flop. *Maybe he is. Maybe,* I'd think, *there is such a thing as born bad.*

This is history now—real life, not the dream. Back then, when I took the undeniable what-was and spun it into the future, I sometimes envisioned myself visiting Peter in jail, him on one side of a glass divider, me on the other; saw my boy's curly-headed beauty turned hard, that strange topaz light in his eyes gone permanently dull. As for his crime, I could not bear to think what it might have been he had done—or to whom—to get himself locked up, much less how long he would have to be in there.

In the dream I'm back neck-deep in it. The police have a say-so in my life, it's the middle of some endless night, Peter's not home yet, and my husband and I are at each other's throats—hysterical. When a child is in trouble, parents all do the same first thing: go crazy. Blind as headless chickens, they do everything books tell them not to, divide the parental front, go mercilessly at each other, scream, yell, flap their wings, meantime ignoring their heads, over on the chopping block issuing warnings, *Don't do this, it's wrong.*

Sometimes to keep busy—at two, three in the morning—we folded clothes. Other times my husband, Glenn, drove out into the night, trying to track the boy down while I kept watch at home, peering out the front window, waiting for his car to turn in or the telephone to ring. I didn't want Glenn to drive out into the night, he didn't want to hear any more of my half-baked theories, it went on.

In the dream, Peter comes up to me and it's as if he's walking out of dreamland into the flesh-and-blood night. He's smiling and he's gorgeous—not surly, not sullen—and I'm frantic with worry and he's trying to reassure me. *It's okay, Mom. I'm fine.* All of this has happened before. I believed him, I trusted in my own inborn inclination toward the upbeat, and it wasn't okay, he wasn't fine.

The dream peaks. Peter goes off with his friends, laughing, some kind of mischief in mind.

At that point, I wake up and lie for a time on the rim of no-telling.

In a dream hangover, I wait in the real night for a sign of him: the headlights of the car we should not have bought him streaking across the ceiling, the sound of his car cassette player up loud, Van Halen, Rush, Bad Company, or his favorite, Foreigner, doing "Feels Like the First Time" or "Cold as Ice," then—once he's in—the smell of his hormonal funk and secret cigarettes. I wake up from the dream as if from real life and wonder: *Where is he now and what has he done this time?*

The fall from dream to blunt, boring what-is is long but over with mercifully fast. In the dark I make my accommodations. I don't have to worry about Peter turning into a state boy, I don't have to try to figure out how to be a good mother to him; Peter is dead.

You get so used to scaling down: okay, so maybe he won't go to college; okay, so maybe he won't graduate from high school this year, so maybe never; so he has a juvenile record, so he smokes dope, *okay,* but—I used to think—do I have to scale down as low as prison?

"Miz Lowry?"

I turned from the architect's rendering. Leaning from an opening in the wire enclosure, the gatehouse guard held out my driver's license. "You'll need to show it again over there," he said. "It'll just be a few more minutes."

I slid the driver's license into my pants pocket. Two days later, I would look for the license in my wallet and, finding it gone, think I had lost it. Since then I have learned. Before stepping from my car in the parking lot of the Mountain View gatehouse, I clip the driver's license to a notepad. If I can see it I won't forget it.

In my second letter, I had asked Karla Faye if I could bring anything—food, I was thinking, maybe homemade bread. Toiletries, possibly clever earrings.

In reply, Karla simply said no, she had everything she could possibly need. "I'm soooooo spoiled as it is," she had written. "Maybe you could just bring some quarters and we can have a soda together while we talk."

What Karla didn't tell me was, I would not be allowed to bring her anything: no food, no gifts, no supplies. In addition to my letter, as a way of introducing myself I had sent a padded mail bag filled

with my books and some articles I had written; the bag was returned with the handwritten inscription "Inmates not allowed to receive packages from individuals." Books in fact could be sent, but only by a bookstore. I could send pictures, but Polaroids would be cut at the bottom in the never-ending search for contraband. My letters would be scanned before being delivered, as would hers to me. I could subscribe to magazines for her. I could have stationery—but not stamps—sent, but the stationery could not be personalized.

In addition to TDC rules, for that first visit Karla had made a few of her own. When I called to set up the interview, the warden warned me Karla had specified no paper, no pencil, no tape recorder, no camera.

"Fine with me," I said to the telephone after I had hung up. "I'm not doing an interview."

Feeling extremely conspicuous and very much in the way, I waited. Soon, a blond, pregnant young woman came in with a clipboard and asked me to sign in. I put down my name and the name of the inmate I was visiting. There was a column marked "Reason for Visit." I had come as media because Karla had instructed me to. I had no idea what the distinction meant in terms of prison rules. Because everybody ahead of me had written in "interview," I did too. I started to leave "Employer" blank, but because the other blanks had been filled in, I wrote "Free-lance."

From behind me, a sandy-haired guard with swingy straight hair said I should follow him in my car, and he made for the front door, clicking his boot heels, jangling a thick wad of keys. I thanked the gatehouse guard, followed the other one out, got in my car, drove to where he waited in a white TDC station wagon, and followed him back to the same parking lot in front of the brick house with the churchy roof.

The station wagon stopped just under the guard tower. With a great impatient sweep of his arm, the sandy-haired guard motioned me out of my car. As I got out and raised my hand to close the car door he shouted—across the road—"You can't take that purse."

It makes you so nervous. You know you haven't done anything wrong . . . or do you? Possibly in a deeper sense the guards and the fences represent moral authority, the policemen of our dreams, the rules we broke, the secrets we keep. I tossed my purse into the car, shut the door, and, hands in big pockets—in which I could have been carrying any-thing—came across the road. In a ground-level guardhouse, I waited for my escort to finish his paperwork. He asked for the driver's license, glanced at it, wrote down my name, returned the license, walked past me out the door, wordlessly leading the way to the first gate.

As the guard fiddled with the lock—which was making a low, buzzing sound—I looked up. The fences. Lord, the fences. Ten feet of chain link, topped by four-strand barbed wire—slanted *in* toward the prison to make it harder to climb—and on top of that, concertina wire, barbed wire looped in endlessly connected *O*'s. Altogether, some fourteen, fifteen feet.

The guard unlocked the first gate and held it open. After I walked through, he closed the gate behind me. There's a sidewalk and then, twelve feet in, another fence, another gate with a buzzing lock, the same arrangement of ten-foot chain link topped by four or five feet of slanted barbed wire and looped concertina. Same locks. The second gate closed. I followed the long-legged guard—my surly cowboy—to a low red-brick building with barred and meshed windows.

The guard tried the door. "It's supposed to be open," he grumbled. He got out some keys, stuck one in; at first it wouldn't open, then it did.

Inside the visitors' center the cowboy's boot heels made sharp clicks like a dog's toenails on concrete. He looked around in disapproval, as if there were bound to be something out of order. The cowboy was my personal bath of fire. In all my visits to Mountain View since that initial one, I have been treated with firm, country courtesy.

The room was plain. Red linoleum floor, molded plastic chairs, gray metal desk, several stacks of aluminum ashtrays, blackened from the endless crushing of endless cigarettes. Beside the door were two identical soft-drink machines offering R.C. Cola, Orange Crush, Ta-hitian Treat, Dr Pepper. Not a Coke or a diet Coke in sight.

That was when I remembered about the quarters. When I bought my diet Coke and Fritos I had asked for five dollars in quarters, to make sure I had enough. The quarters were in my wallet, in my

purse, in the car. So there it was; I was not about to ask the cowboy to let me out and back in again. He stormed around, told me to have a seat. Like a child requesting permission from a teacher, I asked if the restrooms were for the public. He said yes; I went in one, and when I came out he was gone.

I went to a window which faced the prison yard. Inmates walked in pairs, in starched white cotton pants with short-sleeved tunic tops with unflattering open collars. Shoes varied from heavy leather work boots to running shoes. Some women wore sunglasses, mostly mirrored, aviator-style. Haircuts were mostly short, slicked back, butch. The only way you knew many of the inmates were women was, they had to be. The sun was high. There were no clouds. Nothing much seemed to be going on. At the front door of one dormitory two black women in prison whites carried on a lively conversation, one gesticulating wildly, the other laughing. In extremely unflattering, man-tailored uniforms, female guards walked quickly and with purpose. Inmates strolled.

I reminded myself yet again, it was not for nothing that Karla Faye Tucker had been sent here: she had helped kill two people without mercy. She had told about the murders in great detail on the witness stand—had told about them *twice,* in fact, once at her own trial, and again for the prosecution at the trial of her boyfriend and fellow murderer, Danny Garrett.

Hearing voices beyond the door through which I originally entered, I went over there.

Outside the windows, Karla Faye, in prison whites, carried an Army-green padded jacket. I wondered why. The day was warm. Accompanying her were two guards, one male, one female. As the male guard fiddled with his keys, Karla brushed a piece of something from the man's shirt, then—cocking her head—wagged a scolding finger in his face. The guard hung his head, pretending to be ashamed. The female guard giggled. Karla laughed, her head thrown back.

My heart dipped. I did not want to go soft on this girl, I did not want to get *attached,* I wanted to keep Karla Faye Tucker at a safe remove.

The male guard jiggled his key in the lock. It wouldn't go. The flustered man threw up his hands; then, still laughing, the trio back-tracked and disappeared.

Until Peter's death, I guess, I had never wanted my life to be too safe. Not that I was a daredevil, but I did like chanciness, vibrancy, some risk. When the ground was pulled out from under me I lost my nerve. *Just please,* I asked whoever it was up there making things up, *let it be boring from now on. No more surprises. I want it dull.* At Mountain View waiting for Karla, I could only think I had moved on from that request. Otherwise, why was I there?

A key turned in a gray metal door behind me. Attached to the door was a sign: Employees Only, in English and Spanish. My cowboy came through the door, locked it behind him, and motioned for me to follow. After showing me through another door, he went away.

The room he left me in was obviously the visiting room. There were two long sets of counters with chairs lined up on either side of a Plexiglas screen. Chairs were stacked on top of one another.

From somewhere down some hall, I heard them approaching, Karla and the guards, still laughing and chatting. Absorbed in conversation, Karla came straight over to my side of the counter, then—catching sight of me—clapped her hand over her mouth and, chugging back in the direction she came from, smoothly vaulted a low wall.

"I'm not," she said, "supposed to be over there where you are." She nodded toward my side of the Plexiglas. The male guard said good-bye. Karla Faye waved, called him by name. "Now you be good now," she told him. The man said he'd try, and disappeared.

Face to face with Karla, I waited to be told what to do.

The newspaper picture had not made too much of her. Her hair is long, dark, and lustrous, her eyes black as Louisiana coffee, her skin quite dark. Her face was lightly, carefully made up. On her left arm is a large brown birthmark, like splashed mud. She is a bit coarser than in her picture, a bit heavier. "I'm *fat!*" she complained soon after we met. "It's so hard to get this off." And she plucked at her behind. "I do aerobics every day with the television. But I can*not* get rid of this."

Somewhere along the way, I had read or heard that Karla Faye's legal father, the man who helped raise her, was not in fact her biological father. From somewhere I remembered her genetic background was Greek. She looks Greek; like a wild-haired Mediterranean girl, born to water and sun.

Finally, the female guard, a short and pleasant, solidly built woman, motioned me to sit, anywhere I liked, she said. Karla chose a particular spot on her side of the Plexiglas. Karla stood and so I stood. The Plexiglas screen extended a good three feet above our heads. At the base of the Plexiglas is a thickly woven metal grille to talk through. But Karla is small, and if we sat, we would be looking at each other through the listening grille. And so we stand.

Karla folded her jacket on the counter for a cushion to lean on. (Eventually I realized why the chairs were stacked: to be tall enough to see one another through the clear Plexiglas, people sit on several at once. Of medium height, I need two.)

Exercise is one of our topics. During the next year Karla would eventually build up to a fifteen-mile brisk daily walk around a figure eight she's devised in the patch of grass that serves as a yard for the inmates on Death Row. (Twenty-three laps around the figure eight is a mile. I asked her how she knew; she said she took a yard-long tape measure and figured it out. Does she count every go-round? "I used to. Now I time it on a watch so I can get some thinking done while I'm out there. A little over one hour is five miles, a little over two hours is ten, et cetera.") Karla asks me about running, about yoga, about dance, about stretches she can do to help with her shoulders—stiff since she dislocated them executing a dive into a spring-fed pool in Austin from atop an eighty-two-foot cliff. I do yoga stretches for her—sitting on the floor or standing with one foot on the counter, sometimes feet-up doing handstands against the wall—to the great amusement of the guards.

In March 1989, when I met her, Karla was twenty-nine. She seemed more like maybe thirteen, a transitional girl, and no wonder: Karla Faye missed out on adolescence. Prison has given her a chance to go back and, like a learning-disabled child, catch up on the steps she missed. She's up now to, I'd say, maybe fifteen.

In time, Karla Faye got to where she would tell me anything, sometimes—often—more than common sense would have her say.

In exchange, I fill her in on the world beyond the double fences. I send pictures, postcards. When I went to D.C., she asked me to take pictures of the Washington Monument, the Lincoln Memorial, the White House. When I went to New York, she wanted to know, "Will you go to Times Square? Can you go see Baryshnikov dance?"

For her, I have taken pictures of my house inside and out so that she will know how I live; of clothes in my closet, new shoes I've bought, my dogs, cats, horses; of a drawer with plastic dividers in which I keep my precious collection of nonserious, bright jewelry: jangly bracelets dripping with jokey trinkets; a dog-faced watch; a necklace hung with Monopoly pieces; earrings, earrings, earrings— shaped like fish, like watermelons, stars, palm trees, rabbits, snakes, clocks, flamingos, a compass, small pencils. "You know which earrings I like best?" she wrote me in response. "The ones of the world globes. Next time you come, would you wear them?"

When I talk she is intensely quiet and receptive, a sponge. When it is her turn, she is like a one-woman band. Her hands flutter, her hair flies. Responses come spontaneously, and in a gush. She bolts, veers, does pantomimes, covers her mouth when words erupt on their own. Because she has given a full confession of the murders, she does not have to be careful or choose her words; she can talk freely.

That first day we start off awkwardly, like any two people the first time they meet. With my introductory letter, I had enclosed a magazine article that said pretty much who I was, what I had written, and how my life had gone. From the *Houston Chronicle* article and my call to Jackie Oncken, I knew a fair amount about Karla Faye. Still, we are strangers. She doesn't know whether to trust me; I don't know whether to trust my instincts.

When I apologize for having left the quarters in the car, Karla quickly reassures me. It's fine, she says; really, she isn't thirsty, it doesn't matter. (Karla Faye does a lot of reassuring and righting of balances—a quickly learned adaptive reflex, crucial to establishing a tolerable prison life.)

"The thing is," she says, leaning closer, "they didn't tell me you was coming. I was washing my hair when they told me." She laughs at herself. "There I was"—she runs her hands back and forth through her hair as if to scrub her scalp—"with my head in the sink . . ."

The room where we visit is maybe twenty by forty. The guard sits at one end of the counter on a platform, where she can oversee what we do. Since that first visit I have always remembered to put quarters in my pocket. After I buy Karla's drink—usually Strawberry Crush or root beer—I give the can to the guard, who then opens it and hands it to Karla. I can give Karla Faye nothing directly. I cannot touch her. In Texas, Death Row inmates are not allowed contact visits from the time they go to the penitentiary right up to and through the day they are executed. I could not buy a drink for the guard if I wanted to. "I'm not allowed, ma'am," one of them told me nicely when I offered.

It's pointless to try to make prison rules make sense; prison rules exist for the sake of themselves, the same as in any formalized institution, prep school to the military. A clever inmate learns this early on. I take Karla's lead.

In that big room, there are always only the three of us, me, her, and a guard. As Death Row inmates are isolated from general prison population, their visitors are segregated as well. People coming to see Death Row inmates are scheduled for weekday visits, saving weekends for general population. Death Row inmates are allowed one two-hour visit a week from approved friends and family, a maximum of two people at any one time, a maximum four visits a month. Every three months, the inmate makes a new list of ten people for the prison authorities' approval. Because I came as media, my visit did not count as Karla's weekly one.

On the wall behind the guard is a black wall telephone, a clock. Beside her is a floor-to-ceiling wire enclosure, called a seg cage, where lawyers can visit their inmate clients face-to-face. The seg cage is padlocked. Adjacent to the visitors' center, just beyond the wall at the female guard's back, is the dormitory set aside for Death Row inmates; it has room for eight women. Behind me are windows overlooking a small yard where later in the spring Death Row inmates will plant a vegetable and flower garden. In front of the garden is Karla's figure-eight walking path.

I visit for about three hours, from one o'clock until four. If by the end of our afternoons together I am exhausted, Karla is not. She milks the final minutes, performs small tricks for a final good-bye, plays practical jokes—"Wait!" she once said, and turned her head away. When she whipped it back around, she had a foot-long string of plastic snot hanging from each nostril.

That first visit I am entirely edgy the whole three hours, thinking someone will come—the warden, a sheriff, God forbid the cowboy —either to tell us our time is up or to question my reason for being there. I keep thinking maybe other visitors will show up, or . . . I don't know what. Being locked up makes you crazy, even when you're only passing through.

Nothing happens. At two-thirty there is a shift change. Karla has to leave the room with the first guard, then return with the next. The second guard looks very much like the first. She sits there.

I have no idea whether or not the correction officers listen to us; I have no idea if anyone else—say, the warden—asks what we talk about. I expect that the guards have thoughts and lives enough to attend to without paying attention to ours, but of course I have no way of knowing. We are three women on different ends of the Plexiglas.

2205 McKean

The hardest thing about telling a story—fiction, nonfiction, for that matter even a joke—is figuring out where to start. In the beginning was . . . what?

"Endings are elusive, middles are nowhere to be found, but worst of all is to begin, to begin, to begin." Donald Barthelme wrote that.

So where does this one get going—with the murders? Karla Faye was twenty-three at the time, and wired. Texas law requires that the crime first be spelled out on its own, blow by blow, minus mitigating, aggravating, and/or contributing factors. Guilt or innocence must be determined first without reference to sociology, psychology, drugs, and IQ; or to reason, motivation, understanding. Texas law—any law—has its reasons, and certainly when a crime is committed, responsibility must be assigned and accounted for, not just understood. But for a writer used to studying motivations, character, family background, blood ties, social history, such legal requirements make for a tough assignment. Does the nightmare begin with sleep itself or with reasons for the dream? In Karla's case, the windup is long and slow, the culmination of events achingly inevitable (you can see the punch line coming long, long before it arrives), the wrap-up blunt and merciless, two people dead, two others waiting to be.

But to get to it, to *begin,* to make the bare-bones scarecrow picture . . . In northwest Houston, in the predawn hours of the morning of June 13, 1983, Karla Faye Tucker, twenty-three, her bartender boyfriend, Daniel Ryan "Danny" Garrett, thirty-seven, and an occasional chum, James Arnold "Jimmy" Leibrant, thirty, a speed lab operator, drove in Danny Garrett's 1977 blue Ranchero to the apartment of one Jerry Lynn Dean, twenty-six, a man Karla Faye hated. There, Karla Faye and Danny Garrett murdered two people, Jerry

Lynn Dean and his one-night companion, Deborah Ruth Thornton, thirty-two, after which they stole some of Jerry Lynn Dean's possessions—a motorcycle frame, some motorcycle parts, and a car, a 1974 blue El Camino.

A Ranchero is an odd-looking vehicle, half car, half pickup truck. So is an El Camino. In both, the front part of the chassis is a car, identical to the ordinary-model cars of that year, but instead of a backseat there is a truck bed. A passing fad. You see them in marginal neighborhoods.

"Took against him" is a Texas expression. Karla Faye had taken against Jerry Lynn Dean the day she met him; her feelings had not let up since. There were reasons. The day Karla met Jerry, it was 1981, she had just gotten home from work turning tricks for a week out in Midland and she was bone tired; coming home to the apartment on Quay Point she shared with her best girlfriend, Shawn, to find a Harley dripping oil on her living-room rug was not exactly what Karla had in mind that day, not at all. Now she knew if a man had a Harley he kept it in the living room, but there was something about walking in to find it dripping oil on her rug when she was that tired that got to Karla, and besides, Karla almost never turned tricks in her own home; she liked for the place she lived to be special. Home was home, business something else. And so Karla Faye marched upstairs and found Jerry in bed with Shawn in *her,* Karla's, bed. She hated the way Jerry looked, so washed-out and puny, and she threw him out of the apartment. Other things had happened since then to add to the reasons for taking against Jerry Dean, but the reasons don't add up exactly unless you start with the basic, primitive fact that growing up, Karla Faye Tucker was a hothead, a girl of passion, a girl of very clear definitions who when she took against somebody or declared herself for somebody, took against that person or stuck by him or her with fire and purpose and for good.

A child of the Harley-Davidson subculture—big in the South, the Southwest, and on the West Coast—Karla Faye liked street-smart, street-tough manly men. Men who knew how to wear skintight T-shirts, blue jeans, and motorcycle boots, who could hold their drink and drugs, men who would watch violent movies and take her to a gun show and buy her a camouflage T-shirt saying "Kill Them All. Let God Sort Them Out." Although she never much went for tattoos—otherwise she'd have gotten one herself, wouldn't she?—a lot of the men Karla knew had them. They liked pit bulls. They bragged about committing gruesome acts in Nam. They were real men.

For a man to get Karla's full attention he—in other words, her basic requirement—had to be able to "hold his own in any situation." Emphasis on "any."

Although he had a Harley, although he hung out and rode with bikers, Jerry Lynn Dean was not such a man. Jerry Lynn Dean was a pussy, and a man who was a pussy did not deserve to own a Harley. A man who was a pussy would have his Harley taken away from him.

After Karla threw Jerry Lynn Dean out of the Quay Point apartment that first time, what happened but that she came home another time to find the Harley dripping oil on her living-room rug again; Jerry in the bed with Shawn again. Karla tossed Jerry Dean out again, this time with more vigor and clarity; drawing the line in the dirt. Afterwards, she told Shawn that while Shawn was always welcome anyplace Karla lived, Shawn knew that this guy Jerry definitely, permanently was not. Period.

Shawn eventually married Jerry Dean and moved out of Quay Point. Karla moved in with her sister Kari for a time. Somewhere along in there—after Shawn was married—Karla went to New Orleans with a famous rock-and-roll band, the members of which she had known for some time. Shawn came too, but she did not make it to New Orleans; Shawn was with the roadies, not the actual band. Afterwards, Shawn's husband, Jerry Dean, got it into his head that Karla Faye had coerced Shawn into partying with the rock-and-roll band. In retaliation for that and for kicking him out of her house, Jerry Lynn Dean got out some photo albums of Karla's that Shawn was keeping for her until Karla found her own place to live, and he stabbed up some pictures in the album, including one—this is crucial—of Karla's mother.

The next day, Shawn came by Karla's house to pick up a jacket.

This was in March 1983, only three months before the murders. Having found out about the stabbed-up pictures, Karla told Shawn it was fine for her to be there, as long as she didn't bring that guy Jerry, and Shawn said well, guess what, he was right outside in the car. Karla roared from the house and punched Jerry Lynn Dean out again, blindsided him, dotted his eye. Jerry Dean wore glasses. Shawn had to take him to the emergency room to have bits of glass taken from his eye.

One of the things Karla Faye was proudest of was that she could fight. Punch. Closed fists. Could hold her own with a man. Could come up on a man, fast, and hurt him.

Dotting Jerry's eye was not enough, however. Punching him out in no way made up for the fact of his stabbing up her mother's picture; it was Karla's only picture of her mother, or so she claimed at the time. It *might* have been the only picture in that particular scrapbook, but there *were* pictures of Karla Faye's mother to be had elsewhere. That didn't matter. Karla was still hot about what Jerry had done. She couldn't get past it; her disquiet brewed. In early 1983, Karla's mother had been dead a little more than three years, having fought her final battle with hepatitis in the Harris County public hospital in 1979.

Karla Faye thought a lot of her mother. If Jerry Dean knew what was good for him he would keep his distance.

Reasons? It happened. Reasons piled up.

To look for a particular *cause,* to try to figure out why at three or four o'clock in the morning of June 13, 1983, Karla Faye Tucker, Jimmy Leibrant, and Danny Garrett climbed in Danny's Ranchero and drove over to Watonga Street to make a bloody mess of two sleeping people, is about like searching for one particular glob of tar in the whole Gulf of Mexico.

Nobody *decided.* It happened.

At the time, Karla Faye and Danny Garrett were living together in a rented, three-bedroom house at 2205 McKean Street. Living as a couple. They had been together since January. Danny Garrett wanted to get married; Karla wasn't sure. She'd just gotten *un*married from a man she never loved and wasn't sure she wanted to jump right back into the frying pan again—even though except for her father, Danny Garrett may have been the only man Karla Faye had ever truly loved.

McKean Street is off the Katy Freeway in northwest Houston in a suburban area called Spring Branch. When I first moved to Houston in 1966, people were saying that for middle-class white people with children Spring Branch was the way to go. Spring Branch has its own school system; unlike Houston proper, it's zoned: some blocks are designated commercial, others residential. In Houston you can buy yourself the house of your dreams only to have a 7-Eleven pop up next door, people in and out at all hours buying emergency beer and Tampax. When Spring Branch was being built, Houston was still known as an overgrown cow town, essentially and incurably redneck. Spring Branch was supposed to be a step up from that. The school system was supposed to be better. I don't know about better schools, nicer houses. The unspoken issue was more white people, fewer blacks and Hispanics, the middle-class dream.

There are areas of Spring Branch that have the expected, prefab look of the American suburbs, the brick houses on cul-de-sacs, the professionally landscaped yards with the curvy sidewalks and sculpted low-maintenance hedges. But Spring Branch has its pockets. Drive one block from the sculpted hedges and nothing. An empty lot littered with abandoned couches and car seats. A backyard turned into a parking lot for junked Sno-Cone trucks. A front yard gone to seed from dogs and motorcycles. A car up on blocks.

Houston's so new and in such a hurry, much of the city is like that. One block it's cathedral ceilings, a wet bar, and a spa, the next it's vacant lots, burglar bars, and a hand-lettered sign saying I Fix Cars with an arrow pointing to the backyard.

The land Houston is built on is reclaimed swamp, after all. The ooze constantly threatens to rise up and take back its rightful place.

2205 McKean is just north of the intersection of Hammerly Road and McKean. Across the street from the house Danny and Karla Faye lived in is a huge vacant lot, maybe an acre. On their side of the lot, the McKean Street side, there's a ditch, a field, but most of the acre-sized lot is taken up by a sand pit. They draglined the sand out years ago, and now the sand pit is filled with water. Somebody has built an upscale apartment complex next to it. Patios overlook the sand pit. There are piers, willows. A sign saying No Swimming in the Lake.

Karla Faye used to swim in the sand pit. She took her dogs, watched them fetch sticks. Danny Garrett says there's supposed to be a crane at the bottom of the sand pit, sunk so far down in the ooze it can never be located, much less recovered.

On McKean Street, in June of 1983, there had been a lot of talk-talk. Karla Faye, Danny Garrett, and Jimmy Leibrant were thinking about—talking freely about—stealing motorcycle parts from the big pussy Jerry Lynn Dean. Jerry needed taking down a notch. There were rumors of a drug deal gone bad, and everybody knew Karla Faye hated him. The talk-talk was building. They knew Jerry was custom-building a special kind of rigid-frame Harley, piece by piece as he collected the parts from friends and at swap meets, and who was he to think he deserved a Harley? That was an issue, certainly a relevant one, and there were others. There was Karla Faye's having taken so violently against Jerry Lynn Dean, and Dean's having stabbed up Karla's mother's picture, plus the other thing, not exactly an issue but a contributing factor, one that made the whole picture come clear and gave the threesome a definite direction in which to go, which was that the best way to get back at a man building a Harley was to strip his motorcycle and steal the parts. Men that have Harleys, says Karla, usually it's like their kid to them.

So if the talk-talk was to come to anything, if in the early morning hours of June 13, 1983, Karla, Jimmy, and Danny were to do the manly thing, act, do, go after the big pussy, they knew how to do it and what to go for, meaning naturally enough his Harley. Plus, Karla was building her own bike; she needed parts and Jerry had some. Also, Shawn had left Jerry by then, this time she swore for good, and had shown Karla the busted nose and lip Dean had given her and told her she deserved a medal for having punched Jerry out that day and that she, Shawn, didn't care what Karla did to Jerry this time.

Shawn getting punched out by a man who could not hold his own in any situation was the last straw: that was when talk about stealing motorcycle parts started. Revenge was a total necessity. Only the week before, Karla, Shawn, and Kari had taken Jerry's Quicksilver bank-card (provided by Shawn) and, wearing flimsy disguises—hats, sunglasses—to fool the automatic teller's video-camera eye, had withdrawn all of Jerry's cash, some $460. Shawn's mother was saying that Jerry had called her up steaming mad, saying he was going to file charges on Shawn.

"Shawn's ass is mine" is exactly what Jerry Dean was supposed to have said.

How much was Karla expected to take? She and Shawn were close, really close. Best girlfriends. When Shawn came to her with the busted nose and lip, Karla knew she had to do something, she just didn't know what.

On June 13, 1983, Shawn had been living at 2205 McKean with Danny, Karla, Karla's sister Kari, and Kari's ex-husband, a speed lab operator named Ronnie Burrell, for a couple of weeks. But Shawn was still in contact with her husband, and she had brought home to McKean Street the report that Jerry Dean had put a contract out on Karla Faye. Not to kill her—to burn her face with a flare gun and scar her for life. Shawn said Jerry said he could get the job done for three hundred dollars. There were rumors about a group of bikers Jerry had contacted, some guy named Sideburns.

Rumors. Talk.

Jerry kept a flare gun at the apartment, on top of the television set. Shawn said so.

June 11, 12, 13, this is how the talk-talk went, this the company they kept: bikers, dopers, bad cops, whores, rock musicians, titty dancers. Men with tattoos on the heads of their penises, to prove what manly men they were.

In and among that company, there was all this *she said he said.* Karla had her group—it was more like a *tribe*—and even though Karla was the baby in her family she had become, especially since her mother died, the tough guy, the bad-ass enforcer: you wanted something done, you told Karla Faye. Sometimes if you didn't want it done and on purpose didn't tell her about it for that reason, she took care of it anyway. For instance Kari. What Karla knew was that her big sister Kari was consistently terrible at choosing men, always going for one that beat up on her. Kari goes with a guy Karla thinks is bad for her, Karla finds somebody she thinks will treat Kari better—a guy named Mohawk, say—and introduces the two, she knows the type Kari goes for, lets nature take its course. Which it did.

Karla might be the baby, but since her mother's death she had taken over. Kari was vulnerable, Kari had to be looked after, Karla Faye in fact had maybe gone a little crazy over taking control. Maybe that was her way of making sure her mother wasn't really dead, by exerting this iron-hand control. She seemed so tough. She was passionate and sure, muscular and thin; in her jeans and tight T-shirt with her flat chest and lean arms, when she put her hair up she looked like a knotty little Greek boy. Being dark-skinned and black-headed with bowlegs and a definite sense of the boundaries of herself, Karla was different from everybody else in her family. Karla was so different from the others—soft and drifty, cotton-blond, with pale skin, straight legs, blue eyes—that you wouldn't have thought she belonged.

She wanted to be like them. To this day, she thinks of blond girls as the pretty ones; dark ones, never.

They were this tribe; they had been together for years, especially Karla Faye, her older sister Kari, and Shawn Jackson Dean. The three had lived together, traveled together, had gone on the road with rock bands together, had turned tricks together. When Karla's mother was alive she was honorary leader of the girl gang, teaching them by example if not mother-strict words. Mama Carolyn passed johns on to Kari, who passed them to Karla. Mama Carolyn rolled joints with her daughters before they'd had their first menstrual periods. There was nothing one of them did that the others did not know.

Best girlfriends, nothing like it before or since. Most women would understand; we have all been there. Except for the two years Shawn and Karla were estranged because of a fistfight Karla had had with Shawn's sister Shay, Shawn had always been in and out of any house Karla had lived in. Just like Kari. Shawn and Karla, Karla and Shawn. They were stuck together, Karla says, like Siamese twins.

In her teens, Karla Faye had been married for a few years to a form carpenter named Stephen Griffith, but she had grown to despise her husband and in May of 1983, when her divorce was final, Karla Faye managed to get her birth name back, so that she would be rid of all trace of the Griffith in her and become who she had once been all over again, her mother's daughter, Karla Faye Tucker.

Back in her tribe. Outside it she was nobody. Now she was herself again.

June 12, 1983. Karla claims not to have taken seriously Jerry Lynn Dean's threats to pay three hundred dollars to have her burned. She didn't think Jerry had what it took to do anything like that.

This is how they lived, one step outside the law, one breath—if that—this side of violence. Jimmy Leibrant and Ronnie Burrell made bathtub speed for a living. Like their mother, Karla and Kari made money on the telephone.

A doper at eight, a needle freak behind heroin by the time she was eleven, Karla Faye shot up any drug she could get her hands on. Ate pills. Placydils, Dilaudid, Somas. Went for acid. Loved the needle. Liked feeling the needle going in as much as if not more than the drug itself. They all had their prescription doctors. That was where Karla met Danny Garrett, in the waiting room of their prescription doctor, who for twenty dollars and a feel would write you any prescription you wanted. Danny Garrett carried a .38 caliber pistol in a holster in one boot, his drugs in a small paper sack in the other. Every bartender, he assured Karla, carried a gun. In the house on McKean Street there were at least two shotguns, one in the bedroom, another in the living room behind the couch.

Over the line was always—perpetually—only a whisper from now. All it took was a puff.

2205 McKean Street is a respectable-looking tract house, dark brown brick, small, new style, like a town house, the garage the first thing you see and not much yard to take care of. Wall-to-wall, drapes, appliances. Karla and Danny slept in one bedroom, Karla's sister Kari Tucker Burrell slept in another. The reason Jimmy Leibrant hung around McKean Street so much of the time was that Kari had invited her ex-husband, Ronnie Burrell, to move in with them and Ronnie Burrell and Jimmy Leibrant were in business together, making speed.

Danny didn't like it when Ronnie Burrell moved in, but he was outvoted two to one. Ronnie slept in the third bedroom. Jimmy didn't live there but he was around a lot.

Daniel Ryan Garrett was in love with Karla Faye Tucker, had been since he met her. He didn't want to lose her. And if Danny had learned anything about Karla Faye it was that, one, the best way to get her to do something was to tell her not to; and two, you did not come between Karla Faye and her sister. You just did not.

So Ronnie Burrell moved in. Ronnie Burrell was a scary guy. Everybody says: Ronnie would do anything. Ronnie knew things, took care of things, Ronnie was a real enforcer, not the loudmouth hotshot kind like Karla Faye. Nobody wanted to cross Ronnie Burrell. They still don't. I have been warned: Stay away from Ronnie. Ronnie has tattoos; one on his arm is of the Black Rose of Death. On the witness stand, Danny Garrett's brother Douglas said he thought Ronnie Burrell was the devil. Douglas was not kidding.

After leaving Jerry Dean, Shawn moved into the McKean Street house; she slept in the bedroom with Kari.

When they were married, Kari and Ronnie had a child, a son. The boy lived with Ronnie's parents.

Shawn had a daughter by a husband before Jerry. The girl lived with her grandparents.

Jimmy Leibrant camped out at 2205 McKean now and then, slept on the couch, had sex, hung out. Others came and went. The tribe expanded, drew in, stretched, but never shut down. There was a couch in the living room everybody flopped on, plus anybody could sleep anywhere on a given night. People swapped, switched, shared; they chipped on husbands, wives, boyfriends, girlfriends; sometimes there were threesomes, foursomes. Karla Faye, however, made it a point not to chip on a man when she was with him, married to him or not. Turning tricks was one thing; turning tricks did not count as chipping, turning tricks was business.

Their family. Their tribe. Plus two pit bull bitches, Tessa and Tooter. Karla Faye was good with dogs. She had trained them to obey using hand signals only.

At 2205 McKean, sex was like eating. For Karla and Kari that had been the case for a long time. Not that they were without conventional girl-type instruction; their mother had taught them early on to cook and clean ("I mean," Karla says, "not just clean but *clean*") and had stressed the importance of a good education. Words. Good advice. What Karla and Kari could see was Mama Carolyn in her nice apartment, wearing her great clothes, having fun, making money on the telephone. "Do as I say and not as I do," she told them, which didn't slow Kari and Karla down, and as Karla admits, her mother didn't put up that much of a fight to keep them from doing what she did.

And so, by their mother's example if not her words, Kari and Karla learned early on, a snatch was not to enjoy or get private about; a snatch was how you got by . . . no, a snatch got you more than by, it brought you up in the world, gave you your independence plus a great deal of *stuff*. A snatch provided you with full-length leather coats from Neiman-Marcus, great shoes, good furniture, fuzzy chairs, a nice end table. You didn't need brains, plans, or a boring life of punch in/punch out when you had this great asset, the value of which was never in flux or question. The men were always out there.

In the spring of 1983, Kari and Karla were doing fine. Once a month, they went to west Texas, to Midland, to work the Sun Valley Motel. The people who owned the Sun Valley were nice enough. They set things up: dates, times, the money. There was a suite they used at the motel. After a week's work, Karla and Kari came home with anywhere from $1,500 to $2,500 apiece, almost enough money to see them through the rest of the month. This was before the price of oil cratered, of course. In a few years, west Texas men would be scrambling for jobs and money instead of making monthly trips to the Sun Valley Motel to do business with top-dollar whores from Houston.

Karla and Kari had another regular gig, in Enid, Oklahoma; the rest of the time they made their living on the phone, a red telephone no man was allowed to answer. As prostitutes—they prefer the term call girls—Karla and Kari were proud of their independence. They made their own appointments, had their own list of clients. Men called them, not the other way around. And they had all this free time. To lie around. Make plans. Buy clothes. Do drugs.

Danny worked steady, always had. It bothered him, the dopers hanging around, Karla Faye with so much time on her hands. Not that he didn't do drugs, he did them on a regular basis; but he thought Karla would be better off if she had a real job, and he was hoping that his love for her would convince her to quit turning tricks, and in fact he thought she was about to. Then when Karla went to Midland in May, Danny Garrett had gotten into trouble with Kari on the living-room couch. A big mistake. Danny knew it at the time—anybody who knows about sisters would—but he and Kari were both loaded and, well, it happened.

When Karla got home Danny told her. Karla says she wasn't so much *mad* when she heard about it as *hurt*, especially by Kari; after all, Kari was her sister. Then it got worse: Kari bald-faced came out and said she liked it with Danny and didn't regret doing it. Her own sister. As for Danny, Karla threw that off on the fact that he was a man and since she had been cheated on by every man she'd ever been with in the past, why should he be any different? And she went back into her old and usual mode of not trusting men—even Danny—again, the way she'd been when they first got together.

If Karla Faye wasn't *mad,* she also was not above hurting back; she just did it, she says, differently from most women. She gave her sister and her boyfriend the silent treatment. Would not let them talk about what they'd done, never yelled or raised her voice, said the few words she had to say up front, then did not speak to them for three days. "They knew I knew about it and would never trust them again and I didn't want to hear anything they had to say."

Kari had a nervous breakdown over Karla's reaction. Danny sank back into a slump of remorse and depression he still has not pulled out of. When after three days Karla began talking to them again, everything had changed: everything. "I knew Danny and I would never be the same and never make the long haul. I knew I'd never trust Kari again as far as being around any man I liked."

Danny worked as a bartender at what was known as a swingers' bar—you had to have a membership card to get in—called the Jet Set Club. Karla says it was a sex club, which meant you went there to find new partners, swap, switch, chip. Danny had once been a high-class bartender, making fancy drinks at high-class bars like the one on the roof of the Galleria, inside a posh Houston hotel. People liked to watch Danny Garrett at his job, he was that smooth, that good at making it look easy. But he'd gone down. Instead of a Chrysler 300 he was driving a Ranchero. He was working at the Jet Set Club. There had been an arrest. Drugs, a gun. Possession.

Reasons snowballed. When asked why, in the middle of that 1983 June night starting on the twelfth and moving into the thirteenth, she decided to go out and get in the Ranchero and drive with Danny Garrett and Jimmy Leibrant to Jerry Lynn Dean's apartment, Karla says she doesn't think she really decided to do anything. . . . "My mind," she says, "was scattered."

It happened. They went. Events and reasons mesh, briefly make sense, and then fall away. None of it works even as partial explanation without the party, the weekend, the needles, the speed.

Sunday, June 12, 1983, was a dark night, a Sunday, the moon in its first quarter. Not officially summer yet, but from May on in Houston who could tell. The feud between Jerry Lynn Dean and Karla Faye was in the air, all the talk-talk. Beyond feuds and grudges, there was the other issue, the indisputable fact that on that dark June night in 1983, Karla Faye Tucker, Danny Garrett, and Jimmy Leibrant climbed into Danny Garrett's blue Ranchero at three or so in the morning and drove to Jerry Lynn Dean's apartment because—essentially because—they were ripped.

They had been sitting around the house on McKean Street shooting crystal and drinking tequila (Karla liked it mixed with schnapps) and eating pills for three days, from Friday the tenth through Sunday the twelfth. The eleventh was Kari's birthday, it was supposed to be a party. People were in and out of the house all weekend. Shawn had predicted an orgy, but they needed men; so Shawn had gone out the week before to recruit some.

On Sunday morning, four of the weekend participants—Kari Burrell, Shawn Dean, Jimmy Leibrant, and a casual drop-in male—had had sex together; Jimmy had even set up a machine to videotape the fun. Karla was out of commission for personal sex as well as turning tricks because of an ovarian cyst. She was not going to be able to make her June trip to Midland. Danny Garrett, who was coming off a four-week battle with hepatitis, also was not at full potential. Somebody did barbecue. Ribs, Kari says. In the backyard of 2205 McKean there is a gas grill, another hopeful, upscale sign. Sunday afternoon, Karla gave her dogs, Tooter and Tessa, their obedience lesson; had her hair cut, ate pills, drank, shot speed.

Karla remembers "people in and out, coming in and getting high, getting loaded, but that was like it was, in and out, during them days."

By Sunday night, the birthday orgy was pretty much over. By then, "there wasn't too many people around."

Karla Faye and Jimmy Leibrant had not slept in three days.

After eating the ribs she'd cooked, Kari Burrell went out on a job, with a regular client named Sammy. Understandably, Sammy has not been seen or heard from since. Ronnie Burrell was supposed to be home by ten-something; he didn't make it.

Danny went to work, came home.

Only the three of them were left: Karla, Jimmy, Danny.

More speed.

They had sat around the house as much as they could stand to. By the time the end of Sunday rolled into Monday morning, the three of them were wild to get out of the house and go do something, for a very simple reason: "We were very wired and we was looking for something to do."

"Something to do" keeps cropping up. Whatever would take up the slack, move the focus beyond themselves out onto something or somebody else, so that once the action was complete, they could then settle back over the line, back into themselves.

"Jimmy was pacing back and forth down the hallway looking for something to do. Sweating. Real hyped up. Talking. Saying if he . . . didn't find something to do he was going to go crazy. . . . I was probably walking all over the house too. No telling doing what."

No telling doing what. Like hyperactive children, bored, needing more, more, unable to say why they need it or exactly what it is they need, just on the other side of things, *in need* and out of control. Like a baby sucking idly at a tit, not hungry anymore, simply on a roll;

needing more. Still, in the conventional, undrugged world, it doesn't play.

You have to have been there, your nerves that shattered, the mind that numbed, the ante so high.

The participants have to have crossed over into a nightmare reality where anything can happen, anything.

I/Me

Hearing the stories, studying the pictures, I try to find a way to approach some understanding of how that was; try to step over, in imagination and memory, the line between my world and hers.

I grew up fat, my father was fat, my brother was, my mother went up and down, we were all desperate about fat, it was a major issue in our family life. And so my father, a pharmacist, got us diet pills. Diet pills weren't thought of as drugs back then, they were medicine. In college I went with a group of girls to a drugstore in Oxford, Mississippi, to get time-release capsules of Dexedrine so that we could stay awake all night and cram for final exams. None of us had the nerve to ask for the pills except the skinniest one among us, a girl from Jackson who could not have weighed more than ninety-eight pounds. The girl waltzed in and told the druggist she was on a diet and needed oh, say, fifty capsules. When the druggist suggested tablets instead, the thin girl said well, no, she thought she needed the heavier dosage. The druggist counted them out.

I stayed up all night that night with my books and notebooks, I thought I had never been so smart in my life, the next day I aced a bluebook exam in Philosophy 101, writing my head off, composing long discussions of . . . I had no idea what. By the grade sheet posted on his bulletin board the next morning, next to my A plus, my professor wrote a personal message: "How," he wanted to know, "did you learn all that Kant?"

Kant? By then the information had turned to dust. On to history. I had so many bright notions, my pencil could not keep up, I was that full of brainy ideas, answers, sentences, paragraphs, connections, the smart-girl A-plus stuff.

After the exams, on a page of the notebook over which I had sat hunched those three or four nights, I found drawings made with a quivering pencil, senseless notations, something about a boat with a paddle wheel coming to get me. A picture of the boat.

I had no memory of a boat with a paddle wheel and no idea where the drawing came from. I tore up the crazy notes and picture, went home, and, after chewing the inside of my jaw until it was ridged and red, fell asleep, rested, got past the pills. Growing up, I despised being fat more than practically anything, but I never took diet pills again.

No credit to the mind. Nothing to do with willpower or deciding. Fear makes up its own mind.

This is baby stuff, a whisper of what the voices must have been like on June 12, 13, at 2205 McKean. Not even a whisper. The intake of breath before the whisper . . .

Enough to, with imagination, make the leap.

The Insane Root

In the area of Houston where Karla Faye lived with Danny Garrett, there are a lot of apartment complexes, the newer ones of which offer hopeful come-ons for a name: Whisper Wood, Hickory Ridge, Hammerly Woods. The apartment complex next to the sand pit on McKean calls itself Spring Lake; the one Jerry Lynn Dean lived in with his wife, Shawn, was named Windtree (sold since that time, now called Stradford Oaks).

Older apartment complexes are more down-to-earth: Village Park, Skylane. Others get their names from no one knows where. One on Mangum Road is called Burnham Wood.

In *Macbeth*—also the story of the dark actions of one dark night and the bloody consequences that follow—Banquo, the soul of convention and good sense, having seen the sexless witches cavort and make prophecy, doubts his own senses. "Were such things here," he incredulously asks his friend, "as we do speak about?/Or have we eaten on the insane root/That takes the reason prisoner?"

At 2205 McKean, reason was securely locked away. Karla Faye, Danny Garrett, and Jimmy Leibrant had been gnawing on the insane root for days.

Karla remembers a turning point. "Whenever Jimmy said if he didn't find something to do he was going to go crazy, Danny said, 'I know what we can do.' And he pulled out a sheet of paper and started drawing the floor plan to Jerry's apartment."

Washing Shawn Dean's blue jeans a week or so before the birthday weekend, Karla had found a set of keys she recognized as some Shawn had been missing, the keys to Jerry Lynn Dean's apartment and car. Karla reminded Jimmy and Danny she had the keys, then went and got them. Danny drew the floor plan; Jimmy was wild for something to do.

It began.

Karla . . . *was game.*

Jimmy . . . *was overamped . . . to the point of yeah, okay.*

Danny had been to Jerry Dean's apartment, knew where all the rooms were. Karla had been there too, but she was so drugged up that day she had to be carried out.

Even though they had been talking about stealing motorcycle parts, they did not plan to run in on Jerry Lynn Dean or to steal the parts that night. Danny said they had to have a plan, they needed to be cool. Danny was the teacher, the oldest, the one with the car, the job, the sense of authority. The three did not leave the house thinking they would do anything that night beyond casing the place for future reference. Or at least that is what they thought then and continue to believe now.

Karla says Danny said they could go over there and case the place and she and Jimmy thought it was a good idea to see who was up at that time of night, what lights were on in what apartments, wherever they were around the apartment, where windows were, doors were.

Jimmy says he went for purposes of intimidation, in case there was static.

On his way out of the McKean house, Danny picked up a shotgun, probably the one that was kept behind the couch in the living room. Danny had gloves. . . . Nobody thought anything about it.

In Houston, a secret shotgun is not unusual. There are a lot of people living in houses in Spring Branch this very night who have not only a shotgun stashed behind their living-room couch but other guns in other rooms as well: handguns, rifles, automatic weapons, some of which are loaded. These people do not consider themselves criminals.

There was no *formal* plan to hurt anyone that night or steal anything. Still, Danny took the gun. And gloves.

Karla says they were on a—what do you call it?—reconnaissance mission. Danny had been in the military and professed to have certain know-how; this was how it was done. First you did your spy work, then you made your move.

The three of them were not so much on a far edge anymore as beyond it, out where thinking no longer proceeds, it just goes. It's easy to look back and see that now. But in their *minds,* at the time, as they climbed in the Ranchero and set out south on McKean toward Hammerly Road, turned east, and drove the five and a half miles from their house on McKean Street to Jerry Lynn Dean's apartment at 4000 Watonga, they did not plan, these three, to run in on anybody. The stealing of motorcycle parts from Jerry Lynn Dean was still a very real possibility, but that was for some other time, not now; the stealing was to take place later, if it happened at all.

A dark night. Reasons piled up but did not gain sense, reasons only added size and heft in their minds, like scrapped cars in a junkyard.

Jerry Lynn Dean lived in a first-floor apartment on Watonga Street one neighborhood over from Spring Branch in the Oak Forest section of Houston, another on-the-verge neighborhood inhabited by people who are without much of a legacy in education or hope; people trying to leverage themselves up to the next stage of income and social prestige, but rarely doing so. On the main streets, every other business has to do with cars: repairs, tires, upholstery, paint-and-body shops. There are roller rinks, bowling alleys, nut churches. Some of the neighborhoods are pre–World War II and quite pretty. Most of them are made up of apartment buildings where people come and go, quick and easy. The convenience stores have burglar bars. The No Parking signs include the number of the wrecker service to call to get your car back. It's upwardly mobile redneck territory, where up seems a long way off and mobile mostly means feather-footed: one apartment to the next.

The Windtree is set back in a pretty grove of trees, almost what you might call a glade. There are small oaks, hackberries, some pecans. Windtree had two sections of apartment buildings, one for people with children, the other for those without. Because Shawn Jackson Dean's daughter, Jamie Kay, had lived with her and Jerry Dean for a time, Jerry Dean lived in the family section.

The apartment buildings themselves are pleasant enough, if without distinction. They're brick, with aluminum windows, aluminum screen doors. Outside, there are trimmed boxwood hedges, carports, a plain Saint Augustine lawn. Because of the trees and the dip in the landscape at that point on Watonga Street (uncharacteristic, for Houston), it's actually quite pleasant. Clean. Made to look like a little neighborhood. There are thousands just like it all over the city. Hopeful.

Hammerly Road's a wide, busy street, with apartments, strip shopping centers, convenience stores, fast food. Hammerly at Mangum Road is a big intersection where there are larger stores, a traffic light. Traveling east on Hammerly, to get to Watonga you turn right at the light, pass the stores, go over a railroad track and . . .

Mangum changes to Watonga. The street gets a grassy esplanade. The stores disappear. There is a dip in the road. On either side there is the foresty glade and ahead, pleasant houses, a quiet, attractive neighborhood.

Mangum used to dead-end before you got to Windtree, at the railroad tracks. When Karla Faye, Danny Garrett, and Jimmy Leibrant drove to Jerry Lynn Dean's apartment from McKean Street, they had to go north of Windtree, then back south; they couldn't get to the apartment complex from Hammerly.

Windtree has apartments on the left and right sides of Watonga. To get to Apartment 2313, traveling south, you cross the incoming lane of Watonga and turn into the apartment driveway on your left.

In the blue Ranchero, Karla, Danny, and Jimmy turned left into the Windtree drive, then veered to the right. They pulled up and parked, close to the back door of Jerry Lynn Dean's apartment building. Jerry Lynn Dean's front door faced a courtyard. His back door—leading from the kitchen—opened out onto one of the Windtree roads leading to Watonga Street and through the apartment complex. According to Jimmy Leibrant, after Danny Garrett double-parked the Ranchero, he, Jimmy, went off to do his part of the scouting job, which was to look for the El Camino.

Reconnaissance has begun. The mission.

To see what lights were on in what apartments. Where windows were. Doors were.

Karla was Danny's student. Danny was teaching Karla how to do things like develop night vision, carry a gun, wear a ski mask, walk through ditches in the blackest night, cross lakes, jump fences wearing a ski mask, gloves, black clothes. To see in the dark. To watch without being seen, hear without being heard.

He was teaching her to watch people so that you learned how they lived and could pounce on them when they were at their most wide-open and vulnerable, late at night, when they had taken off their clothes, unpinned their hair; when, afloat in sleep, they had let their guard down and their consciousness slip.

All of this was feeding into her dreams: to be in charge, street smart and street tough; to operate in her own world by her own rules; to hold her own in any situation. Was teaching her to stalk the night until she was part of it: perfectly invisible, perfectly silent.

Teaching her until she made the switch.

Became no longer prey.

Become predator.

What's Going On?

Danny Garrett is wearing motorcycle boots, blue jeans, a black T-shirt with an eagle on the front and on the back the words "Harley's the Best, Forget the Rest." He is carrying the shotgun. Karla Faye has on blue jeans, kicker boots, a dark T-shirt. Being a druggy she is bone thin, maybe 105 pounds. In the dark—all hushed tones and whispered conspiracy, the tough talk having now come to an abrupt and necessary end—they make their way from the rear of Jerry Lynn Dean's apartment to the front door.

Back door to front is not far. There aren't many windows. There aren't any lights. The blinds are drawn. Not too much to gain from reconnoitering. Windtree is asleep.

At Windtree, each apartment building contains four units, two downstairs, two up. Jerry Lynn Dean lived downstairs, in a corner building with nobody to the right of him. If he looked out his bedroom window he would see a carport, the drive, the cars. On the other side of his living-room wall there is another apartment. To the left of his building, other four-unit buildings in a U shape around a courtyard.

The front door of a downstairs apartment at Windtree is recessed. There's an overhang, made by the porch of the apartment upstairs. And so the front door is dark, even in daylight. There's a small porch, really only a six-by-eight-foot concrete slab. People put barbecue grills on the slab, weight benches, children's Big Wheels and skateboards. There's an aluminum window. An aluminum screen door. A mailbox. The apartment number.

Standing on the slab of apartment 2313, Danny tells Karla to open the door. Karla digs in her tight jeans for Jerry Lynn Dean's keys.

"I don't think we decided anything, but . . . I don't know but I think from the time we opened the door, after that . . . I have thought back over it and back over it. I don't know why Danny said open the door and I don't know why I did it. I don't blame Danny, Danny wasn't the leader, we were equal, but from then on . . ."

Karla frowns. When her vision clears, she lets the ugly thought run its course. "I think from then on those people in there did not have a chance."

Karla unlocks the front door. Danny brushes past. She follows. The floor of the living room is carpeted (wall-to-wall goes with the territory in Houston apartment buildings like this, as do central air and heat, appliances, and a covered parking space) but the kitchen is not. Beyond the kitchen, down a short hall there is a bathroom and two bedrooms, one on either side of the hall.

Danny knows which bedroom Jerry Dean sleeps in, the spare; the other one, the bedroom designated by Windtree as the master bedroom, having been given to Shawn's daughter, Jamie Kay, when Shawn and her daughter lived there. Danny has drawn the floor plan; he knows where he is going. (We are not talking big here; the entire apartment comes to only 723 square feet of space.)

Just after they open the front door and go in, they hear a voice.

"Jerry said—" Karla begins (this is during her trial). Her lawyer interrupts. How did she know whose voice it was, is Karla certain it was the voice of Jerry Lynn Dean she was hearing when she opened the door to apartment 2313, did she *recognize* Jerry Lynn Dean's voice?

"Well," Karla replies, "it was his apartment, and so I just guessed it had to be him." Anyway, the voice was coming from the spare bedroom, the one Jerry slept in.

"What's going on?" the voice from the spare bedroom calls out.

Last words have a special poignancy, especially if the person about to die—the person about to be murdered; killed—has been sleeping.

What's going on? is friendly, almost flip; it is accommodating, hopeful, the language casual, authentic. Mostly, *What's going on?* is a cry into the night and the unknown, a plea for normality, for a full night's sleep; for a return to one minute earlier, when the night was quiet and without complication, before the owl screamed and the cricket cried.

What's going on? the man about to be murdered cries from his bed, hearing—what? Footsteps on the grass outside his window, as the two people dressed in black case doors and windows to find out what lights were on in what apartment, where doors and windows were? A rustling outside? His front door unlocked and opened? Muffled footsteps on the wall-to-wall, louder ones on the kitchen floor? Perhaps he only senses something amiss, something new, an intrusion into the silence of a dark first-quarter-moon night, the irregular breath of two people so wired they might as well be flying.

It is a moment that belongs decidedly to the victim. The intruders have gone beyond sociology, sympathy, understanding now. They have crossed over into the realm of pure horror-story unthinkable.

Three or so A.M. is morning, of course, but by most internal clocks it is dead dark night, the deadest darkest *thickest* part of the night. The most vulnerable. At three, we have let go. Eleven, the news is finished. Midnight, talk shows still go on. One, in Houston, is last call. Two, bars shut down. Three, most of us are safe at home and blotto.

"You don't want to get a phone call at three in the morning," I heard the father of a murdered boy say in a radio interview. "And if you do you don't want to answer it. Nobody calls you up to ask for a cup of coffee at three in the morning."

What's going on? The key turns. There are footsteps—boots— muffled, then not. On the rim of waking, Jerry Lynn Dean might have thought he dreamed, not heard, a noise; might have, in his half-wakened state, wondered if he had actually heard something real or if reality was perhaps unhinged, was wrapped in the context of a dream. Jerry Lynn Dean might have thought he was asking the question of the dream, not of real people, not of real life.

He had a girl in bed with him, a girl he had met only that afternoon at a beer party. Hearing the real or imagined sounds, did Jerry Dean think of the girl just then, of taking care of the girl or of blaming her; did he wonder who this girl might really be and if possibly she had gone to bed with him only to set him up?

Karla follows Danny through the living room and through the kitchen; they turn down a hall. It is dark, but Danny knows the floor plan. Danny walks to the doorway of the room in which Jerry Lynn Dean sleeps. And Karla . . .

"I was right behind him . . . and the light was out and the window was on the far wall and there was a little crack in the curtains and a little bit of light coming through. And I could see the silhouette of a body that had sat up, was on the floor. . . . I couldn't see detail, faces or Jerry's clothes, anything like that, but I could see the outline of everything, like a shadow on a wall. . . . And I walked past Danny and went and sat down on top of him. Right there."

There?

"Here."

Tell us.

"His lap."

Show me.

Doesn't know why, she just did it, the momentum going in that direction now, going forward. Karla went and sat on Jerry Dean's lap, only that little bit of light coming through the curtains to go by.

The autopsy report indicates that Jerry Lynn Dean was a smallish man, sixty-seven inches tall and 142 pounds. He had a moustache, longish blond hair. He slept naked, on a mattress on the floor. The mattress was pulled out from the wall somewhat, in the middle of the floor, closer to the windows than to the door. A small room. Behind Jerry Lynn Dean's head was a window, curtained, the draperies pulled shut except for a crack. Pictures of the scene show a messy room, boxes all around, two aluminum stepladders, some scaffolding, work tools, garden tools, more boxes. In the living room was the half-built Harley, up on what is called a stand but looks to be only a cheap wooden table.

Karla "went to him, sat down on top of him, told him to shut up."

At this point, it seems, Jerry Dean realized who it was sitting on him. *"Karla,"* he said. *"We can work it out."* Something to that effect. *"We can work it out. I didn't file charges on Shawn. I didn't call her mother."* Referring to the Quicksilver card, the $460, the threats he was supposed to have made. *Shawn's ass is mine.* Jerry must have thought Karla was coming to get back at him for threatening Shawn.

Jerry Lynn Dean wore glasses. How much in fact he could see, waking up to find Karla Faye Tucker, at three or four in the morning, knowing what Karla Faye was capable of, perhaps seeing Danny Garrett behind her, backing her up with a shotgun, is not known. Fearful by now, Jerry Lynn Dean made his plea. Karla, he said, we can work it out. . . .

Q: What was his tone?

A: He was pleading.

Karla told Jerry Lynn Dean to shut up.

Shut up? Other people say there was more.

"Move and you're dead, motherfucker" is what Karla's sister Kari says Karla Faye told her she said . . . a line Karla cannot recall but does not deny saying. "I might have," she says, and closes her eyes. "Might have *said* I said it anyway. Which is just as bad."

Things get hazy here. Because who struck the first and/or killing blow and who picked up the unthinkable weapon is important, nobody wants to remember. Also, fights are messy. People get mixed up about what happened in which order. Jimmy Leibrant had not yet come back from his mission, or maybe he had. He says he had gone back to the Ranchero to sit for a while, nodding off, he says, even though not five minutes before he was bouncing off the walls at 2205 McKean, overamped, wild for something to do. At any rate, what Karla remembers—so mixed up with what Danny told her afterwards that she is not certain what exactly went on and what has become pure story—is Jerry Lynn Dean making a last-ditch attempt at self-protection by grabbing Karla's arms, just above the elbows. Karla naturally pulled against Jerry's grip, they wrestled a bit, and then Danny Garrett intervened, in the process shoving Karla Faye off Dean's lap, onto the floor.

This is what Karla remembers, which is all we have. Jimmy Leibrant was not present, the victims are dead, and Danny Garrett has never said one word. Karla told the story twice on the witness stand, she has told it to me, to her lawyers, the story never changes, she never waffles in order to remove herself from the center of the picture, never fails to make the spotlight of guilt shine on her. Also, lies usually run out: people come to a point beyond which they can do no more conjuring. Karla never gets there; her eyes are clear, she is right there the whole time, and she seems constantly to be asking *What else do you want to know?* Some of it, she says—the blood—is gone from her memory and her mind. This is not unusual. After the commission of horror-story crimes, forgetting blood happens more often than not.

In Karla's case, if the blood has vanished, other grim details have not. "Whenever I was shoved back and I had come up and got to my feet, I seen the silhouette of Danny hitting Jerry in the head with a hammer. When I went back to turn on the light he was already finished. . . ."

The light? Why would she turn on the light, what was it she wanted to see? She does not know. It seemed the thing to do at the time.

Finished what?

Hitting Jerry.

The hammer? Karla Faye says it came from the truck, a ball-peen hammer, she insists, although it might have been a claw hammer, she is not exactly sure she has the terminology right, she'd always called it a ball-peen hammer. There were tools all over the bedroom, which Danny might have used. Not to mention the butt end of his shotgun. No hammer was ever produced. In the Houston medical examiner's opinion, more than likely the weapon used on Jerry Lynn Dean's head was not a hammer but a blunter weapon, perhaps the blunt end of the pickax, maybe the butt end of the shotgun, but then again it might have been a hammer.

Karla Faye is positive. She was there. It was a hammer.

"No, they never found it, because I threw it as far as I could in the sand pit. It had blood on it. I wasn't about to leave it lying around. Jimmy Leibrant wanted to keep it. I went over there, it was about a week later, and I threw it as far as I could."

Karla has dreams about the sand pit, imagines it drained dry, and there on the bottom is the thing she is certain Danny used on Jerry Lynn Dean's head that night, the hammer.

It is an odd scene to picture. Karla Faye says that from her position on the floor she saw Danny exactly behind Jerry Dean, between the curtains and the top of the mattress, hitting Jerry Dean on the *top* of his head. It seems awkward, if not odd, but then Danny Garrett professed to be skilled in such matters; from his time in the military he claimed to have learned where to hit a person to kill them fast and without leaving traces. Maybe that night, Danny Garrett was looking for the right spot. *Why* he suddenly started in on the man in bed is another question, whether it was to protect Karla Faye when Jerry Dean grabbed her arms or if the speed in him suddenly surged up or if maybe it was just time to get the thing started, which they all said they were not going to do but which surely down deep they knew was in the works if not the cards the whole time.

At any rate, after whamming Jerry Lynn Dean in the head with some kind of instrument, Danny Garrett left the room. Perhaps he was tired.

Karla stayed in the room with the dying man with the light on. Jerry Lynn Dean had somehow been turned on his stomach, face down.

Because of the particular placement of the wounds inflicted on him by Danny Garrett, the unconscious Jerry Dean started making a noise. A *gurgling,* by all accounts, as blood and fluid flowed into his lungs. A loud sound.

It is a sound that gets to many murderers. The gurgling, the loud, inhuman gurgling. Murderers wish for that sound to stop. They cannot bear the sound, are derailed by it, as if the sound were an affront, the victim's revenge, beyond the bounds of tolerance. When in 1977 Richard Herrin bashed Bonnie Garland's skull in with a claw hammer because she said she didn't want to see him anymore, Bonnie Garland started to make those same gurgling noises. The noises so infuriated and confounded Richard Herrin that he then struck his victim in the throat, to shut her up. She didn't. Not for hours.

The medical examiner has confirmed the fact that it was the head wound that made the gurgling occur. Jerry Lynn Dean had been hit so hard on the top of his head that his head was unhinged from the neck, just beneath the occipital ridge. When a head is unhinged that way, the breathing passages fill with fluid and blood and . . .

Karla was standing there and "Jerry was laying face down on the mattress that was on the floor and he was making this gurgling noise . . . and I kept hearing that sound and all I wanted to do was stop it. I wanted to stop him from making that noise. . . .

"So I looked, I seen a pickax against the wall. I reached over and grabbed it and I swung it and hit him in the back with it . . . four or five times."

Jerry Lynn Dean owned a pickax because in one of his jobs he worked for a television cable company. One of his duties was to lay cable from telephone poles to a house. To break up Houston's gumbo-thatched Saint Augustine grass in order to dig trenches, he used a pickax. He slept in the room with the tools of his trade and kept his Harley in the living room. It was the way he lived.

But the noise. He kept making the noise.

Somewhere along in here, Jimmy Leibrant comes into the apartment, probably to assist Danny in moving boxes of motorcycle parts into the bed of his truck, or maybe he never left. Hard to say, Jimmy Leibrant was saving his own skin. At any rate the fact remains: he did not participate in the murders. From the front door, Jimmy can hear the noise Jerry Lynn Dean is making, and so he goes back there and . . .

When Jimmy Leibrant saw Karla Faye laying into Jerry Lynn Dean's back with the pickax, he left—or in Karla and Danny's words "tucked tail and ran."

Jimmy says he "burned off . . . because I didn't buy in for that. That's not what it's supposed to be. . . . I hadn't gone for that. It was just supposed to be intimidation and collecting money. That's not my way."

Jimmy Leibrant left Windtree, walked back down Watonga, and called Ronnie to come get him; Ronnie didn't answer the first time, he was asleep, but the second time he did.

While Karla continued to go at Jerry—without much success, as the gurgling continued—Danny began loading motorcycle parts into the bed of the Ranchero. But the noise wouldn't stop, and so finally—probably beckoned by Karla, as she was the one who couldn't take the sound—Danny Garrett came back in, rolled Dean over, and hit him in the chest with the pickax. After that, Jerry Dean was quiet.

Next morning when police came a radio was on in the living room, playing loud music. Nobody can remember turning it on. Nobody can remember a radio *being* on. No one in the upstairs apartments heard it come on, that time of the morning. If Danny Garrett remembers a radio, or if Danny turned it on, he is not saying.

As for the choice of weapon, "Dan said it was right there," Danny's brother Douglas Garrett testified. "It was right there . . . right next to him. It was right there. . . . Dan said that it was a freak thing. They woke up. The pickax was there."

In all the hotheaded what-if discussions at the house on McKean Street, in all the plans made about stealing motorcycle parts, the possibility in fact had been raised, what if they went over to steal the parts and Jerry Lynn Dean was there? What if he was asleep and woke up, then what? They would, they had decided in their talk-talks, have to *off* him.

That would take them to the next level. Up the ante, raise the stakes. From casing the joint to stealing parts to murder. But—they said to one another in all the talk-talk before anybody actually did anything—they would have no other choice.

Once Jerry Lynn Dean was quiet, Danny went back to stealing motorcycle parts.

Once again, Karla stayed.

"Danny had walked out of the room. I noticed that there was a body underneath some covers laying against the wall by the door. . . ."

Someone else was in the room, the girl in bed with Jerry Lynn Dean. Karla says she did not see the other person until after Jerry Lynn Dean was quiet and when that happened, that was when she saw the other person, who was not on the bed at that time but on the floor under some covers, down at the end of the bed, past the foot of the mattress. "I don't know why she was there," Karla says now. "Danny told somebody he saw her when we first got there and told her to get under the cover and keep quiet. I don't know about that. All's I know is, first time I saw her, that's where she was."

Imagination's dangerous, enabling us as it does to move into the mind and heart of the innocent sleeping partner, to in a sense become that girl, sleeping in the bed beside a man she had met at a party only that afternoon, then hearing the intrusion, and then the goings-on, the threats, the sounds, the gurgling in Jerry Lynn Dean's throat. Imagine how long the preceding minutes seemed, from the time of the key turning in the door and Jerry Lynn Dean's calling out into the darkness *What's going on?* through the rest of it, until now. Unspeakable is about to become unthinkable.

A body? Again the examining attorney asks, meaning to make it clear that Karla Faye is not talking about a *body* here, she means a person. A living person.

"Their head was under a pillow and the body was shaking . . . under the covers. At that point my mind was, I don't know where it was at. I picked up the pickax again. I swung it and hit the person in the upper part of their shoulder."

Deborah Ruth Thornton, thirty-two, worked at a mortgage company, Lawyers Title Company of Houston, as a bookkeeper. Karla Faye had never laid eyes on Deborah Thornton in her life, and neither had Danny Garrett. Deborah Thornton had met Jerry Lynn Dean only that afternoon, Sunday, June 12, 1983, at a swimming-pool party at her apartment complex. Dean invited Thornton over to his place. Debby arranged for her stepdaughter and her son to be taken care of and then in her blue pickup truck with the personalized license plate saying "DEBBY" she went to apartment 2313 at 4000 Watonga, the Windtree Apartments, in the Oak Forest section of Houston. She had brought clothes to wear to work the next morning—a green-striped dress, hanging in the bathroom—and hot rollers for her hair. According to the autopsy report, Deborah Thornton was sixty-nine and a half inches tall—two and a half inches taller than Jerry Lynn Dean—and weighed 111 pounds. In bed that night—the mattress on the floor—she was wearing only a T-shirt, with "Teller 2" across the front, a ring, and a gold chain. She was still wearing those items the next morning when the police came.

If you have ever broken up ground with a pickax or a grubbing hoe you know how heavy a tool a pickax is; unless you are terribly strong in your upper arms and shoulders, after a swing or two you have to rest. Karla used to have strong arms, but she had torn all the muscles in both biceps the previous year, doing that daredevil eighty-two-foot leap into the spring-fed pool, and so her arms were possibly tired by now, because when Karla swung at Deborah Thornton with the pickax she only grazed her shoulder.

No feelings anymore; if *we* can imagine what it must have been like to be Deborah Thornton, Karla could not—the victim has to have become without humanity for the murderer to do his or her work. When doing the killing, the murderer has canceled out imagination, feeling. What is left is the job to be done, the mechanics of the thing. Cogs, wheels.

The pickax "did not penetrate. I tried again the second time, and when I did the person came up from under the covers and it was a woman and she grabbed at the pickax."

The light was still on. The radio might have been on. Deborah Thornton came up out of the covers fighting for her life. That she did not want to die was one thing; in addition to her instinct for self-preservation, Debby Thornton simply had more information to go on than Jerry Dean had. She knew that there was no negotiating with these intruders, no "working it out"—these people were *gone*. Also, Deborah Thornton had a son, and though it's hard to imagine her thinking of anyone else at that moment, subconsciously the fact of the boy's existence may have had its effect. In addition to which, Deborah Thornton had size over Karla Faye, a good six inches in height, a good ten pounds in weight.

Karla was struggling when "at that point, just as soon as she got up and grabbed it, Danny came into the bedroom and he grabbed the pickax also. Separated us two. And when I was not holding the pickax any longer I walked out into the living room . . . and carried some boxes out to Danny's car."

Deborah Thornton fought for her life. Later, Danny said at least Deborah Thornton had faced her attackers down, while Jerry Dean "did not even have the nuts to stand up and fight for his life." Karla's sister, Kari Tucker Burrell, quoted Karla as having said, "The girl was a tough motherfucker to kill." Karla swears she never said that.

Time is hard to pin down here, time was not a factor, but at some point Karla Faye came back into the bedroom, and "the girl was sitting down and the pickax was real deep in her left shoulder and she was in a sit position and she had her hands on the pickax. Danny was standing there over her and she said, 'Oh, God, it hurts. If you are going to kill me, please hurry up.' "

On the stand, Karla Faye puts both hands in fists at her shoulder, one fist on top of the other, the way Deborah Thornton did when she was there on the mattress in the sit position trying to pull the wretched thing from her shoulder.

"And Danny kicked her in the head and pulled the pickax out at the same time and when he kicked her it knocked her back flat on her back and he hit her and put the pickax right there in her chest. When I seen that—it happened that quick—I turned around and walked out of the bedroom and Danny was behind me and we got the motorcycle frame, carried it, and put it in Jerry's vehicle."

Danny left the pickax plunged into Deborah Thornton's heart, the head buried some seven inches in her chest, pulling part of her shirt and the "2" of "Teller 2" down into the hole the point of the pickax made.

Danny drove off in the Ranchero, Karla in the stolen El Camino. The two half-and-half car-pickups split, one going south to Douglas Garrett's apartment, the other back home to 2205 McKean.

It was daylight by then, 6:30 A.M.

The Weapon,
the Woman, the Nut

I asked Joe Magliolo, the lawyer who prosecuted Karla, why Karla
Faye's case had received such extraordinary attention that six years
later people still remembered it.

Joe Magliolo did not blink. "The weapon," he said. "The morning
they found the bodies it was all over the courthouse. I heard it
everywhere I went. That was before I was chief prosecutor. I had no
idea I would have anything to do with the case. But I knew about
it the first day, because of the weapon."

A detective on the stand at Danny Garrett's trial testified that the
police force had been extremely anxious to break the case. When his
questioner allowed that this was probably because it was a capital
murder case, the detective corrected him. "No," he said. "Capital
pickax murder."

The weapon is one reason. Then, when they caught the killers and
one of them turned out to be a woman . . .

The weapon of choice for women killers used to be poison, mainly
because a woman's place was in the kitchen, where poisons were kept
and food prepared. Nowadays a woman is most likely by overwhelming odds to use a gun; for that matter, so is a man. You don't have
to get close to a person to kill with a gun.

A pickax is a nightmare weapon, one of those household and garden
tools you know has a useful function, and yet . . . it's the utilitarianism
that makes it chilling, the idea that death is all around, that our own
hammer, the one we use to hang pictures, can kill us, our sewing
scissors, your grandfather's carving knife, this screwdriver I use to

open a cranky drawer; that death tools are everywhere, these commonplace domestic items. In the indictment, the pickax is called a mattock.

When a woman kills it's news. When a woman kills unmercifully and with such a weapon, it's big news.

Lizzie Borden comes to mind. People in Fall River, Massachusetts, knew immediately about the weapon used to kill her parents; when the daughter herself was arrested, so did everybody in the country.

Once Karla Faye's trial was over and she'd received the death penalty, a true-detective magazine ran a story featuring a photograph of Joe Magliolo—smiling, smug, victorious—holding the pickax. It's cheap, but then, he won.

As I sat reading court transcripts in the appeals office reading room one day, a lawyer came in, looking for a file. Seeing the sixty volumes stacked on the table before me, he said, "Must be a capital." I said yes. The lawyer peeked over to see who the defendant was. "Oh, her," he said. "Isn't she the one who . . . ?" And he mimed a pickax stroke, placing his hands in fists one on top of the other over his head, bringing the fists down.

The weapon makes for good copy, so does a woman on trial for her life. But to be really sensational, the story lacks another element, one that Karla herself was to provide.

One month and five days after the murders, on July 18, 1983, Danny Garrett's brother Douglas and Karla's sister Kari Tucker Burrell called on J.C. Mosier, a homicide detective and longtime high-school friend of one of Danny's ex-wives. By that time, Kari had taken one of the pit bulls—Tessa—and moved out of the McKean Street house. Kari Burrell and Douglas Garrett had been an off-and-on couple for some time. After the murders, they became a live-in couple, just like their brother and sister, Danny and Karla Faye. Ronnie Burrell moved in with his parents, where his and Kari's son lived, for a while.

Because J.C. Mosier grew up in Oak Forest, the double-pickax homicides grated on him. The case wasn't his, but he had been keeping a close eye on it as it developed. "It was brutal," he says. "We were all watching it, everybody in homicide. It was just so bizarre. And it got worse every day."

On July 18, 1983, when Douglas Garrett called up J.C. Mosier and told him that his brother Danny and his girlfriend Kari's sister Karla Faye had killed Jerry Lynn Dean and Deborah Thornton, J.C. couldn't believe his ears, especially about Danny. "I said," J.C. remembers, "he did *what?*"

So this is what it came down to: Kari and Douglas turned in Karla and Danny. Sister and brother put sister and brother on Death Row. Douglas agreed to wear a wire, and turned his brother in because he was scared.

Danny and Karla, it seemed, had been bragging about what they had done. They had been talking about offing other people. The talk-talk was getting darker, scarier. Karla Faye's boasts went beyond murder.

"Doug," Douglas quoted Karla as saying, "I come with every stroke." Of the pickax, she meant.

Kari confirmed this: "She told me that every time that she had picked Jerry that she looked up and she grinned and got a nut and hit him again."

J.C. says he knew from the first conversation he had with Douglas and Kari that this case was a capital and that the only way they were going to break it was for Douglas to wear a wire. J.C. told Douglas that right off. They worked it out. J.C. wanted everything on tape, including the part about Karla getting off.

After the trial, the joke around the courthouse was *Cosmopolitan* had called for an interview. There was a new way women in Houston had found to get off, so the magazine had heard.

A woman. A pickax. Two killings. That slippery, now-you-have-it-now-you-don't thing, the female orgasm.

Karla Faye doesn't deny she said "got a nut," she never has.

"I always," she said on the stand, "tried to present myself as a badass. Excuse my language."

Peter

Do I create her by living out her life and through her crime, or is she in some way re-creating who I am by expanding my world, taking me beyond what I thought I knew?

Making stuff up, you go places you've never been, get introduced to people you do not know, stretch yourself beyond limits to include within your own life and imaginative experience new lives, another history, alien geography.

Sitting in the visitors' room on the other side of the Plexiglas, Karla is my narrator.

I feel myself passing through boundaries to where she is and has been.

And then she does it. With the correction officer sitting there watching, the Death Row inmate escapes. Like a Chagall floater, she comes to my side of the counter, beyond the double-careful barriers, to where she is not supposed to be. Into my life.

"So . . . is there anything you want to know about me?"

The clock behind the guard's head says five to four. Karla and I have been talking for almost three hours. Although I'm pretty much exhausted, she's still fired up.

For about the first year, we sat in the same spot, halfway down the counter between the guard on one end and the door leading into the visiting room on the other. One day when Karla had something private to tell me, we moved a couple of chairs closer to the door. The next time we moved down another one. Now, unless the CO tells us not to, we sit as far away from her as we can get, in the two chairs nearest the door. We whisper there together like schoolgirls.

Karla answers my question by asking one of her own.

"In that article you sent, it talked about your son Peter. He got in trouble. And he died?"

With my introductory letter, I included an interview published in a Houston magazine. The interview went into my personal life in some detail, including mention of Peter's death and the fact that he'd been a troubled boy.

I level with her. "I guess I knew," I say, "you'd ask that."

After three hours of nonstop conversation, we faced yet another choice, whether to get closer, keep talking, reveal more, and if we decided to plunge ahead, how far to go. Every step took us into riskier territory; thicker muck, more snakes.

Three hours is short, but we kept crossing the line. I guess the basic state we were both in made things happen fast, combined with the unusual circumstances—no interruptions, no social expectations, nothing to do *except* talk—not to mention the fact that the two of us tended to do that anyway, make the daredevil leap into friendship fast and on the spot and without restrictions.

Up to the time of my question, however, the stories had all been Karla's.

I study my hands, trying to figure out where to begin.

Karla waits.

It had been almost five years, but I was still in a state of needing to let people know. I had the feeling that because Peter's death had forced me to start over as a new person in the world, a woman with whom I was not much familiar, I had to reintroduce people to the new me. And so like an old lady showing her scars, I told my story and told it. I could not get enough of telling it, I told it to anyone who would listen, including those who did not particularly want to.

"My son was killed," I would say, "in a hit-and-run—" sometimes I'd say "incident," sometimes leave it at "hit-and-run," learned never to say "accident," because it wasn't.

Particularity was my speciality: the irony of concrete detail, down to clothes, weather, geography, and exactly pinpointed body hits. I think I thought if I told the story often enough and in great enough detail I'd eventually come to believe, accept, *swallow* it. I think I wanted the story to become old hat and part of the past, so I could move on to better times and look back at the hard part.

People were kind. I don't know how they did it, but friends heard—waited—me out. No timetables, no instructions.

"I have never"—I am telling this now to Karla, my rapt, my *captive* audience of one—"been comfortable with 'hit-and-run accident.' That's how newspapers and most people say it. But . . ."

Retelling is like rewriting. You hone your sentences, you cull the text, you listen for inaccuracies and unnecessary phrases. The slightest misstatement nags like a twitching eye. Next time you try a new phrase, a different beginning, sharper vocabulary. You don't want to lose the story, you don't want to forget or get it wrong, you want to say *exactly* how it was. You have the feeling if you keep working at it, you will eventually get the story right and if you get the story right, you will have made it into a kind of monument to the event itself.

"I tried saying 'when Peter died.' That didn't work; it wasn't true. I finally settled on 'My son was killed in a hit-and-run incident.' "

"A car actually . . . hit him?"

"Something. Car, truck. We don't know what."

Karla blanches, asks the date it happened.

"September 4, 1984. Monday the third was Labor Day."

I can see her making calculations, thinking back: locked up in county, awaiting Danny's trial.

When Karla listens she's right there, a fierce participant. She's quiet, she's attentive, she's focused, she's latching on.

Her eyes fix hard on mine and I go on.

September 4, 1984

Labor Day was rainy that year, after a summer of drought. The grass was burned up, leaves had turned yellow, the river that runs by our house had fallen too low for drifting down in inner tubes. Ordinarily submerged rocks jutted above the surface of the water, to poke at tender tailbones and snag passing bathing suits. Shallow bends had become a trickle.

To mark the end of summer, Peter had planned a party on Labor Day afternoon, a gathering of friends to come by our house to play music, drink beer, eat chips, and swim.

Tuesday, September 4, was the first full day of classes at San Marcos High School. Peter had turned eighteen in January. He should have graduated the previous June. He hadn't. I didn't even know what grade he was officially in.

For Glenn and me, the Labor Day party was a big event. Ordinarily Peter's friends came over only when we were out of town and somebody was house-sitting, or when the house was empty. Other times he went to his friends' houses or they gathered in one of their places—the Kettle, the Sonic, the river—but he never brought his friends to our house except for short interludes, to watch television, talk on the phone, wait to go someplace else.

It is still hard to bring the two parts of his life together. As a child, Peter had seemed such a happy chunk; other people said the same thing, at the time and later. He's just, they said, so active and happy, so determinedly *normal*. When they were little, Peter's older brother, Colin, had been the serious one. Peter lived on the block, played hard, slept hard; pursued unshakable boy-boy friendships; did sports; had a life beyond the family, with his friends.

The fourth grade was his last good year. Fifth, he got in trouble with teachers, his grades went down, he started to lie. Sixth was more of the same; it kept getting worse. So what, I kept saying to myself, junior high's tough for most kids, boys especially. But Peter was starting to go too far. "He can't stop testing limits," a teacher said. "Testing authority." I tried not to get too scared. I thought, what does she know?

In 1982, after we moved from Houston to San Marcos, Peter and two friends had stolen a car—a Trans-Am with the eagle on the hood—and taken it for a day-long joy ride. They took personal possessions from inside the car, including a small cassette recorder they traded for a pizza. Peter had been arrested while eating the pizza—arrested alone, his buddies having decided it was time to split—and had spent a night in jail without revealing to the police the names of his compatriots.

There had been other, less serious but equally as disturbing infractions—with the law, at school, at home. The happy chunk of boy had become, as an adolescent, surly, dour, complicated; prone to making trouble for himself. I don't know why he stopped thinking of himself as a loved child, but there was one incident from about the time the hard part started, somewhere along about the fifth grade, that I have always remembered. I don't know that the event meant that much, really, but to me it has seemed a momentous crack in his life, dividing one piece of time from the next.

We lived in a small-town-type neighborhood in Houston called West University, a place where—then, anyway—it was possible for kids to roam and ride bikes and feel safe. It was a Saturday. Peter was out playing somewhere, then suddenly he was home, bursting through the front door calling for me. He'd hurt his arm, he said. He was sweaty and dirty and alone, his friends having scattered. Although he cradled his wrist with great tenderness, I couldn't see anything except dirt, and so I told him to go wash it. (Peter used to come to me often with small scratches, holding them out for careful examination as if they were serious wounds. When he was very small I used to kiss the scratches away, then he outgrew the kissing cure and . . . it got to be a *thing* between us. I didn't know what he wanted; Band-Aids were never enough.)

"Mom." He turned the arm over and I saw the lump. "It's broken," I told him. He stared quietly at the lump, then looked up at me. He used to have these expressions: *Big duh, Mom,* when I said something obvious. He didn't say it this time, but it was in his eyes.

I know of no job harder than being a parent. To this day, I have no idea what I did for my two boys that was constructive and useful and right and good, and what damaged them, none. It is a puzzle the whole way through, even now, when my son Colin is grown, with his own family. You never know anything, not really. You never let yourself off the hook.

We took Peter to the emergency room. After the X-rays were in, the doctor bent down to Peter's level and said, "You've already set this, haven't you?"

Sitting on the examining table in T-shirt and jeans, his long moppy hair tangled about his face, Peter nodded. Absorbed in and by his own thoughts and his arm, he said nothing.

I can't remember what he told us had happened; some pure accident, I think—tripping over a rock, some unavoidable fall. It took a while for the real story to come out. It turned out he and his friends had fashioned a rope swing, tied it to a tree, and hung it over a ditch. They were riding the swing like Tarzan from one side of the ditch to the other. When Peter took his turn—maybe he went first, I don't know—the knot came untied. (Thinking of ditches in my own hometown, when he told the story I saw him fly through the air down onto mud, dirt, grass. It took several days for me to remember, the ditches in West University had all been paved; when Peter fell he went straight down onto concrete.) Breaking his fall, he broke his wrist. Sitting there, Peter snapped the bones back in place himself.

Fearing trouble if he told the truth, his chums made up another story. It wasn't until the next night, after his arm was in a cast and we were going on with our lives, that he told about the rope swing. The wrong kind of knot. The fall. The concrete ditch bank.

I don't know what all of this signified, if anything much, but it has always seemed to me that Peter's plunge through open air was his great fall into the second part of his short life. As for his setting his own arm—I can't bear even to imagine it.

After that, the happy chunk seemed to feel star-crossed, as if he'd been tripped up by fate, the stars, time, birth sequence, the weather, whatever was not immediately within the sphere of his control.

Waking up the morning of September 3, 1984, to find Labor Day the first wet morning in months, I expected Peter's usual sour attitude of "Wouldn't you know—isn't it my luck." But that day Peter seemed uncharacteristically cheerful and able to make the best of things. His number-one running buddy, Bobby Numbrano, came over to help set up; so did one of his two girlfriends, Cindy Rodriguez. They plugged in his music machine, snapped pictures of one another, watched the rain. Other friends arrived. Danny Longoria, Arthur Contreras, Jesse "Poppo" Machado . . . girls I'd never met, whose names I never knew. Rainstorms drifted by, moved on, then returned. Low, gray clouds blanketed the sky. The air was damp as a used washrag.

The summer had been difficult. In June of that year, Peter had stolen money from Glenn, some three hundred dollars, which he did not even go to the trouble of hiding. It was not the first time this had happened.

We had given him too much, we knew that. Too much freedom, too many decisions to make on his own. Too much pure *stuff*: things, clothes. When his response was to ask for and take even more, we didn't know what to do. We tried the usual things, therapy, boarding school, hard line, soft. Like all parents whose children are in trouble, we weren't up to complicated thinking on the subject. On this issue, we were as primitive as apes.

The morning after the theft, I told Peter he had to move out. "I think," I said, "we are at the end of a road here."

"End of the rope is more like it," Peter replied.

I was used to such statements; he tortured us with them often, deepening their portent with his best dark glare. I never thought Peter would commit suicide. "It's some people's way," he told me once. "Not mine." He said it with such calm certainty —as if he were telling me he wasn't a redhead—that I believed him.

Still, I didn't—couldn't—simply kick him out. I helped him look for a place. He moved in, with, I don't know, a friend—two, a gang? That was in June.

After doing pretty well or at least *okay* for a couple of months, Peter was arrested again in August.

We got the call from Bobby Numbrano one night. Peter had pawned a stolen gun in Austin; he was in the Travis County Jail. We called our friend Jim Pape—our lawyer, Peter's lawyer—who said it would be close to impossible to spring him that late and maybe the best thing to do was wait for morning.

Pape called the next morning. He had made the arrangements; I could go pick Peter up.

August in Austin: the sun was blazing. Downtown the heat gets trapped between tall white buildings and radiates on sidewalks. Peter met me on the street corner in front of the Travis County lockup, at I-35 and Eighth Street. In his surfer shorts and a concert T-shirt, his Oakland Raiders cap bent just so, soft brown curls escaping over his ears and down his neck, his battered white leather Nikes with socks stretched up to the knees to emphasize his long straight shinbones, he looked beautiful . . . and achingly young.

He got in the car. "I need to get to work," was all he said. "I'm late."

He had a job at a local restaurant frying hamburgers, tacos, fixing stuffed baked potatoes, had had it for some eight months, his salary was up a dime or two an hour, he didn't want to lose this, at least one carryover thing he was doing well.

We headed south. By the time we got to Ben White Boulevard and the Austin city limits, his bluff had crumbled. Peter broke down and cried. Before putting him in a cell, the police had taken his shoestrings. His cellmate had to be treated for lice. The temperature was in the hundreds, and the air-conditioning in the brand-new jailhouse had been on the fritz. He told me about the smells and the screaming, the orange medicine they poured on his cellmate's shaved head. He said when the policeman instructed him to walk down a certain hall and they were telling him what a shit he was and he was trying to keep his shoes on without shoestrings, he considered breaking through a window and jumping the three stories to the sidewalk below.

"I did, Mom," he said. "I did."

It occurs to me all of a sudden how nervy this is, to be sitting there telling a woman on Death Row about the horrors of jail.

Karla gets it, and nods: go on. It is one of the first prerequisites of successful adjustment to a severely restrictive life: cut losses, don't rail against fate, don't lose the outsider's point of view. *Compared to what* is the key.

On the way to San Marcos, Peter asked to be allowed to come home. "Nothing," he said, "is being accomplished at the apartment."

I remember precisely where on Interstate 35 we were when he said "Nothing is being accomplished." We had passed Kyle and the rest area. We were approaching the Yarrington Road exit, where the Blanco River turnaround is, a place where Peter once totaled a car. Peter almost never made reflective statements. I don't think I'd ever heard him use the word "accomplish" before.

I told him I thought we could work that out and dropped him off at work. That night we talked. I told Peter he had to apologize to Glenn for stealing the money before he could move back in. Peter didn't want to, but eventually—I guess—he managed it: they talked privately; I never asked. And so, two weeks before the Labor Day party, Glenn and Peter had a tearful reunion, which shook them to their bones, they both wanted so badly to believe that things might get better.

At night, in bed, ever since I have had children, I have measured the safety of house and self by the steady sound of other people's sleeping. When those in my home breathe safely through the night, what can go wrong?

Once Peter was back, I could sleep again. If I needed to I could get up and go watch him, sprawled across his bed, arms flung to one side, head sunk down in the soft feather pillow he preferred, those long shinbones of his scissored and still. His room smelled of him long after his death. Sometimes even now I run across some leftover something and think I smell him again, and remember how my brother had that same smell when he was growing up, secret cigarettes, the teenage crazies.

In September, then, Peter was facing possible indictment by the grand jury. He had returned the gun, moved back home, enrolled in school. Pape thought that Peter would not be indicted, but. . . . My God, the legal system was the smallest part of our concern.

The day of the Labor Day party, Peter and his friends didn't come inside except to use the bathroom or to get something they needed. They set up in the garage—there were eight or ten of them, often more. They came and went. I didn't offer to fix food; I'd done that too often. They preferred quick-fix junk: generic chips, generic dip, peanut M&M's. When it came time for hot food, they went to Burger King, McDonald's, Wendy's, where friends worked, and would throw in an order of onion rings or fries, free of charge. Anyway, I had sworn off trying to fix things.

Glenn and I sat in the living room reading. I watched out the front windows as the group headed to the river for a swim in the rain. The boys wore river clothes: ratty cutoffs, torn black concert T-shirts, either rubber flip-flops or worn and beat-up athletic shoes they didn't mind getting wet. Peter's friends were all Hispanic. (The population of San Marcos High was about 65 percent Hispanic; still, it was unusual all the way around for an Anglo boy to have that many Hispanic friends.) Their dark, heavy hair swung when they walked from beneath the bandannas they had carefully folded and tied horizontally around their heads. Peter put his music machine under the overhang on the deck and played music that was old to them, Foreigner, Bad Company, Rush, Cheap Trick. I heard "Cold as Ice" rewound and replayed a number of times. Nostalgia was the theme. The end of summer, the beginning of their last year in high school.

"Peter and his bad friends," I said, looking out the window. And I laughed. Laughter was rare by then, lightness unheard of. If I hated becoming so grim and heavy where Peter was concerned, I didn't know what to do about it. That day, I don't know, maybe I thought we were coming out of the hard part. Even Glenn, whose thoughts tended to be blacker than mine, laughed a little.

For a long time, Peter had talked about these years as if they were an assignment. "It's the teenage life," he used to tell me with a shrug, when I'd badger him about smoking. When he was out of the teenage years, he had vowed, he would change. On Labor Day of that year,

I think he had the feeling that now that he had moved back in and was starting on what he swore was his last chance to finish high school, he was marking a change, having a party with his parents in the house.

I remember what we ate that night. We broiled a steak, tossed a salad, put Peter's steak in the oven so that he could eat it after his friends were gone. After dinner Glenn and I watched preseason football. The Cowboys were playing and at one point Peter stuck his head in—his mind clear, his speech normal—and asked the score. We told him Dallas was losing. He cheered; we hated the Cowboys. We reminded him that Tuesday was a school day and the party shouldn't go on much longer. Peter agreed and went back to his friends.

At ten, the game was still in progress. Peter said Cindy had to be home soon, and that since it was her mother's birthday, would I sign one of my books to her, he wanted to give her something. I signed a book, Peter showed me a funny card he'd bought, said he was going to take Cindy and the others home and he left.

Normal. Not stoned, not drunk.

"We never saw him again."

"Did he . . . do you know if he was doing drugs?"

This is Karla's standard first question when she hears of young people going off one or another kind of deep end.

"He smoked dope, drank beer. Afterwards, I asked Colin to tell me the truth about anything else, and he said Peter's crowd didn't do serious drugs, but I don't know."

Keeping her thoughts to herself, Karla nods.

When the football game was over, I wrote Peter a clever, loving note—we left lots of clever, loving notes to one another, adorned with clever, loving drawings—telling him his steak was in the oven and to sleep well. Glenn and I went to bed.

Since that night, I cannot stand not knowing the end of a story. Is it happy? Is it sad? Who dies? The end of this one is, the boy dies. The boy is killed. We are telling this story from the perspective of the future as the future re-creates, relives the past, from a time in which there is no boy anymore, the boy is dead.

Kate

It was time to go. The first guard said someone would come to let me out, but first I should go make sure the door to the visitors' center was unlocked. It wasn't. The guard came around, fiddled with keys for a long time, mumbled, fiddled, finally found one that worked.

I went back to tell Karla good-bye. From behind the wire mesh, she called out "Bye!" and waved her hand, flopping it wildly, like a child. I told her "Bye" back.

A second guard arrived. The two flanked Karla closely, escorting her down a hall to the room where she would be strip-searched.

I went out into the other room where the drink machines are.

On her way down the hall, Karla yelled "Bye!" again in a two-note singsong.

I raised my voice, yelled back, said next time I'd put quarters in my pocket. Karla said "Bye" even louder, as if I were moving off into the distance and she had to keep raising her voice.

As I opened the front door and stepped out into the hot afternoon air, we were still shouting. Then the thick metal door slammed behind me, and our first visit ended.

Our farewell reminded me of childhood visits to my grandparents—before all the arguments, when my father and his brothers were still on good terms. Driving away in the car, my brother and I used to wave out the back window until aunt, uncle, cousins, and grandparents were specks. My father would honk the horn all the way down the block and after we turned a corner headed for the boat that ferried us across the Mississippi. Even when we couldn't see people anymore, my brother and I waved.

Standing by the double fences under a sycamore tree waiting to be let out, I thrust my hands deep into my pockets to make sure I had my car keys and driver's license.

The sycamore provided little shade and no breeze at all. I wondered if anyone knew I was there. A new guard was in the tower; he did not come out of his box. The prison yard was mostly empty.

You feel so alone. You know in a thinking way that you are not going to be left there, but your heart races.

"Sorry it took so long," a very pleasant Hispanic guard said when he finally arrived, probably fifteen minutes later. "It's count time." He opened the first gate.

"Count time?" He unlocked the second.

"We count every single inmate."

I thanked him and walked through the buzzing outer gate. In the parking lot, my car was an oven. I tried to grease my lips with moisturizer; the stick had melted.

On State Highway 36, for company I turned on the news. By the time I got to Interstate 35, I had switched off the radio. I listened instead to Karla's stories once again. Saw her eyes. Heard her warm, bright voice.

Try this. Life had nothing to do with it this time. This time it was me. Making choices, taking risks. *See how you like it.*

The next morning—March 10—dawned cool and foggy; standard for March in Texas. We'd have peeled to shirtsleeves by noon.

Glenn and I had two horses then, a mare, Shatterproof, and her yearling filly, Buy the Glass. Shatterproof was in foal. Every morning, the first thing I did was look out the window to see if she had dominoed during the night.

On the morning of March 10, the horses weren't in sight. We went to the barn and found Shatterproof lying on the ground, a large yellowish mound at her tail. Behind her, the early morning sun sent soft shafts of pink through the trees. Fog from the creek drifted through the trees, the mare's warm breath made fast clouds in the air, steam rose from the mound of yellow. It was the new foal's head, wrapped in birth sac.

Glenn shut Buy the Glass out of the pen and went back to the house to call the vet. I stayed and snapped pictures (I had brought my camera, in case) and watched, encouraging Shatterproof.

The foal's head rose, then fell. Shatterproof struggled to expel the shoulders and front legs, panted, pushed, stood, walked in a circle, lay back down in a new place. I snapped pictures, pushed with Shatterproof, commiserated, crooned, and when the foal was safely out, helped pull the afterbirth off so she wouldn't keep slipping on it as she tried to stand.

When Glenn got back, it was over. "It's a girl," I told him.

The dogs hung close, waiting for a shot at the afterbirth.

Snapping pictures, I thought, Karla will love this. Karla's going to have a fit when she sees this. I wasn't taking pictures only for her. I was taking them for friends, for myself, I was taking them because it was a momentous occasion, I was taking them because I was taking them. But mostly I was taking them for Karla Faye.

When the filly had finally found her mother's bag and was sucking, when the sun was up and the tension had eased, I stood looking at the new, amazingly fit and strong creature and thought how strange life was, how unpredictably—if nothing else—*engaging*. Not fifteen hours earlier I had been on Death Row hearing of unspeakable murders, telling in turn my own story of grief and loss. Now life was reasserting itself, strong and hungry all over again.

None of it made sense. Maybe it was the sheer unlikelihood that made me feel hopeful. Next day when the film was developed, I sent the pictures to Karla.

Because the foal was sired by a horse named Ponti Bars, we named her Pontificate. A sleek sorrel filly with a white star, Kate is feisty and muscular; she's spirited, if not to say downright *mean*.

Dreams

April 4, 1989, a week before I was scheduled to make a second visit to see Karla, I had a dream.

I had gone to see her and she was in a standard movie-type cell, gray stone walls with bars, so we visited through the bars, then I went to talk to the warden and she was Karla too. We had a brief conversation; big suspicion on Karla-the-warden's part that Karla-the-prisoner was about to try to escape. I went back to the cell to ask; inmate Karla said nothing, looked inscrutable. I ate lunch in the prison cafeteria, where the food was lousy.

Next I'm home and this person is coming across the field in front of my house. It's dusk and I can't quite make out who it is, but my heart speeds up and then she's there, hair cropped blunt-short as if she'd taken scissors and chopped it. She's in a swirly-print clingy gold blouse, a tight black skirt, and flimsy shoes, a small purse over her shoulder . . . whorish but plenty cute. I can't believe she has made it out, I'm thrilled she has come to see *me,* and I am afraid. She on the other hand is completely nonchalant—as if this happened every day.

We talk. When a car comes down the road, she takes off. Watching her go, for a flashing moment I become her—think her thoughts, feel what she is feeling, understand her reasons: *I won't be out long, I know they'll catch me, meantime I have this and it's worth the risk.* I wonder how much time they will add to her sentence for escaping and why if she was going to cut her hair for a disguise she did not dye it too, say, blond. I also know where she is headed, to Houston to see her mother.

When nothing else happens, I assume she is okay. But I am worried. The dream is filled with suspense, like a chase movie.

Blurry scenes. Questioned by the warden, I say I haven't seen Karla. I worry more; wonder if she has any money; go at myself for not thinking to offer any.

Time, a big pause, and I am in the town where I grew up. Karla's there and I'm showing her around; we go to the Dairy Queen. I ask if she saw her mother in Houston, she says yes, and I am filled with admiration to think what a clever girl she is, to go exactly where authorities expect and not get caught. I drive her around, take her past a house I used to live in, it's nighttime or at any rate dark. I am both scared and excited by the danger.

At some point we change places and I become the one trying to escape. Not being as canny as Karla, I am immediately captured. They take away my blouse and tight skirt. I am dressed in only a white cotton slip and ballerina slippers. I look down at my legs and I have skinny calves, Karla's calves. It has happened, I have become her. I don't mind being taken back to prison, it's part of the game. Being of prison mentality now, I have this feeling of great smugness, as if to say, "Well, at least I got to see my mother."

The next scene is of my own mother in bed in a nursing home. She's wearing a lavender nightgown and she has very large, swingy breasts. She seems druggy and confused. Her nursing home colleagues are trying to get her to eat. Somehow I have the sense of her drunkenly swaying, even in the bed. My position is above her, to the left of her head; I am looking down on all of this, wishing she would get out of this place and get well. She wants to get up and go with me. I take her by the hand and she starts to get up to go. She looks very determined, the way Karla did in the beginning of the dream, and I want very much to help her but it's hard and I'm not sure I can do it . . . and that is all.

I did not quite know what to do with the dream except write it down, share it with Karla. She wrote back and said she thought it was *neat*.

My mother's death in 1982 had been quite as sudden and un-expected—she was sixty-three—as my father's, in the summer of 1988, had been long and lingering, from alcoholism and complications connected to diabetes. It was he who had been confined to a nursing home, where in his last days he refused to eat anything except corn-flakes sogged up with milk and sugar, which I spoon-fed him. After a time he refused even the cornflakes. He only wanted milk thick with sugar.

When I am writing fiction, dreams come to tell me when I have something wrong. About character, motivation, vision, pure thinking. I always pay attention.

In the months following Peter's death, I dreamed about him all the time. Mostly he was alive in the dreams. The ones about him dead were nightmares, especially those about the mechanics of death, the gradual disposition of the flesh, what time had done to the physical shell of him. From those I awoke in breathless horror. Others were a sweet treat, as if Peter himself had dashed over from the other side to say hello.

In one, I had gone to a sideshow that promised a glimpse of heaven—actual heaven—inside a carnival tent. The barker said Virginia Woolf would appear. He pointed to a picture of her writing desk on the side of the tent. Vita Sackville-West might come too. *Virginia Woolf?* I bought a ticket, went in. There were bleachers, I took a seat up high.

It was heaven, all right, but in place of writers, an ethereal baseball game was going on. Peter was playing the outfield. His soft curls inched out of his cap—bill folded just so, as in life—and he stood in a half-squat, awaiting the ball, yelling encouragement to the pitcher, and he was not surly and shut down as he had become those last years in real life, but happy, wide open to life, and beautiful. He looked at me once. I wasn't sure he saw me. I called out to him but he did not respond. When the game was over I went to the place in the stands above the tunnel leading into the locker room. The team filed by. I watched Peter walk by beneath me without trying to make contact, as by then I knew he could not. He disappeared beneath the stands, making small talk with his teammates.

I woke up from the dream feeling refreshed and lucky. He had looked so calm, so peaceful; beautiful, like a real angel.

In the dream about Karla, was she my mother, was she Peter, was I trying to save her life, rescue her from prison, *become* her? Or what?

When I told a sociologist friend whose field of expertise is criminology and deviant behavior that I was going to make a second visit to see Karla, she looked surprised. She understood making the first trip, "but why," she asked point blank, "are you going *back?*"

I told the Karla dream to a psychiatrist, also a friend. He said the dream indicated unresolved issues concerning my mother and a great deal of ambivalence on my part about going to Gatesville. "You may not have gone there *as* a writer," he warned me, "but you certainly went because you are. Maybe you need to get clear with yourself not so much why you went in the first place but why you are going *back.*"

That was Sunday, April 9. By Monday the tenth, the night before I was scheduled to visit Karla, I had made up my mind to call in the morning and cancel. *You do not have to go,* I said to myself. *No one will lower your grade.* Too many times in my life, I told myself, I had let events and plans catch fire on their own. Surely by now I was up to doing a little research and plain hard thinking. Possibly I should make lists: reasons to go on one side, reasons not to on the other. Wasn't isolating the variables as a route to making decisions an important part of becoming a grown-up?

It was too late for lists. While I am not a wildly impulsive person, and often take a tediously long time before acting, once a decision has lost its dust and come clear in my mind, I don't question the sense of it or make lists. Don't pause, don't think, just go. I'm out there by then. I can see myself on the move, as if I were somebody else.

Good sense and the variables said to wait. Tuesday morning I set off, due north up I-35. As if for a reward, fields of bluebonnets carpeted my way. After I turned west on Highway 36 at Temple, new wildflowers appeared, kinds which do not grow in my part of the state. There was a white cup-shaped one something like a poppy but not. I had never seen one before and have not since.

Halfway between Temple and Gatesville, I had a conversation with myself. *All right, Beverly. If this is about your mother, then this time get it right. Don't flutter. Be there. Let her live her life through you if she needs to; you can afford to be generous.*

When I walked into the visitors' center, Karla Faye was at her same window, looking toward the door she knew I'd come through.

I jingled my pockets. "Quarters."

Karla said she'd been thinking about a Strawberry Crush all morning.

Weak with relief, thinking how close I'd come to disappointing her, I went out to the drink machine.

She had curled her hair. It was looped in fat waves and piled on top of her head in a fancy arrangement—I was certain especially for today. Her skin was several shades darker and she had curled her hair.

I bought myself a full-fledged sugar-sweetened drink, handed the guard Karla's Strawberry Crush, commented on Karla's hairdo, and asked if maybe she'd been on a Caribbean cruise.

Karla threw back her head and laughed. "I've been taking sun baths," she said. "We're all getting tan."

Toward the end of the visit, I made my commitment. I told Karla Faye that unless some unshakable something came up, I would visit her once a month; that way she could relax and not waste time wondering if and when I'd come back, and I wouldn't sit around wondering whether I should go, and if so, why and when.

We talked through red lips on the Plexiglas. Somebody before us had kissed hello or good-bye from my side. Sometimes the kiss was on Karla's cheek, sometimes over her eye.

We have our rituals now. When we say good-bye, we press our palms against the Plexiglas until our fingers turn white, then pull back and cross our arms over our chests and, holding tight to our own shoulders, rock back and forth, hugging ourselves as a substitute for one another.

II / Caney Creek

They say you're the center of the wheel. Everybody else is spokes. They say you're number one.

—DOUGLAS GARRETT, 1983

They got nothing, Doug. No fingerprints, nothing.

—DANNY GARRETT, 1983

Danny and Karla were proud of theirself. . . . She didn't act remorse. . . . They were giggling and smiling and saying they were famous. . . . We were scared for our lives.

—KARI TUCKER GARRETT, 1984

They're just digging. They ain't got shit. . . . They want to know any more about this, they can call our lawyer.

—KARLA FAYE TUCKER, 1983

Locked Up

In the five weeks' time between the weekend of June 11, 1983, when they got overamped and went over and made a mess of Jerry Lynn Dean and Deborah Thornton, and July 20, 1983, when they were arrested, Karla Faye and Danny Garrett did a lot of boasting and bragging and throwing their weight around.

In those five weeks Karla and Danny were going around saying that since they had gotten away with murder, they might just have to off somebody else. They hadn't yet decided who that would be, but they mentioned some possibilities. Homicide detectives coming around cut no ice with Karla. Karla agreed to be fingerprinted, she even said she'd take a polygraph test until Danny called up and said, "Are you crazy?" after which she told the Houston Police Department she'd changed her mind, her lawyer said she shouldn't. Karla didn't care, she was in charge of her own self now; anyway, the police didn't have anything, they were just digging.

What Karla and Danny did not know and probably would not have believed if someone had spelled it out was that on the night of Sunday, July 17, and into the next morning, in the hours Kari Burrell refers to as the "wee hours of the morning when after midnight it goes Monday," Douglas Garrett and Kari Burrell were making a decision. High-strung Kari was getting more and more nervous. Homicide had been asking questions; they had shown Douglas and Kari pictures of the bodies—Jerry Dean hacked up, Deborah Thornton with a pickax in her chest—and Danny was talking about finding a way to off other people who knew about the murders, like Jimmy Leibrant and Ronnie Burrell. It was getting too close and too weird, in addition to which both Kari and Doug had played a part in the crime, had known about the murders from the beginning, had helped their sister and brother wipe down and hide stolen goods. Douglas was going around with a .38 in his robe pocket. Douglas had had this dream, people with guns, closing in.

In the middle of the night, in the wee hours after midnight when Sunday goes Monday, Kari Burrell and Douglas Garrett decided to put a stop to the whole thing by turning their sister and brother in.

Monday, July 18, HPD homicide detective J.C. Mosier gets a phone call from a person he describes on the official police report as "a personal C.I. who I have used many times." According to the police report, the confidential informant tells J.C. that a mutual friend of theirs needs to talk. J.C. asks the C.I. who the friend is, the C.I. says Douglas Garrett and . . . however all of this actually went, the upshot is that eventually Douglas informs J.C. Mosier that his friend and Douglas's brother, Danny, was involved in the pickax murders. Involved how? J.C. asks. Well, says Douglas, he committed them.

That was when J.C. Mosier said, "He did *what?*"

Douglas Garrett said he was ready to tell all, but J.C. had to proceed with care; after all, the pickax murders were not his case. When Douglas balked at talking to anybody except J.C., however, they set it up. J.C. told Doug to bring Kari and they met, for two hours or so. J.C. Mosier says he has never seen two scareder people in his life.

On the afternoon of July 20, Lieutenant Kenneth Rodgers of the Special Crimes Bureau of the Houston Police Department wired Douglas Garrett up, explaining as he went how the equipment worked: a tiny reel-to-reel Nagra tape recorder was placed in Douglas's boot, a transmitter taped to his chest so that police officers could monitor his conversation. Meantime, J.C. Mosier coached Douglas on his performance. He told Douglas how to act (be casual, act natural, make small talk), what information to get (intent to murder, intent to steal, Karla getting off), what to say in case he got into trouble and needed to be rescued.

Mostly he advised Douglas Garrett to keep his mouth shut. "Let the people talk," J.C. Mosier told him. "We want to hear them talk . . . just be quiet. I want to hear what they have to say." Or as he described it during Danny Garrett's trial: "Our best hope was . . . that he went in, conversation ensued, words spoken, he leaves and then, warrant executed."

According to Sergeant Ted Thomas, one of the homicide officers assigned to investigate the murders of Jerry Dean and Deborah Thornton, "this was a really complex case. There were a lot of suspects, as many from the girl's side [Thornton's] as the man's [Dean's]. We didn't know where it was going to end up. And you know, we never know if a case is going to break. We just keep following leads. Then one day there it is."

With the reel-to-reel in his boot and the transmitter taped to his chest, Douglas Garrett rode his motorcycle from his garage apartment on Fairway Street in southeast Houston to 2205 McKean Street in northwest Houston off the Katy Freeway, close to where 290 crosses Loop 610, a distance of some 23.7 miles. To conceal the wires, Douglas wore a long-sleeved black shirt.

When, a little before 5:00 P.M., Douglas walked in the front door at 2205 McKean, three people sitting on the living-room couch greeted him. The first question Douglas was asked was why he was wearing a long-sleeved shirt on a hot July day. Douglas got himself off the hook by saying it was the only clean shirt he had. Then he asked if there was anything to smoke or drink.

No smoke. Douglas allows as how the city's gone bone *dry*.

Within blocks of that conversation, inside an unmarked police van parked along a side street, HPD officers hover over a transmitter, listening, waiting. If Douglas Garrett says "Jesus Christ," it means he is in trouble.

Ted Thomas was listening that day; so was homicide detective James Ladd. Thomas and his partner, William Owens, had been assigned to the Deborah Thornton side of the murder case; Ladd and his partner, Carolyn Newman, to the Jerry Lynn Dean side. And so Ladd and Newman had been putting the pressure on Karla and Danny. Because of her well-known antipathy to Dean, Karla was a suspect before Danny. During the week before the arrest, Jim Ladd and Carolyn Newman had been going by the McKean Street house every day. But until Douglas Garrett called J.C. Mosier, the case was wide open. As suspects, Karla and Danny weren't any hotter than some others; in fact in the beginning there were more suspects from Deborah Thornton's side. Thornton's father, William List, was a well-known wealthy homosexual who made a practice of picking up young boys in Houston and taking them to his huge, ugly Seabrook home to work for him and do no telling what else. Both Deborah Thornton and her brother had changed their last names to cut themselves off from their father. List also had a questionable reputation in his professional life. At the time of her murder, Deborah Thornton was set to testify against her father at an IRS hearing. As she was the only person with the information to blow the lid off her father's shady activities, there was plenty of reason to examine Deborah Thornton's side of the case with a fine-tooth comb. (During Danny Garrett's trial, William List was ambushed and killed in the hallway of his home by four young boys he had picked up and taken home with him.)

J.C. Mosier was listening to the conversation going on at 2205 McKean; so were Kenneth Rodgers and another officer from Special Crimes; Assistant D.A. Ted Wilson; Carolyn Newman; Thomas's partner, William Owens; and four uniformed patrolmen.

Probable-cause warrants had been prepared and signed for the arrest of Karla and Danny. Everything depended on Douglas Garrett.

Ronnie Burrell is on the living-room couch when Douglas enters; so are Marla Leibrant, Jimmy Leibrant's sister, and, as Douglas says, "a girl named Cookie who I don't know her last name." Cookie turns out to be Ronnie's current girlfriend, Mary Lou Moore. Douglas jaws with the trio a bit; Ronnie says Doug should take a beer from the sack on the floor there. Ronnie had been mad at Douglas for losing his temper and kicking Ronnie's bedroom door in, but the offer of a beer makes Douglas think Ronnie has gotten past the door incident. He grabs a beer.

After not much time, Douglas wanders into the bedroom to talk to Danny and Karla.

There was a lot of talk during and after the trials about what favors Douglas Garrett might have been granted in order to convince him to wear a wire and secretly tape his brother's confession. To most of us, turning in your kin is one thing (you can come up with reasons for that, stark fear for one), but to actually record a damning confession while pretending to have a friendly conversation quite another. Douglas and the police of course say no deals were made, but the fact remains that Douglas had helped Karla and Danny store goods stolen from Jerry Dean, and he might also have helped them get rid of stolen property, and yet Douglas was not read his rights and was never arrested. Douglas had a police record: a number of felony arrests, no indictments. The "personal C.I." whom J.C. Mosier had used many times might in fact have been Douglas himself. July 20 might not have been Douglas's first time out as a confidential informant.

When Douglas walks in in his black, long-sleeved shirt, Karla and Danny are lying on their bed not doing much of anything. Danny has to be at work at six-thirty. Karla's eating pills. In the bedroom Doug acts natural, he's low-key, he makes small talk about Ronnie offering him the beer, he listens. When the time is right he zeroes in on the subject at hand, with the grace and pure undistractable focus of a purple martin swooping up a mosquito.

"I been wondering. Did y'all go over there with it in mind to kill them people? . . . Were them people asleep? . . . Did you wake them up?" His voice flat, his accent nasal-twangy. Pure Texas.

Answering his brother's questions, Danny Garrett holds nothing back. "It was a freak thing," he says. "It happened. . . . We freaked out. We just freaked out." Between eating pills neither does Karla. "It was there," she says, explaining why they used the pickax. "It was there." When Douglas says detectives have been coming by to question him and Kari, Danny cautions him to stay cool. "What the lawyer told us," he warns, "is, it's just like a fish. You open your mouth, they set the hook."

Karla and Danny do not hesitate before answering Doug's questions, they have nothing to hide from Doug, they've already told him they're the pickax killers, and besides, as Doug assures Danny on the tape, "You know I'm your brother and I'll take care of you."

Jimmy Leibrant was not at 2205 McKean when Douglas Garrett arrived that day. Jimmy hadn't been seen for days, who knew where Jimmy was, Douglas Garrett didn't even know Jimmy Leibrant's last name. Jim Ladd thought that Jimmy Leibrant might already have been murdered by Karla and Danny by then; after all, Karla Faye and Danny had been talking about offing other people, so why not their accomplice? But on July 20, 1983, between five and six P.M., while Douglas was in the bedroom talking to Danny and Karla, Jimmy Leibrant inadvertently—amazingly—showed up.

The C.I. is ready. "There's your eyewitness," Douglas casually observes. "In the other room."

Flurry in the police van. Nobody dreamed Jimmy Leibrant would fall into their laps. Ted Wilson turns his attention to the task of trying to get a warrant signed for Leibrant's arrest.

All this is going on within blocks of 2205 McKean, which nobody in the house knows except Douglas. Danny and Karla believe this is just a normal everyday conversation. Maybe it seems strange that Douglas keeps asking pointed questions about the murders, but then Douglas is in a state. The police have been nagging him, Kari is terrified, she doesn't take stress well, in a lot of ways she's a fragile girl; plus Douglas has had this dream, people with guns coming to get him, the guns going off out on Telephone Road, the shots getting closer and closer until he, in the dream, finds himself hunkered down by the window expecting to be shot.

In the bedroom, Douglas tells Karla and Danny the dream. "It was so real," he says, and his voice trembles and soon he is weeping. Douglas is a strange man, known to be hair-triggered, to fly off the handle from time to time, to go a little funny. He has even spent time in a mental institution. Karla Faye and Danny are not talking about murder at this point, they're not even bragging. They are trying to calm Douglas down.

"They got nothing, Doug," Danny keeps assuring his brother. "Nothing."

"They're just digging," Karla reiterates. "They ain't got shit."

When she speaks up loud enough and enunciates clearly enough to be understood, on the tape Karla sounds chillingly hard and tough, with a bone-hard Texas accent. She is cold and unfeeling, nothing at all like the girl she is today.

Listening, you have to wonder, so where *were* her feelings in those days—lost, buried, or what?

When Douglas gets to the end of telling his dream—"right out on Telephone Road," he keeps saying, the guns were right out there, getting closer—and says, "It was so real," there is a pause, and then Danny says, "Time. Time will take care of it." And Danny's voice is so quiet, scary, and cold it takes your breath: like dry ice, smoky and cold at the same time; touch it, your skin peels away. It is at that moment that it becomes clear why a jury would think perhaps it was not in a community's best interest to offer this man mercy. You know why jurors had more feeling for Douglas, even though he signed his own brother's death warrant, than they did for Danny and Karla.

While Danny showers and gets ready for work—he is going to be late but that doesn't matter; he is going to have to leave work as soon as things settle down anyway, probably some time after midnight, to drive to Austin and testify before the Texas Alcohol Board of Control the next morning—Karla walks Douglas outside to his motorcycle.

Douglas is upset, is why Karla walks out to his Harley with him. She wants to comfort him. As Douglas Garrett gets on his bike, Karla rubs and pats his wide, muscular back—warm and damp beneath the long-sleeved shirt.

It is past six. Douglas has been in the house an hour and fifteen minutes. After Doug roars off on his motorcycle, Karla goes back in the house. Danny gets dressed.

In the HPD vans and cars, policemen and detectives gear up. The case has been broken. It's time.

Jimmy Leibrant left the McKean Street house in his sister Marla's tan Ford Pinto before police had a chance to get the warrant ready. Then—incredibly—just after Douglas's departure, the tan Pinto returns. Jimmy gets out, goes in the house, comes back out. Nobody in the house much notices. People are always coming and going. Certainly the police take note. Jimmy gets back in the Pinto, drives north on McKean to Emnora, turns into the parking lot of a storage shed, where you rent small storage rooms by the month. Jimmy is going to a party, but first he has to get something. When Jimmy Leibrant looks up from unlocking the padlock, he finds himself surrounded: police cars, and homicide detectives, special crimes detectives, and patrolmen, their guns drawn.

At 6:30 P.M. on July 20, 1983, in the parking lot of the storage shed at Emnora and McKean, Jimmy Leibrant is read his rights and arrested. The person in the Pinto with him, a girl, is hauled in to police headquarters as well.

Meantime, inside 2205 McKean, not a clue. Danny Garrett backs up his blue Ranchero and drives north on McKean to Emnora, headed for work. By then, Jimmy Leibrant is in custody. At Emnora—the same corner where HPD popped Jimmy Leibrant—Danny Garrett comes face-to-face with an army of police cars and—emerging from one of the cars—his old friend J.C. Mosier, gun drawn, reciting Miranda. It is 6:44.

You have to wonder: When he saw the squadron of police cars, did Danny Garrett know that it was his brother who had turned him in; that it had to have been; that all those questions Douglas was asking in the bedroom had a purpose, not to mention listeners? Or was Danny Garrett still in a high state of bluff, thinking, *They won't catch me, not me; they've got nothing, they're just trying one?*

Danny Garrett offered no resistance when he was arrested. J.C. Mosier says when he came to the window of his car and told him he was under arrest for capital murder, Danny turned to him and said, "J.C., you think I'd do a thing like that?" When J.C. told him to get out of his car, Danny shrugged and said, "Well, I didn't want to go to Austin anyway."

J.C. Mosier snorts in disgust. "Arrested for murder and all he's got to say is 'I didn't want to go to Austin anyway.'"

J.C. says he had no problem arresting a friend. "Professionally?" he says. "No. I had a problem with the fact that he'd done it."

Nobody inside the McKean house knew that within blocks of the house, arrests were being made. Once Jimmy Leibrant and the Garrett brothers left, the people inside the house went on about their business, the business about which they seemed to have been more serious than any other: sitting around pal to pal and buddy to buddy in endless, bragadocious, and very manly congregation. Beer, drugs. Talk was only talk. Congregation was everything.

Ronnie Burrell is on the living-room couch with Jimmy Leibrant's sister, Marla, and the girl called Cookie. Ronnie is at one end of the couch, the girls side by side. They are drinking beer and watching television. In all the testimony and stories, the primary setting for action in the McKean Street house seems to be the living-room couch. People smoke dope on the couch, get wired on the couch, shoot up on the couch, have sex on it. Danny Garrett got in trouble with Kari Burrell on the couch. Ronnie Burrell appears to have set up permanent residence there.

When Karla went out to tell Danny good-bye, she left the front door ajar. There is no need to lock it, people are always in and out. Karla Faye walks through the living room, past Ronnie and the two women, into the kitchen to get something to eat. She had shut Tooter up in the bedroom.

From the refrigerator she takes a piece of leftover fried fish and some ketchup. She is sitting on the couch eating when Ronnie all of a sudden goes to the front window. She doesn't know why; maybe he suspects something. At the window, Ronnie opens the curtain. "Whose van is that?" he asks.

Karla goes to look. There is this big, dark van parked across the driveway, blocking it, but Karla doesn't think anything, maybe somebody having car trouble; she goes on eating. They are all going to a birthday party later on. They have this giant chocolate-chip cookie for a birthday cake. The cookie is on the table. It is about the size of a medium pizza.

The dramatic moment has arrived, time to dance the pas de deux, sing the aria, and here Karla is on the couch eating fish with her hands; her last minute of freedom and there she is in her spaghetti-strap tube-knit T-shirt, snakeskin cowboy boots, and blue jeans, dipping fried fish in ketchup. It's one of those times: afterwards you wonder what happened to the cookie and did anybody go to the party and who took care of the dog.

Standing at the front window looking at the van blocking their drive, all of a sudden Ronnie Burrell gets it. "It's the fuckin' law," Ronnie says, which he probably figured out from having been busted all those times. And Ronnie takes off out of the living room and down the hall toward the bedrooms so fast it would make your head swim. Wasn't dressed in anything but a bathrobe. Went to the back bedroom, opened up the window and . . . jumped out. Just jumped out. In his robe.

Quite naturally, HPD was out there too. Brought him back in

laughing their heads off. "Hey," they said, "this dude's near-bout *nekkid.*"

The front door is open. From all the times he's interviewed her, Jimmy Ladd recognizes Karla standing in the hallway by the living room holding a plate of food. Ronnie's out the back window by then; the other two girls are on the couch. Guns drawn, police push the door open—"Police! Don't move!"—and everybody starts screaming, yelling, policemen all over the house, everybody afraid of getting shot. Tooter is shut up in the bedroom barking her head off and one of the policemen is shouting, "Will this goddamn dog bite?" and Marla's saying, "Don't shoot the dog, please don't shoot the dog," and Cookie is saying, "I'll take Tooter outside, please don't shoot the dog," because they both know if the police open the bedroom door and storm in, Tooter will attack and they will kill her. The next thing Karla knows she's face-down against the wall and ketchup and fish are flying all over the place and there's a big gun at her temple.

Karla shakes her head. "I see these television shows where people get arrested and it's embarrassing, you know? Because it happens just like that. I don't know, ketchup all over the place. They kicked my feet apart, patted me down, and . . ." She shakes her head and laughs.

On the tape Douglas keeps reminding Karla and Danny that the police have been by his house asking questions. "They say you're the center of the wheel," he says. "Everybody else is spokes. They say you're number one." And over and over, Karla and Danny try to calm Douglas's fears. "They got nothing, Doug. . . . They're just digging. They ain't got shit."

I ask Karla if she knew what the police were arresting her for that day.

"I didn't know nothing," she answers, "except for that gun." She cocks her thumb, sticks the point of her index finger at her temple.

Karla didn't think the police had anything, really; she believed, as she said on the tape, that they were just digging—even when they arrested her. Besides, she was loaded. (At one point in the tape you can hear her shaking pills out of a bottle.) And when she was loaded, which was all of the time back then, she was wire-tough and snappy, cold and smug. Karla Faye didn't find out that Douglas had a reel-to-reel in his boot and a transmitter taped to his chest that day in the bedroom when he asked all the questions—"Tell me something, Karla, is it true you got sexual gratification?"—until almost a month later when she went in for her pretrial hearing. She walked into the room and there stood her accusers, Douglas and her sister Kari. When things got under way, Karla learned what had gone down about the tape and all.

July in Houston it's still boiling hot at six o'clock, with as much daylight left in the sky as at noon.

Everyone in the McKean Street house was taken in that night, including Ronnie Burrell, Marla Leibrant, and Mary Lou "Cookie" Moore.

At 9:04 P.M. on July 20, Jimmy Leibrant began making a seven-page statement to Houston homicide detective James W. Ladd. "Let's do it," he said, like Gary Gilmore out in Utah before he was shot. Still hot. July in Houston it's hot until midnight.

9:55 P.M. Ronnie Burrell made a statement about how Danny Garrett came home early on the morning of June 13 asking Ronnie to help him with the motorcycle frame and parts and the El Camino, and how they drove to Doug's apartment on Fairway and threw Danny's gloves out the window on the way. Said he helped pawn the shotgun Danny took to Windtree that night; helped Jimmy Leibrant burn the serial numbers off the stolen Harley frame.

Around that same time, Marla Leibrant was still holding out. Marla told police she had never seen Karla angry in her life and that Karla, Danny, and her brother, Jimmy, could not and would not have committed the murders. She also said that in her opinion Ronnie Burrell was not very smart.

At 10:00 P.M., Karla asks to talk to Ted Thomas alone, and says if he will let her go to the bathroom—her stomach was acting up, her usual diarrhea—and have a smoke, she will tell him everything. Ted Thomas agrees. When Karla finally comes out of the bathroom, all she will say is that she got loaded the night of June 12 and could not remember a thing, but that Jimmy Leibrant had told her she went crazy. When Ted Thomas asks Karla what "crazy" means, she says when she shoots up she gets crazy, then doesn't remember a thing, and Jimmy Leibrant had said nothing else except she went crazy. One time she shot up and went so crazy she tried to choke her sister. Didn't remember a thing about that, either.

When he tells this story now, Ted Thomas chuckles at the ruse Karla pulled, promising to tell all in order to go to the bathroom. He inquires about Karla's health. "She had stomach problems," he says.

At 11:45 P.M., July 20, 1983, Danny and Karla are locked up in the Harris County Jail. Since that night, Karla and Danny have never not been in custody. They have been out of jail only for court dates and to see about medical problems. When Karla is taken off the prison grounds to see a doctor she is shackled hand to foot.

"If we could have pled guilty in exchange for a life sentence," says Mack Arnold, one of Karla's two court-appointed attorneys, "I'd have advised her to take it. Like a shot."

"We had so little," says the other attorney, Henry Oncken. "They had color pictures, a videotape. . . ." He lifts his hand from the table—we are sitting in his very comfortable home in Spring, Texas, north of Houston—as if to brush the memory away. "And the tape." He shakes his head slightly. Henry Oncken is a superbly controlled man, a man ill at ease with any undue show of emotion. And so when he makes that slight movement of his head and looks up at you with those sad, pale eyes, it's memorable. "Our only chance to save her life," he goes on, "was to try to humanize her. And the only way we could do that was to let her tell her story."

Henry Oncken's blue eyes fill with the kind of sorrow and frustration that settles in for good once you've done your best to help improve a situation and it wasn't even close to being enough.

Mother

"I don't think any of this"—Karla gestures, waving her hand in the direction of the barred windows behind her head—"would have happened if my mother hadn't died."

Surprised at her own words—she does not like even to give the appearance of excusing or justifying what she has done—she hesitates, leans closer.

"Not that I blame Mother, I don't blame nobody but myself, but when she died, I don't know . . ." Her voice drifts off.

"She died when I was twenty and I don't know, it changed me. I turned stone cold to the world."

I ask if Mountain View has a resident psychiatrist who might help her explore this kind of speculation.

She snaps to. "Sure," she says, "but we've got a little Peyton Place out here, you know. Word gets around fast. You ask to see the psychiatrist, it gets reported. Anyway . . ." She waves the thought away. "I saw a psychiatrist in County; I knew then it wasn't for me. If I was going to talk to anybody I'd rather it be my chaplain."

Karla Faye sits with her eyes down for a few seconds, but when she raises them to meet mine, they are clear. She is in no way backing down from her statement about the effect her mother's death had on her. She just hadn't been quite prepared to hear herself say it.

"She had hepatitis three times. The last time she died. It was a horrible, painful death. And I don't know . . ."

I already knew a fair amount about Karla's mother. Jackie Oncken had told me some things. The *Houston Chronicle* story had told of Karla Faye's early life with a prostitute mother. Up to this moment, no one had had a kind word for Carolyn Moore.

Karla hesitates.

"I idolized my mother something fierce. I don't think I can put into words how her death affected me back then, but I'm sure you know what I'm talking about because of how Peter's death hit you. It's like it took a link out that can never be replaced."

When two years after Peter's death I decided to quit going to the therapist I had been seeing twice a week since right after the funeral, I had no illusions of being cured. By then I could at least breathe, drive, make my way through the day. I was tired of talking about myself; it was time to move on. Which was an admission of defeat, in a way. I was terminating a particular process of discovery because I knew I would never be much better.

"She died on Christmas Eve, 1979. My whole life was shattered that day. The pain comes and goes now, but the guilt is there to stay."

Carolyn at 17

The earliest picture I have of Karla's mother is a black-and-white snapshot, on the reverse side of which someone has written, "Carolyn at 17."

Someone? The hand is old-fashioned, careful. A woman's hand. Who but an adoring mother would make such a record, who else but Carolyn Moore's mother, Zelda Donaldson, the woman Karla calls Granny B.?

Carolyn Moore was born in Houston in October 1936. An only child, she grew up in Houston. So did the first man she would marry, Lawrence Earl Tucker, also an only child. Houston was barely a hundred years old in 1936. Just starting. Even in 1963, when my husband and I were living in the East and he was trying to get back to Texas and we asked people which city to move to, "Dallas" was the solidly unchanging answer. Houston was a big cow patty of a town, we were told, hopeful but . . . There was no city there really, no real cultural life, just a lot of people, a lot of guff; the ship channel, the oil industry, the fat stock show. A lot of flat, flat land. It was still a reclaimed swamp, we were reminded. A city that started out as a bright idea in the back of a couple of hawksters' cunning minds, it hadn't gotten much beyond that.

Studying the writing on the back of the black-and-white snapshot, I imagine Granny B. penning the caption as soon as the picture was developed, so as not to forget how old. After all, Carolyn Moore was the only child Granny B. would have. It was important to keep records.

I was born two years after Carolyn Moore, in 1938, in Memphis, Tennessee—my very young mother's first child, the daughter she longed for, a girl whose life would be, if she by God had anything to say about it, better than her own. My mother recorded date, age, and occasion on the backs of photographs of me, just like Granny B.: "Bev takes a step," "Bev at 2."

My first year of school, my mother polished my white high-top shoes every night. Every morning she curled my hair. Every night she ironed my dress. I was my mother's hope for her own future— I always knew that—and so she kept meticulous records. In my baby book she wrote in the first person, as if . . . either she and I were one, or I was a made-up character she was creating:

"I started shaking my head for no-no when I was eight months old. I patty caked when I was 10 months old. I have a pink teddy bear. I tore his legs and arms off and I still love him. . . . I love water. . . . Mother tells me I'm going to have a baby sister soon. She talks about Susie and I want to know where Susie is. . . ."

Susie always turned out to be a boy.

I don't remember ever calling her Mother. She was always Mama to me and my brothers. Her real name was Dora Lee, which she hated. Everybody called her Henry, which she spelled "Henri," liking the fancifulness—the Frenchiness—of the *i*. Henry was short for Henrietta, a nickname my father picked up from the "Andy Gump" comic strip.

My mother liked to do things she thought of as *different:* be called by a man's name she spelled the French way, fix curry when nobody in town had heard of it, spray the Christmas tree pink before anybody else ever dreamed of spray-painting a Christmas tree. After the tree was pink, she stepped back and admired her work, jaw clenched, as if to say, "That'll show them."

After my mother died we found notebooks, meant obviously for us to read after she was dead. In the notebooks she left a record of how it was when each of her three children was born. What time of day or night, how it went. In my section, my mother revealed the fact that she had named me for a debutante whose picture she saw in the Sunday Memphis *Commercial Appeal* the week I was born. "Beverly": it was different. Hopeful.

1954. Carolyn at 17—a slim, very attractive girl—is sitting on the front steps of a sturdy brick house in a summer dress. The sun is in her eyes. Her arms are bare. The fabric of the dress is medium-dark and gauzy and the dress has a full skirt which comes to the middle of her slim calves. The girl sits on the second of three concrete steps with some confidence, her left foot on the sidewalk, right one tucked under the left knee, hidden in folds of skirt. Carolyn Moore's spine is straight, her shoulders back. She has rocked her left heel so that her weight rests on the very tip of her leather shoe. Her hands are folded. The dress, tightly belted, has a shallow V-neckline with a wide white choirboy collar. There's a floppy bow at the center of the collar. The look is that of a 1950s Christian Dior knockoff: wide shoulders, slim waist, soft, full skirt.

Carolyn Moore wears the dress well. She holds herself well. Her leather pumps have sensible heels—not spikes but not old-lady-nurse heels either; something in between, the kind of shoes we wore when we were sixteen or seventeen and it was 1954, the kind we could manage to get around in and still feel smart and snappy. There's a bracelet on her right wrist, around her neck a chain with something at the end, maybe a cross or a locket. Cluster earrings; short, dark-blond hair brushed behind her ears; a clean and open face, young, clear, and she's smiling. Her teeth are large and slightly irregular. They might be ever so gently bucked, or she could be overcompensating for an underbite. Her eyebrows are carefully arched, her lips brightly colored, but then of course it is 1954—they would be.

She knows what she's doing, Carolyn at 17. How to sit, what to do with her hands. There's a dancerly grace and rightness to the line of her, from shoulders to toe, the way she has positively *arranged* herself on the steps. She looks loose-hipped and sure, the all-out kind of girl who could walk on out and down that sidewalk taking whatever kind of steps she by God felt like; there is something open-jointed and decidedly unsouthern about her. She's a Texas girl, all right.

Still, Carolyn at 17 exemplifies what we all did back then, arch our eyebrows, sit—we hoped—like Suzy Parker, darken our lips. We dressed like if not old then middle-aged ladies—girdle, stockings, leather pumps—and we carried old-lady purses. We didn't learn to dress young until we were up in our twenties and had a couple of kids. By then the tone of life in America had changed and we who had grown up in the fifties were hot and ready for it—to dress young, act the fool, move our feet.

Beside the stoop on which Carolyn at 17 sits is a low, spreading evergreen bush, some kind of juniper. The bush laps over the concrete stoop, filling in a gap. A professional landscaper's idea of something to do, an evergreen bush like that flanked the front door of every other postwar middle-class house in America. It made the house look polished and hopeful and absolutely *House Beautiful.*

The brick wall of the house behind Carolyn Moore is recessed in broad sections. The front door is too far to her left to be seen, but the frame is not. There is a vertical wooden beam and beside it, two rows of those bubbled-glass bricks which were so popular back then. A solid, sturdy house with a solid middle-class air. The stoop, the bricks, the glass bricks attest to it. Fashionable. Hopeful. Not half-baked or white-trash. Upwardly reaching, like the city of Houston.

When I was twelve, my family built the only house I lived in that we owned. We were living in Greenville, Mississippi, where I grew up. The new house was to be our dream house: no more renting, no more moving house to house all over town as landlords called up one night and demanded their property back the next; finally, we would be settled. My mother ordered two sets of house plans, one from *Better Homes and Gardens,* the other from *House Beautiful.* Both were two-storied, which seemed more exciting than maybe anything.

In our new house there was to be all this fancy *stuff.* A bay window. A Dutch door. Wood floors, redbird-and-magnolia-print wallpaper, a half-bathroom. (Who ever heard of a half-bath?) When only the studs were up in the new house, after supper we'd go over there, leaving dishes on the table at the rented house on Manilla Street.

It was always my father's idea. "Let's go see the house," he'd say, and we'd up and drive over there.

In the fading light of dusk, among nail barrels, stacks of lumber, and sawhorses, we played pretend. "Play like you're outside, Bev," my father would say, and he would mime opening the top half of the Dutch door, yelling for me to come on in the house. "Let's go sit in the living room and listen to the radio," "Let's go eat a steak in the dining room, Bev—right here we're going to have a chandelier!" At his request, I pretended I was going up the stairs to my very own bedroom; I sat at my dressing table, I looked out my window at the grassy esplanade running down the center of Washington Avenue—our street, an old street, a good old street. Talk about *House Beautiful.*

I don't know who planned what kind of plants would go where in the yard of our dream house, but beside our front steps, we had that same spreading juniper as Carolyn at 17.

When we moved into the new house we thought this was the way things were going to go from then on, more hopeful, more settled, easier. Thought we were now part of the uptown country club gang, the Greenville Who's Who.

Lost cause. Within three years of moving into our dream house, we lost it. There was all this *talk.* Lawsuits, defaults. My father had a business for the first time, a moving and storage company, and him a traveling detail man for pharmaceutical companies practically all his adult life. The moving and storage business opened the door to respectability, but something went wrong, I don't know what. Lines were drawn, enemies identified so that we could despise and blame them forever. There was a lot of talk about cheese in storage going bad. I didn't understand how a bank could take your house and I still don't exactly know what the man my mother blamed and hated for their troubles until the day she died had done, or even if he did it; but in fact they, whoever "they" were, did take our house plus some furniture and—for my father, the lowest blow—my mother's Baldwin piano, on which she used to play "Trees," "Träumerei," "Deep Purple," and a very snappy "Darktown Strutters' Ball."

Back to our old life, renting, on the move. Renting was exciting in a way. All those houses. Those secret dark corners, the smells and surprises, the funny notions of the people who'd lived there before, of what a house should be. My brother and I always thought we'd find—who knew?—secret stuff. Every time we moved, the first thing my father said was "Okay, now where are we going to put the Christmas tree?"

"Carolyn at 17" is a hopeful picture. A pretty Texas girl, the Eisenhower years. Korea was over, peace upon us.

In the next picture I have of Carolyn Ann Moore, it is 1956; she is about to become Carolyn Moore Tucker. A black-and-white photo, this one is of Carolyn in her wedding dress, standing before light-colored pinch-pleat draperies with a print in the fabric, flowers and something like an Oriental pagoda. The wedding dress is two-pieced. The top's a white lace bodice with a stand-up collar, long sleeves that come to a point at the wrist, a fitted waistline. Below the waist, the bodice flows out into one of those crisp, saucy little skirts called peplums. (The polka-dotted suit Lauren Bacall wore in *To Have and Have Not* had one.) Beneath the lace bodice, Carolyn Moore is wearing a boned strapless satin slip. The full skirt emerging from beneath the lace peplum is made of tulle, as is the fingertip veil attached to the crown of flowers on Carolyn Moore's head. In her hands she's cradling a bouquet, a white orchid and a spray of stephanotis, tied up with a satiny bow.

Very pretty. Whose dream, I wonder—Carolyn's? Granny B.'s? Somebody's. The reason weddings make people cry is, they are so excruciatingly *hopeful.* "Going to the chapel and we're going to get married. . . . Never be lonely anymore" was not camp when it was written and recorded and is not now.

Carolyn's hair is more tightly curled than in the first picture, she's wearing pearl earrings, and she's tipped her chin to one side so she's looking to her right and slightly up, eyes focused on a point just above the lens of the camera. Her lips are pressed demurely shut. I get the feeling she is uncomfortable posing with her lips together, maybe because of that slight irregularity about her mouth, which in this picture looks like an underbite. She has pale eyes, pale skin, the red lips.

She's a girl full of secrets, but then most brides are. She's pert, she's bright, there's a knowingness about the way she's cut her eyes, and she's holding something back.

Early on, Karla told me that both her parents went to college. "They were/are," she wrote, "very intelligent people but I guess it stopped there! 'Cause none of us girls got it. Ha."

She says her father quit college to join the army, but she thinks maybe her mother got a degree. Later on, she asked her father about that, and he corrected her. "He says Mother was going to go to college, but something came up and she didn't go." Carolyn Tucker's first daughter, Kathi Lynne, was born in 1957; her second, Kari Ann, in June of 1958; her third, Karla Faye, on November 18, 1959. "All K's," Karla says proudly. "All K-a's."

Carolyn Moore's husband, Lawrence Earl Tucker, was two years older than Carolyn. A large, squarish man, Larry Tucker was a longshoreman. He worked on the Houston ship channel, odd hours, nights, days—shift work. Eventually, he would manage to buy into a company called Gulf Motorships. "One-third owner," Karla boasts. "For a while, my dad was a bigwig."

The next picture I have of Carolyn Tucker is in color. It is later in 1956, and Carolyn is pregnant with Kathi, her first child.

Sitting with her husband on a rust-colored couch with a shiny fleck in the fabric, Carolyn Tucker has pressed the left side of her face into Larry Tucker's chest and shoulder, that cheekbone against his chin. She is resting her swollen belly on his rib cage. Her right arm lies easily on her husband's chest. Larry Tucker is fairly sprawled across the couch, left arm across the back of the couch, right arm cradling his young wife's shoulder, large hand resting on the curve of her rear end. His legs are crossed in manly fashion, left ankle resting on his right knee. He has on dark trousers, short dark socks, lace-up shoes, a black shirt with a narrow white stripe. A couple inches of very white skin show between the cuff of his trousers and his sock. Larry Tucker's reddish hair is combed sleekly back in a widening fan, fifties fashion, and he is kissing his wife's forehead at the point of her eyebrow. His complexion is as fair as Carolyn's. His eyes are closed.

A sweet picture, newlyweds, two only children already on their first child. Carolyn's dark-blond hair is in soft waves off her face. She's still wearing cluster earrings and painting her lips red. She's in a white maternity top and a dark skirt. Her waist has thickened but has not yet ballooned. Her arched eyebrows are up and she's still looking full of secrets. Behind the couple are the same pinch-pleat draperies with the flower-and-gazebo print as in the bridal portrait. Beside the draperies, there are open venetian blinds. Outside, the night is pitch black.

I ask Karla what her mother and father's wedding date was. She doesn't know. Didn't they celebrate anniversaries? She shakes her head. Her parents' courtship was never a part of the ongoing family narrative? No.

"Only thing I can think of is, by the time I was old enough to ask, she was—it was . . ."

Over?

"Yes."

Nothing is written on the back of the picture of Larry and Carolyn Tucker snuggling on the rust-colored couch, but the draperies give the setting away. Surely Carolyn had her wedding picture taken at her mother's house. Married now, pregnant, she is back there with her husband, in front of the pinch-pleat draperies with the flowers and the pagodas. Perhaps they had come to Granny B.'s house—the sturdy brick house with the spreading juniper and the bottle-glass bricks—for supper. Larry Tucker's shirt is dressy. They both look spiffed up.

When that first child was born, Carolyn Moore would name her Kathi Lynne. Not Katherine or Kathleen but Kathi with an *i*, Lynne with an *e*—a modern, hopeful version of Kathleen. The next year she would name her second daughter Kari with an *i*. Then—the K-trend was set—Karla Faye with an *e*. Now, Carolyn is an elegant, old-fashioned, middle-class name. But in the late fifties, hopeful, all-out women were challenging authority and the past by giving their children, particularly their daughters, not so much new names (this was before the rush of Tammys and Ambers) as old ones with new spellings. In Karla Faye's and Kari's tribe, there were all these girls with *i* names: Kathi, Kari, Shari, Debi. Girls with boys' names, often with a new spelling: Shawn, Shay. Alliterations everywhere: Kathi, Kari, Karla; Shawn was the youngest of three sisters, girls named Shay, Sherry, and Shawn. Talking to some of Karla's old friends, I once sat in the room with a Debby, a Debbie, and a Debi. Meantime the guys were mostly regular joes: Danny, Douglas, Joe, Ronnie, Jimmy. A number of Richards, Steves, Jameses.

In the color picture taken in front of the pinch-pleat draperies, things look good for the newlyweds. The way Carolyn leans her cheekbone and belly against Lawrence, that relaxed arm on his chest; the way he has placed his hand gently but very possessively on her rear. Their very posture indicates mutual consent. He will be the bulwark, she his soft and lovely flower, his girlfriend forever.

Karla: "Dad was always in love with Mother and never would get serious about anybody else as long as she was alive."

This might have been okay, you have to think. *She likes him. He treasures her.* They might have gone on to live a quiet life. Not necessarily happy, but quiet and decent and basically okay.

When my husband and I moved to Houston in 1965, the very quality by which people meant to put it down was the one I responded to with the greatest enthusiasm. Having been raised in an Old South, class-conscious Mississippi town, I liked the rodeo mentality of cow-patty Houston, where it didn't matter who your daddy was, much less your grandaddy; whoever stayed on the bucking bronco longest won the buckle. Crass, yes; unkempt, certainly. But alive; ready for whatever came next—the space program, art, opera, heart transplants, whatever—and so was I. In such a no-holds-barred atmosphere it was easy to start writing. There was no tradition to live up to. Nobody was watching; you could just do it. In a way, I think Houston's raucous wide-openness allowed me to come into myself, to discover and then stand by my own past and voice.

I made a place for myself to work, in the bedroom, against a blank white wall.

Outside, things were going on. It was a time, that was all; time to get out of the house, go meet new people, take off your bra, loosen up your standards, drink Lone Star, smoke dope, wear wild clothes. The price of oil was sky high. White men in banks were loaning money to other white men on the promise of a leaky promise. Rock and roll. Time for an all-out Texas girl to shake her butt and go to clubs and concerts and take advantage of hot times while they were still hot.

Possibly Larry Tucker should have kept his eyes open while he was staking out a claim to his wife and kissing the tip of her prettily arched eyebrow.

Possibly it wouldn't have done any good: the girl was *ready*.

. . .

We wanted to be pals to our children, Carolyn Moore and me, not policemen standing over them with a stick; wanted them to learn new things, not stodgy old stuff, at their own tempo, in their own way.

I read *Summerhill;* all us educated parents did; we thought *Summerhill* was the way to go.

My older son, Colin, was born in New York in 1961. He started school in Houston. Not wanting to be dictators handing down old-hat rules, we never taught Colin to tie his shoes. Eventually the boy devised his own finger-flying method.

Colin's a decent, loving young man, he doesn't like to be pushy, but in his twenties he asked why nobody ever taught him this most basic act.

"We were," I said, "teaching you better things."

I didn't believe it. He didn't believe it. But being a decent, loving boy, he *pretended* he believed it.

Times. Carolyn Moore and I were out on the same limb, loose tits, tight T-shirts, no old-lady purses or girdles for us. Only, I held tight to the trunk, and Mama Carolyn was way, *way* out on the thinnest, thinnest twigs, which never had the least chance of not snapping.

Miss Tough Guy

I don't know that men do this—immediately get into a friendship, plunge in as if they'd known each other forever, tell one another love secrets and life stories. Catching up on the past, going over and over details, filling in gaps, saying who our mothers were, our fathers. Confiding which boys we went for and which girls and women betrayed us or kept our deepest secrets.

"Mother used to tell me I had rare qualities." Karla bats her eyes, then chuckles to herself. "Rare qualities!" As if to say, "Now look."

The earliest picture I have of Karla Faye is a professional shot taken with Kari when Karla was about six months old, her sister close to two. The two little girls are posing on a large pillow set against a painted blue background, like sky, with clouds rising to heaven.

Karla's fat with chubby cheeks, dark hair, and startled black eyes. She's wearing a pale blue smock-top and matching bloomers. Kari's an Ivory Snow baby with wispy white hair and pale skin, a precious upturned mouth, a squint in one eye. She's in dark blue with red and white rickrack kind of trim around the neck and sleeves. There's a toddler's sore on Kari's elbow, and she's laid a protective arm across Karla Faye's chest. Karla's arms are up, one reaching toward the camera, the other one lifted straight up—palms cupped, as if to catch rain.

Two chunky babies. Well fed. Immaculately dressed. I don't know where Kathi is. Kathi Lynne was older and . . . different.

Karla sends inscriptions with every photograph. About this one she says, "It makes me cry to look at this picture. . . . I don't know why but everytime I look at it I get tears in my eyes."

Hope, promises.

I had a similar picture taken of my boys when they were small. Peter was born in January 1966, the year after we moved to Houston. For about fifteen months, the four of us lived in a furnished apartment in a huge apartment complex where people stayed only until they could manage to move someplace better. The furniture was Motel-6. Plastic covers on the mattresses. I don't know exactly why we did this, but we did. One day, a door-to-door photographer came through. Colin was about six, Peter not yet two. The photographer sold me on a special deal and the picture turned out wonderfully, both boys looking sweetly out as if at all time to come: Colin, the serious firstborn, in navy blue turtleneck and wheat-colored jeans; chunky barefoot Peter in red knit overalls and white animal-print knit shirt, on his face that beatific look, aura of total faith in his position in the family as a loved child, which in his baby years he had with him wherever he went, like a favorite blanket.

Behind my boys is the same background as in the early photograph of Karla and Kari. Blue clouds, heaven-bound.

The first place Karla remembers living is "in Genoa out by the Almeda Mall."

This is how directions are given and understood in the outlying parts of Houston, by shopping malls and freeways. Out by Gulfgate. Off 45, by the ship channel. Up the Eastex Freeway past Northline. Genoa's south of Houston down the Gulf Freeway, which eventually leads to the Gulf of Mexico. Working-class territory. Refinery country. Great silver tanks define the horizon. Gas flares light up the night.

"Dad and mother split up once while we were there and got back together and then we moved to a house on a street named Fisher . . . lived there for about a year, then moved to the house in northwest Houston on Hewitt Street, where I lived until I was about thirteen."

These are upward moves, sociologically speaking, Genoa to Fisher to northwest Houston. The Tuckers were not poor. They started out as by-the-hour working people looking for time and a half, double time, trying to get a leg up. And for a while they did. On the surface things improved—not real social status but the advantages gained in neighborhood terms like schools, lawns, churches, police protection, streetlights, general tone.

"As a child and all of us living together as a family, I remember it being pretty normal. We had a bay house that we went to a lot and I learned how to drive a boat and truck at the ripe old age of about seven or eight. . . . We fished and crabbed and did all the normal things a family does when they go for a week or a weekend at the lake house. We had the family dog. Her name was Ladybug. She was with us for about thirteen or more years."

Granny B. says Karla and her sisters used to go to church all the time. Karla remembers going twice in her life, but Granny B. says she went a lot until she was nine or ten. Karla doesn't argue the point. Granny B. has her own way of remembering things.

The family dog, the bay house; according to Granny B., church. *If I just work hard enough,* Larry Tucker must have thought. *Put in enough hours. Make enough money . . .*

Another studio picture I have is a waist-high shot of the three sisters lined up side by side like a singing group. They are about eight, six, and five. Kathi's hair's a blond pageboy, perfect as a Barbie doll's; Kari's is cotton white. Karla is on the end with her mop of black curls, that dark, dark skin, those bright black eyes. . . .

They look adorable, like three stuffed bunnies on a bed.

Two bunnies from one planet. The youngest from another.

For a while, at Jackie Oncken's suggestion, she and Karla exchanged family anecdotes: stories of happy times, sad times, funny occurrences. It was a way of catching up on one another's past; also, Karla had asked Jackie to help her with her spelling and vocabulary, and Jackie thought that that might be more fun if they did it telling stories. This is from a letter Karla wrote Jackie Oncken in 1985.

I will tell you another story that I love from when I was little. I was about 8 yrs old and we (my family) had a bayhouse in Cany [*scratched out*] oops . . . Cainy Creek out by Brazoria (sp?) and Sargent. We had a boat that ran about 30 or 40 miles an hour and we took it with us every time we went to the bayhouse. Well when I was about 8 yrs. old my Daddy taught me and my sisters how to drive the boat up and down the lake in front of our bayhouse. I realy enjoyed it and every morning I would get up before anyone in the house and put my swim suit on and go jump in the boat and drive it about three miles up the lake (the lake curved all the way, actually it was a creek I think) and gass it up and drive back to our pier and get my sisters and we would pull each other on the ski's all day long!

One morning our nextdoor neighbors at the bayhouse saw little ol me come driving up and pull the boat up to the pier and tie up and they almost dropped their teeth out! HA. They asked my Dad if I should be driving the boat alone and he told them I could drive it better than he could. That made me feel so grown up. I just grinned from ear to ear and jumped back in the boat with my sisters and took off and started skiing. I realy used to love going to that bayhouse with my family! There are *alot* of warm and happy memories from there. I cried last year when Dad sold the place. But no one ever goes there any more so he had to sell it. I'll tell you some more about it in my letters to come. There is alot to tell from there!

Caney Creek's about forty-five miles southwest of Houston, toward the Gulf of Mexico, near the town of Brazoria. For Karla, Caney Creek when she was eight and nine was the great time of her childhood.

Karla loved the bay house especially because it had stairs. As far back as she can remember she loved places with stairs. Also, the owner of the local store knew the Tucker girls and their daddy, and so when the girls came in on their own to gas up and get goodies he always knew it was okay when they said, "Put it on Dad's bill."

"I swear," says Karla, "that was *the ultimate!*"

I have a photograph of Karla at the bay house, in a two-piece red bathing suit at the top of the stairs. She looks cocky and tomboyish, skinny and dark, wound up and ready to fly.

At Caney Creek, all three girls learned to drive. Karla was so tiny she had to sit on the edge of the seat to reach the clutch and brakes and accelerator and even then she almost couldn't see over the dash, but she drove anyway, long before she was old enough. Larry Tucker told his daughters not to drive the truck but they did it anyway, and he probably knew it, but he indulged his girls; after all, what else was a bay house for if not to have fun doing things you couldn't in the city? When the girls got old enough to be allowed to drive to the beach or to town, well, that was a really big step.

On the tape Douglas Garrett made, he and Danny spend a lot of time talking about what to do with the stolen motorcycle parts Douglas says he still has. Douglas says that since he's going to Waco for three months to train for a new job and the police are coming by so often to question him about the murders, he needs to get rid of the parts. (Actually by then he had already thrown the parts in the Brazos River. And he wasn't going to Waco to train for a job.)

"Them parts," Douglas keeps saying. "We got to do something about them parts." Danny makes various suggestions, including putting the parts "in the fucking ocean if we have to." In the background, during this discussion, Karla is steadily mumbling.

"We can drive out to Brazoria," she says. "Put them in Caney Creek. . . ." Her voice fades out, then comes back clear: "Caney Creek."

It happened. It's back there. At Caney Creek, the Tuckers were a happy family living the normal happy life with the normal family dog.

Trouble, however, was in the works. Like me when I think about Peter's life, Karla likes to divide hers up in two parts: the good, happy time and afterwards, when things went haywire. In fact, for the Tuckers during those Caney Creek years, trouble was background music the whole time. For Larry Tucker to have said the things he did about his wife once he divorced her and got custody of the children—calling her whore, bitch—Carolyn Moore had to have been fooling around for some time. It was about this time that Karla Faye started smoking dope.

"I was eight or nine. Everybody was doing it—older kids, my sisters, kids my age. Mother, when she found out, said, 'If you're going to smoke, little lady, you're going to do it right.' And she went and got some papers and made me stand there and roll joints until I could do it right. Mother was like that: if you were going to do something you had to do it right. That's why I've always been able to roll a joint just perfect."

I have a picture of Karla, Kari, and Kathi taken in 1967 at Christmas, at one of Granny B.'s many apartments. Karla's a wiry mosquito. The other two girls are soft and pale, blond; and like their mother, Kathi and Kari always look wavery, a little blurred at the edges.

It's the sixties. Mama Carolyn has dressed her daughters in trendy flared pants, floppy shirts. Kari's in a turtleneck. Her shoulder-length hair's as silver-white as spun-glass Christmas angel hair, and she's smiling shyly—with the same irregularity about her mouth as her mother. Kathi's in autumn colors. Her long hair is limp and without much shine or color. Karla Faye is in front of her sisters in a pale pink cotton shirt with balloon sleeves and matching pink plaid flare trousers. Her pants are what were then called hip-huggers, but because Karla Faye is as slim-hipped as a boy, the pants are hiked halfway up her belly. Her skinny legs are so bowed a cocker spaniel could crawl between them; her hair is cropped short over her ears, the kind of haircut you give an active child.

It's Granny B. again who took the picture, again in one of her apartments. Granny B.'s been married several times—twice, according to Karla, to the same man. I have two pictures of Granny B. She's plenty cute, with a proud pigeon-strut way of holding herself. Her hair's dyed red and she wears it puffed up in a racy pompadour. Plenty sexy.

Behind the girls in the 1967 Christmas photograph, cheap white Fiberglas draperies cover part of a wall. Across one corner is a console television set, the wires and plug of which stick out from behind the draperies. On one side of the girls is a stack of wrapped Christmas presents, on the other a door frame with a chain lock.

Karla says Kari was already fooling around with boys when this picture was taken. Karla was smoking cigarettes and maybe some dope.

She shot heroin the first time when she was ten.

"I was sitting on the front porch. My sister's boyfriend rode up on his Harley looking for Kari. I said she wasn't there and he said, 'You want to go for a ride and get high?' I said, 'Heck, yes' and got on."

The guy on the Harley took her out and asked did she want to do some stuff that would make her feel good. Karla didn't know it then, but what Kari's boyfriend was really after was, he thought if he got her good and high he could get him some ten-year-old *stuff*. He didn't; Karla got too sick from the dope. Kari was furious, but Karla was proud. More than maybe anything else she wanted to be like her sisters and her mother—blond, pretty, and high—and with the guy on the Harley she had passed one test anyway. She had shot up. Maybe she got sick, but she was fine afterwards.

Where was the custodian of these girls, their keeper, the grown-up saying "Stop—no! You're too young!"? There is no one in charge. No one thinks they are too young. Nine was Karla's best year, then it was over—the same as it seemed to be for Peter after the fifth grade when the knot in the rope swing came loose and he went down on the concrete ditch bank, broke his arm, then set it himself.

Karla says people get the wrong idea thinking she was doing drugs to escape something, she says everybody is always talking about "escape," she doesn't think she was trying to *escape* anything, she thinks she was a dope fiend because she liked the way drugs made her feel, period. And after she started heroin that was basically when she started doing just about every kind of drug there was. When she was younger she thought she knew everything and as she got older she learned how much more there was, pills and acid and speed and prescription drugs, and so she just kept going, figuring out how to balance this with that and that with the other.

The force of Karla's certitude has a terrible appeal. You want to believe her, even when you know better. At Mountain View, I listen and nod and get carried away, then come home, come to, and say— out loud, to the pictures on my wall—"Who says a ten-year-old child has any idea when she's facing a problem and when she's trying to escape it or even if she knows what the problem is?"

From the time she was ten until the night she was locked up in County four months before her twenty-fourth birthday, Karla Faye figures, she was on drugs solid, all those thirteen, fourteen years, except for two weeks during the time she was married when she kicked everything.

I have seen the house Karla lived in when she was thirteen, the one on Hewitt Street. It is a pleasant, small brick house on a clean, wide street flanked by other small brick houses with tended lawns, trimmed bushes, a two-car garage. A clean, safe neighborhood. A former-doper pal of Karla's told me point blank, "The good thing about this neighborhood is, no blacks." (When I quoted her friend to Karla, she got extremely upset. "My mother," she said, "may have been wild, but she was never prejudiced against anybody. She taught us never to hold it against anybody what color their skin was. And I never have.")

In 1969, eighteen months after Carolyn Tucker moved out the last time, the Tuckers' divorce became final.

Larry Tucker got custody of the three girls, and it was horrible.

"If you can imagine seeing a movie about the parents divorcing and fighting over the children in the worst kind of way and then the father getting them and separating the mother from children and children crying and hanging on to Mother at the courthouse while they are being taken away, then you get the picture of how I remember it. . . . I remember one night Dad took us girls to the movie and when we got home Mother was gone and all of her stuff. We were devastated. We didn't see her for a long time after that. I don't remember ever being told where she went or why she left. . . . I do remember several times when I'd ask about Mother, Dad would tell me how bad she was, she was a whore and bitch and the like. Those are the two descriptions he gave that I remember well. . . .

"I also remember getting very hurt and upset and mad when my sisters would talk bad about my dad when we would be out with Mother. The first time Mother noticed it she made them stop talking about Dad in front of me and she told me how good Dad was and not to take what Kathi and Kari said seriously."

For two or three years, Karla lived with her father alone at the house on Hewitt Street. Larry Tucker got custody of his daughters. But when Kathi and Kari got old enough, at about twelve or thirteen years old, they were allowed to decide for themselves where they wanted to live. Both moved in with their mother. Karla remembers being especially close to her father during her time alone with him. Going to all-you-can-eat Pancho's Mexican buffets. Throwing the football. When she wasn't blown out of her mind, she says, her dad and she had some of the best times of her life during those two or three years.

Karla's father worked on the ship channel. The ship channel is a long way from Hewitt Street. He was gone a lot. When asked at Karla's trial why he allowed Karla to go and live with her mother, he cited this as a reason: When a ship came in he worked long, unpredictable hours; Karla was on her own too much, going wild. He couldn't control her, didn't know what to do. He had to work.

Karla likes to talk about how strict her mother was in the early years, spanking her girls, making them behave, teaching them table manners and how to cook and clean, always drawing the line, having the final say-so. Karla says in the early years her mother was the perfect homemaker/worker according to societal rules and standards: always cooked breakfast and dinner, made the girls' lunches, cleaned the house *spotless,* taught her daughters to cook and clean and be good homemakers as soon as they could walk. Played games with them: dominoes, Monopoly.

While Carolyn Moore may have seemed a strict parent to her daughter, she also had a fatal flaw: an irresistible attraction to the dark side, to men who skirted the law, to a life that was exciting and unconventional and above all not judged and run by ordinary rules and regulations, a life in which she could walk with an all-out stride and go wherever she wanted. . . .

Her life was out there, not at home; her primary allegiance to living life to the fullest.

Great clothes, a great apartment. Independence. She could hold her own in any situation.

One of those people who craved the inside track, Carolyn Moore liked the crossover zone where lawlessness and law enforcement intersect and people work both sides of the law, where a person of any intelligence can stand and see into both sides and find out what *really* is going on: who's doing what to whom and who the *they* pulling strings really are. For a time Carolyn Moore worked at the Houston Police Department during the day, did dope and turned tricks at night.

There are a lot of Baptists in Texas. Baptists have a very strong lobbying position in the state legislature. As late as 1966, you couldn't buy a mixed drink at a bar in Houston; you had to have a card to get into what was called a private club. Bars were beer joints. The parking lots of the bars out near the Almeda Mall and the ship channel were—still are—ringed with pickup trucks fitted with gun racks. In 1966 the city was still raw, the Baptists held sway, the dark side was easy to come by. "Good" was strict fundamentalist behavior. Everything else was bad.

The court gave Larry Tucker custody of his daughters.

When I ask Karla why she thinks it happened, she wavers, then says, "I guess they thought Dad had a more . . . stable life."

But Larry Tucker was way over his head when it came to his wife and children; there was no way Larry Tucker could handle his wild daughters—who could? First the older ones gave him trouble, and when Karla started in he didn't know what do; he thought maybe her mother could do better. He didn't want to send Karla Faye to live with Carolyn Moore, he knew what his ex-wife was up to, but Karla was strung out, shooting up, getting into fistfights, getting kicked out of school, while he was busy working the docks at all hours. How much worse could it get?

Famous last words; time now for the downhill slide to go really fast.

"Mother had a lot of power. She had a ten-year relationship with a man; he was . . . people would call him a, you know, bad cop. He walked that line, he knew things. They all walked the line. Mother would call up people when he told her a drug bust was coming down, she'd warn them. People called her to find out things. My mother knew how to *operate*. I used to watch her and want to be like that. I wanted to have my own way of doing things. I wanted to be the first female quarterback in the NFL."

Throughout the years of uproar, Larry Tucker seems to have maintained his basic sense of decency. And if occasionally he made unfortunate remarks to his daughters about their mother, well, he had been provoked.

Tucker's decency may have been a big part of his problem. To Mama Carolyn and the girls, decent meant square.

Debi Bullard, a junior-high buddy of Karla's, says, "I loved going to Mama Carolyn's. It was exciting there. I mean, compared to Larry's house. And, well, compared to mine. Mama Carolyn was a high-dollar whore. That's exactly what she was, a high-dollar whore. She ran a good business. She dressed her girls in good clothes. It's hard raising three daughters. She knew how to run a business. I loved that lady. I smoked my first dope with Mama Carolyn. She was sitting on the couch and she cracked a pound."

One Saturday when she was about thirteen, Debi says she was at Mama Carolyn's in bed with the covers up watching cartoons—it was Saturday afternoon, which she knows for sure because she remembers which cartoons she was watching. "Mama Carolyn came in and said, 'Debi, there's a man out here will pay two hundred fifty dollars for you, if you want to.' When I didn't say anything, she said, 'Baby, you don't have to. It's up to you.' I said absolutely not, and she left. I pulled the covers back up and went on watching cartoons."

I asked Debi Bullard why she said no.

"I was scared. I was a virgin, and I was scared shitless."

"Of what?" I asked her.

"Just scared."

Karla says Debi's story is "bull-*corn*." Karla gets upset when anybody trashes her mother, particularly somebody who is not family, and especially when that person goes so far as to imply that Carolyn Moore might have done something as reprehensible as to make a deal to, in Karla's parlance, turn a girl out.

The girlfriends of this story—Karla, Kari, Debi, Shawn—still have an adolescent girl's sense of one another and probably always will; their friendships were formed early on, developed into adolescence, got stuck there. The friends get hot at one another quickly and without warning. They challenge one another's veracity and intent. Each thinks she has the real skinny on whatever story is up for grabs. They are all feisty. And a bit jealous of one another.

Whatever the truth is, Larry Tucker at any rate could hardly compete with the excitement. There were all those bad guys out there and he was not one of them. Rock and roll. The bad guys were the exciting ones.

"Daddy was—is—a good man" are Karla's last words on the subject.

Debi Bullard, who lived within blocks of Karla Faye's house on Hewitt Street, remembers going to school altogether wasted. "One day, Mama Carolyn called. We had a hundred Valiums. Mama Carolyn said, 'Your daddy knows y'all got those pills, now get rid of them.' Me and Karla took thirty-three apiece. We were loaded for days."

Debi figures she and Karla were about eleven. Maybe twelve.

It was about that time that Karla tried sex for the first time—eleven, maybe twelve. It happened at a house where Kari was staying, after running away from home. There was a guy there, Karla thought he was cute, they went back to the bedroom. Everybody else in the house was a lot older than Karla and a lot older than Kari, but nobody thought anything about Karla going back to the bedroom with the cute guy and what Karla knew was, everybody else was having sex and she wanted to be in on whatever it was everybody else was in on.

So she and the cute guy went back to the bedroom, but the guy could not get it in. He tried and tried; it wouldn't go. So finally they gave up and he came back out to where the others were and he said—to everybody—"Hell, that thing's so little you couldn't get your big toe in it."

Everybody laughed. Karla was humiliated.

"I couldn't wait till I got big enough to be with a man."

When she did get big enough, "I was a little sex fiend. I wanted to know everything there was to know."

But the sex was not for her and she never had orgasms. And she was still a child. She just had this way of convincing people she was not.

Good and Bad

We didn't want to be like our mothers, our mothers fluttered, and had no fun. . . . Our daddies shot the moon. . . . What rascals. We wanted to be like them.

I wrote that, in an essay about Southern girls and their daddies. In my family, our father was the wild one. He drank too much, danced to dangerous music, gambled with stakes he didn't have, borrowed against not only his own future but ours. Playing his high-stakes games, he could never afford to be wrong; he didn't have the margins or the resources. He was—and, by extension, we were—always in the hole. From time to time, deep down in it.

I adored him. He was bigger than life, brighter than music; he sang and danced and told stories. He enlarged my sense of pure possibility. I once wrote about him in a novel: "He brought a lot of life to the party. A whole lot of life."

Karla fears I am casting her father in the role of wimp: not man enough to hold on to his wife or keep his daughters in line. Karla keeps telling me what a big man Larry Tucker was, how people were afraid of him, how, coming home once to find her sitting on the toilet stoned out of her mind, he knocked Karla off the toilet seat, into the tub. Tells me how Mama Carolyn threatened Larry Tucker when they divorced: "Lay one hand on my girls," she said, "and I'll take you to court." And so, Karla says, Larry Tucker was hamstrung. The girls were wild, getting wilder, he was afraid if he used force Carolyn Moore would . . .

"Daddy just loved Mother so dadgum much," Karla says.

We are all so frighteningly frail.

My mother was not a wimp either; she had a hot temper, she could lay into the designated enemy with the ferocity of a cornered cat. But she was essentially good; a person of warmth and kindness, whose needs, when it came down to it, were simple. My mother wanted a home. Period. She didn't, however, get one she felt safe in until the last five years of her life.

I tell Karla, it's a problem if she thinks that "decent" and "hardworking" seem unmanly descriptions, and the problem is hers, just as it was a problem for me that I thought my mother was boring when all she wanted was for life maybe to be a little calmer, a lot safer. Meantime, the rascal danced his upbeat dance.

We are on opposite sides of the Plexiglas in one sense here—the good/bad mother/father—but the effect is the same.

I tell Karla she should think about this, long and hard, because I don't think I got it about my mother until after she was dead.

Next to the picture of Karla in a bathing suit at Caney Creek but light years away in experience and tone is one of Karla as a pouting, sexy thirteen-year-old, lounging on a furry brown chair. It's 1973 and the chair's one of those soft, shapeless things that were popular then—Karla calls it a round love chair. Behind the chair is a wall of vertical blinds. Karla's in red flare plants and cork-heeled sandals; she's doing a centerfold pose, hugging a fuzzy pillow to her chest, one leg hiked up. The expression on her face is one of sullenness, boredom, and utter adolescent disdain.

Curtain down, curtain up, Act II. Karla's a juicy girl, having periods, running wild. The wiry mosquito has become a black-haired Miss Tough Guy—a fighter, muscular, athletic; a wild girl.

Radical, she calls herself, referring mostly to the drugs she did, the fistfights she got into.

Kathi and Kari already had a reputation in school. When Karla came along, teachers were expecting trouble. Karla Faye made sure they got it.

In the snapshot, Karla looks exactly like what she was at thirteen, a sullen scrapper about to be kicked out of school, not for grades—even though she had already flunked the seventh grade twice—but for fighting.

When the picture in the love chair was taken, Karla was living in an apartment in Spring Branch with her two sisters and her mother; her mother's best friend, Adele; Shawn; and Laura Sue, another friend of Karla and Kari's.

"Seven of us women in one apartment, four bedrooms, two baths. We had a blast! I wasn't in school that year because I had gotten kicked out. . . . I turned fourteen in November of that year. . . . Mother was working her secretarial job during the day and her and Adele were making money at night off their phone. We always had plenty of money and anything we wanted! I spent that year doing a lot of acid—that was the year I started to get pretty heavy into acid—experimenting with sex outside the missionary style. Kari met Ronnie that year. Adele, Laura Sue, Kari, and Kathi (some) titty-danced at different clubs, so I got into that scene some. I never danced because I never looked old enough but I did get to go into the clubs and see the others dance and do the drugs and stuff. . . . We lived at this apartment for about a year or maybe six months and then we moved to Genoa where this man lived that my mother married for his money."

Carolyn Moore shot her first shot of dope at the apartment in Spring Branch; that was when everything started to go seriously downhill. Mama Carolyn started getting strung out and kicking and strung out and kicking. . . .

By the time Peter was thirteen, he also was affecting a tough-guy stance in every picture we took. He was a pretty boy, but turn the camera on him and he scowled as if to say, "Who the fuck cares."

We thought we were doing right by our children, Carolyn Moore and me, being such *pals*.

Anyway, who wanted to be a policeman, for God's sake?

Mama Carolyn

1974. A color snapshot, the setting the Spring Branch apartment where all the women lived. Karla and her mother are at a card table playing Spades. Karla is fourteen. She's dealing.

She has been kicked out of school for the last time. Been shooting heroin. Been on the road with a couple of rock bands. Is heavy into acid. A boyfriend of her mother's best friend, Adele, a six-foot-seven-inch former Green Beret, has been giving Karla lessons in martial arts and sex "outside the missionary position."

In the picture, Carolyn's wearing a greenish rib-knit tank top. Her hands are palm-down on the card table, her hair is long and loose —blonder, a honey-gold color—and she's looking over her left shoulder, cutting her pale eyes, which turn out to be closer to green than blue, at whoever's taking the picture. There's an open can of Lone Star beside Carolyn Moore's left hand ("Lone Star was Mother's beer"), a pack of cigarettes and an ashtray by her right. Two bottles of different-color fingernail polish are on the card table.

Carolyn's thinner. Her spine's still erect—she does not need to use the chair back for support—but her shoulders are slumped and her arms are slack and there is something slatternly about her—open-jointedness gone too far, the Texas girl having taken wider strides than she can handle if she's going to keep her health. Still, she's pretty, if fragile. Her face a flower, her skin startlingly pale.

Karla's in a sleeveless dark blue shirt. Her black curls mop down to her shoulders. Her arms are muscular, her forearms covered in dark downy hair. She's a sturdy, healthy-looking girl, with an athleticism about her—a muscularity, a definition—that her sisters and mother don't have. She looks younger than fourteen.

Doctors performed a hysterectomy on Karla when she was fifteen.

She'd always had problems, an unusually heavy menstrual flow, cysts on her ovaries; when she was thirteen she had to have a D & C. When she was fifteen, doctors went in to see what they could do to help her condition, ended up taking out her womb and one ovary. Karla says she didn't care, in a way she was glad. At least she didn't have to worry about getting pregnant anymore.

It was all one big *joke*. A big party. A story she was born in the middle of.

Meantime, among her friends, Karla was assuming the position she would hold on to, of badass enforcer who lived by the tough-guy code and saw to it nobody, but nobody, harmed the people she loved.

Debi Bullard says the first time Karla saw her with bruises on her arm from shooting dope, "she whipped my ass. She saw them bruises and she whipped my ass."

"What," I ask, "do you mean by 'whip my ass'?"

"Beat me up."

"Closed fists?"

"Yes."

"To the jaw."

Nods yes. "She whipped my ass."

"Why did Karla think it was okay for her but not you?"

"I never have figured that out."

Karla says she didn't actually hit Debi but only threatened her—neither of them will back down here—and that since she had plenty of other fights she was proud of and in a lot of them she really hurt people, bad, why wouldn't she claim this one? Nobody, Karla says, taught her how to fistfight. They didn't have to.

"I think I squirted out knowing how. I was always strong. And I knew how to fight."

By this time, Houston was on the map. We had the Astrodome, the Astros, Jones Hall, a new wing on the museum. The price of oil was up; so was real estate. We had passed Dallas in population long ago. We had a what was called free school, which let kids learn to read when and if they wanted. We were starting to think about a new museum, a ballet company. . . .

A city like Houston, one sociological theory has it, can be a crueler place to live than one more sharply divided according to social class. A seemingly wide-open city gives people on the margins hope: the line is right there, all they have to do is work hard, wear the right clothes, do the right thing, step over, they'll be accepted, acceptable, *in*. All you need is the money. No zoning. It's all right there.

Upward moves and good times at Caney Creek Estates notwithstanding, trouble was in the background in the Tucker household all that time. Trouble had been in the works since Karla's birth, if not earlier; all you have to do is look at the pictures. There is this family of four Germanic types. Carolyn, Larry, Kathi, and Kari all have light-colored hair, light eyes, pale complexions, that blurry softness. Then comes this black-eyed, almond-skinned baby who would grow up to be a flat-chested, bowlegged, skinny little hotheaded tomboy.

Look at the picture of the three stuffed bunnies on the bed. Two cotton-top Easter bunnies. One wild black hare.

Larry Tucker is Karla Faye's father, and yet biologically Karla is the child of another man. It doesn't take a lot of intelligence to suspect as much. As Karla was born in November 1959, this means that Carolyn Moore was fooling around as early as two years after she got married. Karla's the result of one of Carolyn's liaisons, this time with a Greek, a fireman.

When Karla was thirteen, Carolyn Moore tried to introduce her to her biological father. Called him her real father. The man looked like Karla but Karla wasn't having it. "I already have a father," she informed her mother, and stormed out of the house.

Being given this information made Karla feel like her whole family had been snatched right out from under her. She didn't know what to do about that and never realized, until recently, the effect of being told and how mad and isolated and scared it made her.

Karla and Larry Tucker have never spoken of this touchy subject. After all, as Karla says, "My father is and always has been *Dad*." The Greek fireman only provided the dark hair and bowlegs; her looks, the discrepancies in her life, she had to have noticed the first time she looked in a mirror.

"Soon as I squirted out . . ." she says, speaking of her birth, in

other matters. Everybody had to have known. But Karla leaves it,
goes back to an easier story to deal with: drugs.

"My mother and I were really close. We used to share drugs like
lipstick. She was against heroin at first because she hated needles.
Back when I was twelve and living with Daddy on Hewitt Street, I
started shooting up regular. Skipping school. He couldn't figure out
what to do with me so he called Mother and said you come get her
I can't do anything with her. So Mother came over, I was lying in
the bed buck naked, I remember it perfectly. She knew I was strung
out behind basically the needle, just shooting whatever kind of dope
I could in my arms and she snatched me out of that bed and said
get up and get out of here, you're coming with me, and I said, can
I put my clothes on? and I went to live with her. And I promised I
wouldn't do it anymore but you know a dope fiend's going to find
a way to shoot dope and I did."

Granny B. thinks Karla's too hard on her mother. "She's always
telling me," Karla says, " 'You didn't have it that bad.' " Karla screws
up her face. "I'm not *saying* it was that bad."

Doubtless, when her granddaughters talk in public about sex like
it was oat bran, Granny B. can feel the ground shake beneath her
feet. Granny B.'s a middle-class lady; she knows implied criticism
when she hears it. All that talk about turning tricks. One reason
Karla studies other people's reactions with such intensity is, she's
trying to fill in the gaps in her upbringing by seeing how she's coming
across in the respectable world.

"Our life may not seem normal to other people," Karla says. "And
maybe I see it different when I look back on it now. Not because it
seems different but because of how other people react. It didn't seem
strange to us at the time, it seemed normal. You know?"

Carolyn Moore made her daughters mind their manners and not
talk back, ever. Karla thinks maybe she did it once and Kari did it
twice and she doesn't know about Kathi. Carolyn Moore knocked
Karla Faye out of her chair. As for smacking your lips at the table,
forget it. But the worst was lying. Carolyn Moore told her girls as

long as they told the truth she'd stand up for them. She used to say, "Now I'm not promising what I won't do when I get you home, but as long as I know you're telling the truth I'll stand up for you." And she would. And she had to a lot, because the Tucker girls were really bad and the school was always calling.

"My mother, I don't know, she was always there for us, that's all. She was just there for us. Until she got strung out shooting up."

In a studio shot I have of Carolyn at thirty-eight, she is in a black velvet photographer's drape, tinted up and airbrushed. Her hair falls in loose curls around her long, thin face, she's smiling wanly, her eyebrows are carefully plucked, and she's wearing a gold locket. The drape is low, revealing lush, largish breasts.

Carolyn Moore had just gotten out of the hospital from having a hysterectomy when this picture was taken. This was before she got hepatitis, but she was not in great shape.

In the studio picture Carolyn Moore is still pretty, but she's lost her shine. She's thin, washy, her smile pasted on. It's going . . . her health, her looks, the erect spine, her spirit . . . fading fast.

The first time Karla took money for anything close to sexual favors, she was hitchhiking. Guy picked her up, told her he'd pay her twenty dollars if she'd show him a titty. She did. He paid. Said he'd pay her twenty dollars more to show him the other one. She did. He paid again. Karla got home, told her mother and the other women what had happened, held up the forty dollars. Mama Carolyn took some of the money and kept it, saying if Karla was going to do that kind of thing, she could help pay the rent.

Karla blames herself for getting her mother started shooting up.

"She told me after I moved in that the reason she hated heroin was she knew if she ever used it she would love it and then she'd be hooked and that was why she wouldn't do it. Also she hated needles; but see, I was a needle freak. I liked the needle as much as I liked the dope."

Anything Karla could shoot up she did. She wasn't as bad as some people, like this one guy she remembers who kept sticking the needle in and sticking it in, twelve or thirteen times. Getting off on sticking it in. She wasn't that bad. But, "I got as much out of the needle going in as I did the drug." She covers her mouth. "Makes me sick."

One day Karla went in the apartment and there her mother was, lying on the couch, trying to find the right place in her arm to put a needle in, poking and poking. She asked Karla to help her. Karla said, "No, you're not going to do that," and her mother said, "Fine, then I'll do it myself." And she went at herself again. And Karla remembered one time she was with her cronies in a dope house; a guy tried to shoot up and he didn't know what he was doing and he hit an artery and his arm blew up and the guy died, right then and there. The dope house emptied in a hot minute. So when Karla Faye saw her mother poking at her arm with that needle, she remembered that and said okay, she'd help, and she did, and that's how Carolyn Moore got started on the needle behind heroin.

"I hate that. Everything went downhill after that. . . ."

Karla never much had to pay for dope. Everybody she knew was doing drugs and dealing. Drugs were always around. When she was dealing that was part of it, that she would get drugs for herself.

It was at the Spring Branch apartment that Karla Faye learned about oral sex and karate from Scott, the Green Beret boyfriend of Carolyn Moore's friend Adele.

"Scott showed me the kicks. We worked on the heavy bag. We practiced together and I got pretty good at it. Also the speed bag. That was what I was really good at, punching the speed bag. I can't remember anybody teaching me; I could just do it. I mean, I was always pretty good at athletics. I've been able to stand on my head as long as I can remember. I used to be able to walk on my hands a good ways until I hurt my shoulders. . . . The first apartment I had on my own, I didn't have no furniture, no bed, nothing. Just my radio, my speed bag, and some clothes. I loved it."

I have a picture of Karla doing the splits in the air, legs straight out from her hips, fingertips reaching beyond her toes. Her eyes are closed in concentration, her hair is flying up over her head, she's about four feet up. Her legs are straight, and you can see the definition of muscle in her calves and thighs. She calls this the Russian splits: "It's not perfect. I should've had my back straight."

In addition to martial arts, Adele's boyfriend gave Karla other kinds of lessons. She was fifteen. She had seen one of the women in the house perform oral sex on Scott—taking the whole thing in her mouth, deep-throating so that the semen came out beyond the taste buds and you couldn't taste it—but Karla hadn't done it herself. The Green Beret thought it was time for Karla to learn how to give head. And he taught her. And this ability was something all the women she ran with were proud of.

I have a picture of Karla Faye's instructor. He's wearing army fatigues, a black undershirt. He's holding a pit bull by the chest. His green beret is in his pocket, he has on aviator sunglasses and has bulged his bicep. His jaw is set. He appears to be gritting his teeth.

Then Scott and two other guys decided it was time for Karla to learn how to get what she now knew how to give. All the women kept saying Karla didn't know what she was missing, she'd never know what getting off was until she'd gotten head, and so three guys and a woman took Karla back to the bedroom and . . . nothing. One of the guys was supposed to be an expert. They had honey. Even Adele tried.

It wasn't until Karla went to bed with Danny Garrett in January of 1983 that she learned really to enjoy sex. "Before that I think I'd come twice. And both of them was an accident. I was with a trick. They slipped up on me."

As for her formal schooling, Karla did poorly, every year except the year she got kicked out. She was doing well—straight A's—that year and really wanted to try, but got kicked out two weeks after school started. She had already almost got suspended three times before she got kicked out, but her mother talked the principal into letting her stay in. The rest of the time she flat never tried, never applied herself. She failed the third grade once; the fifth, too, but they passed her. Teachers told her she had the potential to be a straight-A student and she thinks they wanted to encourage her, but her mind was on everything but school and finally it got to where they wanted to pass her just to get her out as fast as possible. Same with sixth grade: she failed but they passed her on to the seventh.

Failed seventh twice, went two weeks the next fall, got kicked out, went out on the road with the Allman Brothers. Karla, her mother, and the rest of the girls were pretty close to a rock group called Dr.

Hook and the Medicine Show, so they were seeing a lot of them.

"I just never was interested in school. I hated the teachers, I hated them telling me what to do, I always got loaded and fell asleep in my classes. I had a reputation before I ever got to a lot of my classes, and you can believe I lived up to their expectations."

After waiting a few beats, I say, "The Allman Brothers?"

Her eyes switch on like a light bulb.

"When I was twelve or thirteen, I went to a concert at Jeppeson Stadium, me, my mom, my sister, and some others. I got in front of the stage and I was dancing and this guy comes over . . . and gives me a backstage pass. He was the roadie, and he took me with him. I rode in the Allmans' limousine to the hotel where they were staying and everybody was there and it was *neat!* The next night I called my mom and told her where I was and she said, 'Well, I figured you must have done something like that when you didn't come home.' "

My father-in-law used to use this expression when he was talking about a child—usually a girl child—who was both adorable and incorrigible. "She's cute," he'd say, and he'd shake his head and chuckle. "But she's a outlaw." And he'd usually repeat himself. "A outlaw."

To be fair to Carolyn Moore, sitting on one side of the Plexiglas watching this animated child-woman on the other side laugh and gush and do her outlandish gestures, I can just imagine what a outlaw she must have been when she was young.

With a outlaw in the family, things get rough. In the end Carolyn Moore may have been as much under Karla's influence as Karla was under her mother's. Karla was a hothead; there was nobody else like her in the family. Carolyn Moore said Karla had rare qualities because she did; she treated Karla Faye different from the other two girls because she *was* different.

So the Allman Brothers' roadie told Karla they'd be back in six or seven months, and when they were, she should come back to such-and-such hotel to get a backstage pass and all. And when the band came back Shawn and Karla went to the concert but not the hotel, because Karla thought, "Oh, they won't remember no little girl like me." So she and Shawn were sitting in seats behind the stage when this guy setting things up looked up and saw them and said, "There you are! Now don't move." And he went and got backstage passes and splats them on the girls' chests and after the concert they go back off to the hotel with the roadie.

After that, once a year regular when the Allman Brothers came to town, Karla would leave with them for anywhere from a week to longer. "There were times when we would go on the road with them in their bus and fly back from wherever we decided to drop out at. Sometimes I'd fly to meet up with them. Flying-wise I went to San Antonio; Macon, Georgia; New York. We rode on their bus to New Orleans. Shawn was with me on all of these, and Mother was with us on the New York trip. It was one of the most incredible feelings I have ever had! I felt very important, like some kind of fantasy world where everything was so perfect it couldn't be real. The first time I ever flew was in '73, I think, and it was Shawn and I flying back from Kansas City, Missouri, where we had been on the road with the A.B.'s the first time.

"We were kind of like the roadie's little girls, me and Shawn. He was about thirty. And he looked after us. I didn't go to bed with him for about a year. We partied together and he took care of us. Then after about a year, I don't know, we'd been drinking and getting high, and it just happened. It was always Shawn and me with him. Not"—she emphasizes her words carefully—"Shawn and me to-gether." She uses her index fingers to indicate two people side by side. "Shawn and me *with* somebody. So then I was with Dickie Betts, you know who Dickie Betts is, he was really cute—I mean! Then it was just Dickie and I was Dickie's girl, and it was 'Watch out, Dickie will kill you if you get close to his girl.' And . . . the thing about going with a band is you have to go with one person, be his girl and nobody else's. If you're with everybody they use you up. The band passes you down to the roadies' bus and then they don't want you back." That's why Shawn didn't make it to New Orleans with Karla that time. She was back on the roadie bus.

How long, I ask, did it take her to figure out the sociology of the rock-and-roll life?

She waves the question away. "I knew it the first night."

Her eyes light up. "I did," she says proudly, "sleep with Gregg Allman. Once."

Shawn was on that trip too. "We were close, that girl and me," Karla says of Shawn. "There wasn't anything I couldn't tell her. If you could imagine the two closest, best friends in the world, that was her and me. We were stuck together like Siamese twins.

"Shawn dreamed about having Gregg Allman's baby. His baby boy. I remember lying in the bathtub after I was with him and Shawn was in there with me and I told her, 'I'll never douche again.' Of course," she chuckles, "I did."

So, I asked, did Shawn ever sleep with Gregg?

Karla shakes her head. "*No*," she says, and that's all.

To have slept with Gregg Allman. To have bested her best girl-friend. At last, she was *operating*. Karla Faye had surely by now fulfilled her mother's expectations as a girl of the very rarest kind of qualities.

And hey. She was only thirteen, fourteen, fifteen years old.

Two other snapshots of Carolyn Moore. In the first, she's at Granny B.'s with Ronnie Burrell. Ronnie was at that time married to Kari.

Ronnie's got his arm around Carolyn Moore; they're sitting on a couch together and she's leaning her head into his, lovebirds-style. She and Ronnie both have long, loose hair and they are smiling. A handsome, strong-jawed man, Ronnie Burrell looks extremely fond of Carolyn Moore. Carolyn's smile looks equally genuine—maybe because she is simply too sick to pose or keep secrets.

"Mother got sick from needles. Then she wouldn't give up the booze. They told her to, but she wouldn't. . . ."

Recuperating from her first bout with hepatitis, Carolyn Moore's in a blue-flowered robe. Her face is puffy, her eyes weak, her hair dark and stringy; she's not wearing any makeup, and I would not have known who it was if Karla hadn't told me. It's a pathetic parody of the 1956 picture of Carolyn and her husband snuggling on the rust-colored couch with the silver fleck in the upholstery.

The seventh and last snapshot of Carolyn Moore was taken in

November 1979, two weeks before she entered Ben Taub Hospital, where, after a two-week stay, she died.

"Mother couldn't stand up on her own. We brought her out and held her up. We're in front of Granny B.'s apartment. Me and Kari are holding her up."

The three women are in dappled sunlight, in front of some bushes and a brick building. Carolyn is wearing tight faded blue jeans and a yellow sleeveless Eagles T-shirt. Her arms lean heavily on her daughters' shoulders.

In tight flare pants and a T-shirt, Karla's got her hand on her hip in her usual Miss Priss pose. Kari's in wide-legged pants and a plain white shirt. Her hair—loose—still looks like spun-glass angel hair.

Carolyn and her daughter Kari have the same mouth, the same nose. They are smiling the same smile. But Kari's the one who looks all-out now. Carolyn Ann Moore's head is a skull. Death is all over her.

For Granny B., Carolyn Moore and her daughters have lifted their chins. It's a brave pose. *Everything is fine,* the posture of the three women says. Carolyn Moore has let her hands dangle from the wrist, as if she doesn't need to hold on to her daughters' shoulders for support. *We are these three lifelong girlfriends, stuck together, who will make the world fine for one another the whole way through, or at least until—I don't know . . . whatever.*

There is one other woman here but she is not in the picture: our photographer, Zelda Donaldson, otherwise known as the plucky Granny B.

"Let me tell you about a dream I had the night my mother died. . . ." Carolyn Moore was in Ben Taub Hospital, where people in Harris County go who have no money. She hadn't wanted to go to the hospital, but Granny B. finally said she could not take care of her anymore, so Kari, Kathi, Granny B., and Karla were taking turns staying with her. Karla could not believe her mother was going to die; she thought her mother would always be there for her.

Karla had gotten married when she was about sixteen, to a form carpenter she met in the park. Steve Griffith was a hunk—her type—and at first Karla liked being with him; then the liking ran out, fast. She was married to Steve Griffith when Carolyn Moore was in Ben Taub. Steve Griffith resented and despised Karla's family; Karla in turn hated Carolyn Moore's third husband—whom to this day Karla refers to as "the Old Man"—and so for the last couple of years of Carolyn Moore's life, Karla had not seen her mother as much as she was used to.

December 22, 1979, Karla had stayed the night with her mother; next morning, when Kari arrived to take over, Carolyn Moore asked her daughters to take her to the bathroom so she could sit on the normal pot, smoke a normal cigarette, and take a normal shit one last time. The sisters said they would, and together they walked her, her IV, and its rolling holder to the bathroom. As they did, blood ran out of their mother's mouth.

Karla had started to protest when her mother said "one last time," but Kari gave her the high sign and Karla kept her mouth shut. Then, when blood from Carolyn Moore's mouth dripped onto the floor, Karla started to go seriously nuts, but Kari again nodded for her to cool it and so she did. They got their mother to the pot and let her do her thing and got her back to the bed and cleaned her up.

Karla still refused to believe it was her mother's last cigarette and she left and went home and told Steve Griffith about what had happened at the hospital and he said he was sure everything would be okay. That was the night Karla had the dream.

"In the dream I was at the hospital and I was standing by her and she took off the ring I had gotten her (I won a foosball tournament and went and bought Mother a mother's ring for her birthday and us girls gave it to her while she was in the hospital after her hysterectomy) and handed it to me and told me she wanted me to have it. As I was slipping it on my finger she died. The next morning I got woke up with the phone. It was Granny B. telling me if I wanted to see Mother alive again I needed to get on down to the hospital in a hurry."

Karla and Steve jumped in the truck and drove up there, and as she walked in they told her Carolyn was dead. Karla broke through the nurses and ran to her mother's bed; her mother was already cool to the touch.

"I fell to my knees and cried my heart out. A little while later Granny B. handed me the ring and told me Mother gave it to her before she died and asked her please to give it to me. You talk about eerie. . . ."

Carolyn Moore died at forty-three, Christmas Eve, 1979. Karla Faye was twenty.

"All the dreams I have about Mother she is alive. . . . I wake up with tears rolling down my face. . . ."

In a picture taken soon after her mother's death, Karla is wearing a big straw cowboy hat with the brim smartly rolled up on the sides, coming to a point between her eyes. Her sunglasses are perched on top of the hat, cupped saucily around the band. She's in jeans and a plaid shirt. Her hair's draped down over her chest, to her breasts.

Karla doesn't look bored anymore. She is in a *rage*.

Her description: "Me at 20. This is right before I left Steve. We had moved to our own house and were actually starting to do good for a few months and then I left him. I was through, period."

I asked Karla why she married Steve Griffith when she never loved him and after the first blush of being with him did not like having sex with him ("It got to where I'd just give him a blow job and go on to sleep") and he was pathologically possessive and they fought— fist-fought—all the time.

Karla took a long time responding. "I never thought about it before now," she said, "but I guess I was looking for a home. Mother had started to go down pretty fast. She was shooting up regular and so . . . I don't know, but I guess I needed someplace to go. . . . Steve hated my family, so I didn't see much of them, those years. He was my family."

Karla and Steve spent most of their married life living with Steve Griffith's parents. Karla hated that. Steve Griffith should have done better by Karla. She soon lost respect for him.

The one bright aspect of her married life was a two-year-old girl named Jeannette, who had been left with them by a father who couldn't take care of her—the mother having hit the streets long before. Jeannette was with Karla and Steve practically the whole time they were married. Karla was strict, making Jeannette mind her manners, not letting her talk back; she took her to Bible school. I have a picture of Steve, Karla, and Jeannette sitting on the floor in front of a Christmas tree. Steve has a scraggly beard and no moustache; he looks far-off and essentially ordinary, nothing special. Jeannette's a cuddled chunk of roundness, maybe four, nestled in Karla's lap. Karla's got her head back; she's smiling a big smile.

The mother eventually came back for Jeannette. Karla never saw the child again. She says she sometimes wonders where Jeannette is and if she knows what happened.

After Carolyn Moore died, Karla Faye left her husband. And then she proceeded to go seriously, uninterruptedly wild.

Once Carolyn Moore was dead, nobody slapped Karla's wrists anymore, nobody said no to anything. There was no Jeannette with child schedules to keep to. Miss Tough Guy was in charge.

Meantime, curled deep in her heart lay the young Karla Faye, the small tomboyish hopeful girl whose life from the moment she squirted out, black-headed and dark in a family of blue eyes and pale skin, was a lie.

Who wanted more than anything to be a *son* for her father, but how could she do that unless she became some other person who was not a girl at all?

My mother died fast; had a stroke, lived a few hours, then, rather than live a no-kind of life hooked up to machines—I am convinced—said "To hell with this" and died. Fast is good for the dying, not so easy for survivors. We never thought she would be the one to go first; my father was the one with the kaflooey heart.

She knew. Had known. Left notes and diaries all but saying so, a letter to me, stuck back in a drawer she knew I would eventually empty. All those stories. My mother, a woman of many names, was also a woman with a secret life, right down to her very dying.

Once she left, except for a far-off niece I rarely saw, for me family life came down to me and the guys: a father, a husband, two brothers, two sons.

My second brother was born when I was twelve. Once again, my mother and I awaited the arrival of Susie.

No Susie.

Brothers, sons.

No Susie.

III / Trials

It is one of the great sensational moments in our civilization, the trial of a woman for her life.

——EDMUND PEARSON,
The Borden Case, 1924

What one did . . . hope . . . was that the doctor felt . . . he could afford . . . to try to put it across the way it was, try to tell: it was like this and like this and you must believe me because I know, it was me, I was there.

——SYBILLE BEDFORD,
The Trial of Dr. Adams, 1962

I wanted to tell the truth. I wanted the real story to be told. I had to do something about how sick-minded we must have been to think about something like this.

——KARLA FAYE TUCKER, 1984

Players

1. Kathleen

I knew that one way to find out what had gone on in 1983 was to read transcripts of Karla's trial. Until October 1989, I had avoided doing that. The story I was interested in was not who said what on the stand or what happened when they did. A trial's about winning and losing; what does or does not come out is geared to that. Somebody wins, somebody loses.

The story was Karla's voice. Her gestures, emphases, choices; which information she considered crucial and which beside the point; the order in which she brought some things up and avoided some others. The story was what I was doing on Death Row, what questions I asked and avoided and what her story did to and for me.

Other than Henry Oncken, with whom I had two brief visits, I had also avoided lawyers. And so it took a little longer than it might have to get to the transcripts, but with help I found my way.

In Texas, once a trial is completed and the notes transcribed, it is the court reporter who maintains rights over the transcripts and profits from their sale—as if the reporter had actually written the trial instead of simply taking it down. To some extent this is fair. From the givens in a trial the court reporter fashions a text. There are decisions to be made: how to punctuate so that the sense of the testimony comes across, how to spell odd names, what actually the witness, judge, attorney, or prosecutor is saying, when to mind the judge when the judge draws a line across his or her throat meaning "Don't take this down."

Late in October 1989, I called the 180th District Court—Judge Patricia Lykos presiding—and asked to speak to the court reporter.

Kathleen Powers, I was told, was Judge Lykos's reporter, and she came on the line.

With the case number before me, I introduced myself to Kathleen. I said I didn't know if she was the person I needed to talk to but that maybe she could help, I was looking for the transcripts of a case that had been tried in Judge Lykos's court some five and a half years before, and I gave the number, 388428.

What, Kathleen asked, was the defendant's name?

I told her.

Silence on the other end.

"I wondered," Kathleen Powers finally sighed, "when somebody would do something with that." She was quiet for another brief piece of time. "I'm surprised it took this long."

Turned out, Kathleen Powers had been the court reporter for Karla's trial, then had gone on a four-year leave shortly afterwards. She had returned to work only the week before I called.

I asked if she remembered the trial.

"I wish I could forget it," she said. "I don't think anybody who had anything to do with it can. I'm responsible for taking the exhibits in and out of the courtroom. Every day I carried that pickax in. The shotgun, the motorcycle parts. . . . At the end of the day, I took them back out again."

I thought I could hear her shudder over the telephone.

"Karla and I were exactly the same age. We grew up listening to the same music. The first album I ever bought was *Eat a Peach* by the Allman Brothers. And I don't know . . . I kept thinking . . . I don't know, it just got to me."

When I began asking questions, Kathleen pulled back.

"I don't think I should say much. You should talk to J.C. Mosier, I'm sure he'll talk to you, and . . . some other people. There was a lot of talk."

It was as far as she would go. When I asked if she wanted maybe to have lunch, she said no.

As for buying the transcripts, Kathleen said she didn't think I wanted to do that; transcripts cost two dollars a page, and capital cases tended to run on—in Karla's case for some two thousand pages not counting voir dire.

"But," she said, "you can come to the courthouse and take all the notes you want."

Kathleen told me who to call to get the case pulled. "If you have any problem, call me back," she said.

Kathleen Powers was unshakable. Her tone indicated her firm intention to help as well as her equally firm resolve to get off the phone and out of any more conversation having to do with *State of Texas* v. *Karla Faye Tucker*.

The following July, I finally met Kathleen. I was in Patricia Lykos's chambers having coffee. Kathleen was late for work, having been delayed by a chemical spill on I-10. She arrived in a flurry of nerves—blond, attractive, big glasses—and flopped down in a big chair to recuperate from her troubled commute. Judge Lykos introduced me.

At the mention of my name, Kathleen looked sharply up.

"I've had your name on my bulletin board since October," she said. "I wondered if you'd show up. You didn't sound too sure back then."

"I wasn't."

"I knew," she said to Patricia Lykos, "somebody would eventually get around to writing about this."

Judge Lykos told Kathleen Powers we had been discussing the tape Douglas Garrett made.

"State 56." From the big chair in the corner, Kathleen called out the exhibit number, and her response was as ingrained a reflex as the memory of an old telephone number you try to forget but can't. "State 26 was the pickax."

Kathleen got up, walked past me, poured herself a drink of water.

2. Miss Rebecca

According to Ted Bundy, if you can make the first six months of jail you can handle the rest. Florida finally executed Ted Bundy, so there's no way of knowing if he included electrocution within the scope of "the rest," but still . . .

About his implication—that the first weeks in jail are the toughest—Karla Faye agrees, except she says she might shorten the time, maybe down to six weeks.

I have one picture of Karla locked up in County in the fall of 1983, some months after her arrest. She's in a medium-blue shapeless button-up jail dress with tight short sleeves and that unflattering open-neck collar jail uniforms everywhere seem to require. Not everybody in County wore blue; this dress just fit Karla—in jail when you find something that fits, she says, you swipe it if you have to, and keep washing it—so she wore it all the time.

If there's a before-and-after aspect to the family album on my wall, the picture of Karla in County belongs square in the middle. It is, unquestionably, the hinge.

In the before pictures, Karla Faye has her look down pat, the surly pout, the cocky Miss Hot Stuff come-on. Even at seven, she looks so *sure.* Here she's pale, she's smiling softly, her chin is tucked slightly, her arms hang clumsily unposed by her side. She looks incredibly, uncharacteristically *tentative,* if not to say downright shy. You get the feeling that for the first time in her life Karla Faye Tucker is backing off from the camera instead of challenging—seducing—it to come closer.

She has the look of a quiet child, that's all. A normal child, feeling her way through the world, peeking out from behind a curtain of uncertainty, wondering *Will I do?*

She's heavier, but that's not it. She'd quit smoking. The only drugs she was taking were her hormone pills and, when she went to court, Lomotil for her stomach to keep her bowels in check. The guards took her to the infirmary every day to get her hormone pills.

In the Harris County Jail, at first Karla "laid around on my bunk most of the time, real, I don't know, depressed, I guess. It was the first time I'd been alone in my life. I had always had people around me."

Separated from her tribe, no biker tough talk to fall back on, no tricks to turn, no friends and sisters to protect, no guys to impress or—her great pride—give expert head, Karla lay on her bunk, wrote long juicy letters to Danny, made all the phone calls she was allowed, and ate ice cream, as much as three pints at a time.

Her comment on the picture in the blue jail dress: "Up to 135 pounds! When I had quit smoking. *Porky.*"

In November, she faced her first birthday in jail:

In the County in 83, I turned 24. I was having a pity party in my cell and noticed it got real quiet but thought nothing of it. Soon here came Mary and told me to come here. Reluctantly I followed. She led me to the empty cell in the tank and everyone (all 11 gals) jumped up and yelled HAPPY BIRTHDAY! and started singing. They had written all over the walls and strung toilet paper all over the place. They took and filled one bleach bucket with lemonaid and one with hot chocolate; they used honeybuns as the cake and stuck matches in for candles; there was sliced up candy bars and life savers on trays. They had gotten some books from Miss Rebecca and wrapped them in toilet tissue and gave them to me as gifts. I cried and so did most or all of the other ladies! It was the best party I've ever had because of where and how. Here were girls that were in jail for who knows what, not really caring about someone's birthday—or so I thought.

Locked up, Karla Faye began to inch out of the drug fog. It goes slow. Rusty Hardin, who prosecuted Danny Garrett, says he thinks Karla Faye was still a little fuzzy when she went on trial in April 1984. He says she was clearer-headed when she testified in November. "She was more," he says, "in the world by then."

You can see it in the picture taken in County; she's a blurry girl, not the sharply defined one we're used to. Her nerves are capped, emotions in sight but still *out there* like a prize she's after but can't quite get to. In a way, it's lucky they gave her a number, because I'll swear, this girl does not know who she is. There's a positively sweet look about her. Now that she's locked up away from all the talk-talk, the sweetness—vulnerability—can emerge.

I watched as, toward the end of his life, my father came up out of the swamp of alcoholism. He looked like some slime-drenched bog-movie creature, rising from the muck. For close to a year, he looked worse not drinking than he had when he was putting away vodka like a chocolate freak doing M&M's.

In the beginning of jail time, you are a caged rat. All you can think of is getting out; it doesn't matter how, just out. You weep, rail, curse your fate, bang your head, mope, go on food binges, stop eating. . . . That's the six months Ted Bundy was talking about.

Karla calls it holding up the brick walls by yourself; let go and they tumble in on you. Somewhere along in there comes a decisive moment: you either yield to the situation or don't, adjust or refuse, make something out of what's left or don't, make a move toward creating a life within the terms handed down—no matter how reduced or unpalatable the circumstances, no matter how appalling the choices—or do not.

After my mother died, my father went on his last serious binge. For weeks he ate practically nothing, just drank; poured vodka down his throat until he could neither walk, talk, nor sign his name. I signed him into a hospital for a twenty-eight-day period of drying out and counsel. Diabetic, he was in such terrible shape it took six weeks instead of four. The alcohol and the stress from my mother's death had ruined his system for good. His sugar count was way up. For the first time in his life he had to inject insulin; doctors noticed gangrenous spots on his big toes. Beginning of the end.

When in July 1983 my father was going into surgery to have his second leg amputated, the surgeon assured him that the operation would not be complicated and that he would be fine—an easy promise to make, as it turns out; amputation is as simple as sawing off a tree limb. "What's more," the surgeon said, "I know this is hard for you to believe, but there will come a time when you will be happy again."

We were in the hall just outside the operating room. My father— on the gurney, waiting to be rolled in—just looked at the surgeon. My brother and I were too stunned to speak. The loss of one leg was one thing. But to be ungrounded like a puppet?

The surgeon was right. For a time there, as my father learned to walk with a rolling walker and to get in and out of cars and bed and then to go to work and to AA meetings, he was not only pleased as a child with himself, he was—relatively, *compared to what* being the issue here—happy. Working within the givens, he had a life.

On December 6, 1983, less than a month after her twenty-fourth birthday party, Karla attended her first AA meeting, an hour-long open drug session. It was at AA that Karla met a woman who would prove to be as important to her as anyone she had or has met in her life, Chaplain Rebecca Lewis, whom Karla calls Miss Rebecca.

AA became a constant in Karla's jail life, then Bible study classes.

She counseled individually with Miss Rebecca. Miss Rebecca listened to Karla, advised her, heard about her life, her mother. Rebecca Lewis came to like Karla Faye Tucker—probably more than, for professional reasons, she's now willing to admit. In the summer of 1990 when I went to see her, the chaplain had only one photograph tacked on her bulletin board, a snapshot of Karla Faye, squatting in the small yard outside Death Row.

In time, Karla lost the weight she had gained in County. She inched up out of her sulk and began to make friends, encouraged others to attend AA and Bible class. Eventually, she was allowed into Miss Rebecca's elite corps, the advanced Bible studies class, reserved for a select group of inmates the chaplain trains to go back into the tank and hold Bible studies classes on their own.

Consistency is the trait Rebecca Lewis looks for. The chaplain knows about inmates playing church; she does a thorough screening of an inmate before she allows one in her advanced class. Karla was not, Rebecca Lewis is convinced, playing church. She was consistent, in her beliefs and her attitude.

I went to see the chaplain expecting hard-shell fundamentalism. What I found was an extremely intelligent and articulate woman who has studied sociology, psychology, criminology, religion, and the law.

We visited in the chaplain's tiny office upstairs in the Harris County Jail. I had come without an appointment. The phone lines to the jail are always busy; they put you on hold, play a tinkly version of "Greensleeves" until you want to choke somebody. I kept hanging up.

Rebecca Lewis is a very pretty, very young-looking woman in her early thirties. She wears her dark blond hair girlishly long and loose, she has pale smooth skin, full pink lips, and clear blue eyes that fix on the light of God with practiced alacrity. The day I met her, she wore a pale blue belted dress with a big white lace collar; small earrings; no rings, faint makeup. She's quite lovely, in a completely uncomplicated way. If central casting needed a new Aimee Semple McPherson, they would do well to check out Chaplain Lewis.

Like all deeply religious people, the chaplain is nothing if not certain. When she says "the Lord," for her he's real as a window. When she says "I was raised in a Christian home," she is standing on the rock where Jesus stood, her tone blessedly assured.

Overwhelmed by her clarity and her luminosity, I felt certain Rebecca Lewis disapproved of me, I could not say whether because of my hair, my shoes, something I had said, the book I was writing. Maybe nothing. Maybe I imagined it.

When Karla was locked up in 1983, Rebecca Lewis had been working at the Harris County Jail for a year. She is now head of chaplaincy there, the first woman ever to hold that job.

"People come in here," Rebecca Lewis said—by "people" she meant inmates—"they want to *be* somebody. They don't know how to do it or really what they want. They don't know how to work with or in a group, they have no social skills; they almost always *have* a group, but what they really believe in is their own independence, their ability to take care of themselves and to operate *on their own*. That's what they rely on. This usually means their ability to manipulate others."

The chaplain was angry. The source was hard to pin down.

"People come in here, they have had bad experiences as a child— government figures suggest that 85 percent of all inmates have been sexually molested; that's *government* figures. They are looking to please someone, quite often the mother. They will do *anything* to have their love returned to them, anything. We try to help them become a complete person on their own, whether or not that love is returned—which will probably never happen, no matter what they do. We show them that the *Lord* can provide that completion. We tell them, you can't be loved any more than *totally,* which is how God loves you. The *Lord* provides completion."

She was angry at mothers for lying down on the job, at lawbreakers for needing mothers, at the government for supplying lousy figures. . . .

"For many of them this is the first time in their lives they have slowed down long enough to look at themselves. . . ."

Angry at outsiders for not understanding how tough this all was?

"I don't know how much Karla has told you about her mother, but, you know, she was a bad mother."

I nodded.

"Karla needed the Lord for completion. I served as a character witness at Karla's trial because she was *consistent* in her attitude and actions. I said that. But it doesn't help to be a character witness. Sometimes it does just the opposite. The prosecutor turns it around, he says, 'But you only know her in jail, in special circumstances, you don't know her outside and you didn't know her when she committed the crime.' And that's true. The way it's set up, if you tell the truth, they manipulate it. I did it for Karla. That was the first and the last time I testified for anybody."

When I suggested that perhaps the chaplain was a force for good in Karla's life, maybe one of the few ever and probably the only one she'd ever paid attention to, Miss Rebecca backed off. It wasn't her influence, she says, but the Lord's. The *Lord* deserved all the credit.

Growing up, considering a career, Rebecca Lewis leaned toward a helping profession, something to do with the law, she didn't know what. Then . . .

"I had a dream, of locked-up women. The women weren't necessarily in jail, they were just locked up. But I could see how they could get out. And I didn't understand why they didn't. I asked one woman, 'Why don't you leave?' She said it wouldn't matter if she did; 'I'd only be back,' she told me. I couldn't get that off my mind. 'I'd only be back.'"

Eventually, Lewis combined the two strongest elements in her life, the Christian home and the need to help locked-up women avoid going back.

When my time with the chaplain was up, I felt wrung out, as if she'd been the one asking the questions. In the hall, waiting for the elevator, Rebecca Lewis bantered with a fellow employee, her comments lightly barbed and witty, his a little wary.

When I got to my car, I discovered I had left my reading glasses on the chaplain's desk.

Rather than face "Greensleeves" again, I decided to write her a note.

I never went back. Odds are, the glasses are still on her desk.

3. The Judge

The Harris County district attorney's office announced its intentions. Karla Faye Tucker and Daniel Ryan Garrett would be tried separately, Karla for the capital murder of Jerry Lynn Dean, Danny Garrett for killing Deborah Ruth Thornton. Each could be tried for the other murder later on, depending on the outcome of the first trials.

Prosecutors often see themselves as benighted champions of goodness and order, out doing the Lord's work. Prosecutors can be overly earnest; they have to be diligent. Diligent, earnest prosecutors take it badly when you talk about the strategy of a trial as if it were a game. But it's a game, all right, one in which the state has the first move. The Houston D.A.'s office, while generously funded, does not often open its pockets to a capital case against a woman. Capital cases cost. Women don't often get the death penalty. The D.A.'s office likes to win.

Karla was tried for the murder of Jerry Dean because the state had more evidence against her in that case. As Danny Garrett seemed to have inflicted most of the damage done to Deborah Thornton's body, the state would try him for her murder. If in either trial the prosecutor didn't come up with a death penalty verdict the first time around, another prosecutor would have another shot later on.

Assignment of a case to a particular judge goes by luck of the draw. To decide which case goes to whose courtroom, Harris County uses the Ping-Pong ball method, like a bingo game. A clerk announces the case, whirls the Ping-Pong machine, a ball pops out, marked with the name of your judge.

In the lottery for judges, people think Danny Garrett lucked out. His case would be tried in District Court 232, Judge A. D. Azios presiding. In Texas, judges are elected, which means they are politicians first and, often, foremost. Known as an easygoing fellow, Judge Azios keeps his constituency happy by emphasizing his record as a war hero and by being a lovable kind of guy—tough on crime, yet affable—and also by being Hispanic.

Karla Faye's Ping-Pong ball said number 180, Judge Patricia Lykos presiding. No one who has appeared in the 180th District Court of Harris County in any capacity comes away feeling lukewarm about Patricia Lykos. Among the comments I have heard from prosecutors and defense attorneys alike are "bitch" . . . "Greek tyrant" . . . "inconsistent" . . . "unpredictable" . . . "the complete political animal" . . . "publicity hungry" . . . "grandstands for voters" . . . "bitch." One defense attorney simply said "my favorite judge" and let the iciness of his tone speak for itself. A prosecutor quickly clammed up when questioned, then smiled sweetly, as if to say, "You won't hear it from me."

"She'll do anything"—this from an attorney who had tried several cases in her courtroom.

"Like what?"

"Like keep the courtroom waiting an hour and a half, then waltz in and say to the jury, 'If I could get these attorneys to show up on time, ladies and gentlemen of the jury, we wouldn't have these unfortunate delays.' Like that."

These comments do not surprise Pat Lykos.

"I'm not popular with attorneys," she says. She shrugs. "That's okay. I'm not in tenth grade."

The judge is an extremely attractive woman, late fortyish, olive skinned, with lush Mediterranean features, dark-haired with some gray. She has a great comb-back haircut, colors her lips deep burgundy to complement her skin tones, wears bright-colored suits in place of a robe, drinks coffee and smokes from the bench, taking deep draws, then blowing the smoke to heaven via the air-conditioning vents. She allows jurors to smoke in the jury box as well, with this admonition: "I would ask that the smokers sit on the back row. I find that that is least offensive to the nonsmokers."

Very early on in Karla's case, during the pretrial proceedings, Patricia Lykos interrupts to ask Karla's lawyer Mack Arnold point blank, "What are you doing standing up?"

Danny Garrett is on the stand at the time, taking the fifth.

Mack Arnold says, "I would like to see the witness in the face, Your Honor."

"Swap places," Lykos advises.

Mack Arnold thanks the judge for her good advice. He and Henry Oncken switch chairs. And Lykos makes her speech:

"I want all attorneys advised that questions will be asked while they are seated there at the counsel table, unless there is a reason for them to approach the witness and they ask the court's permission. No attorney in this court will be permitted to waltz around the courtroom throwing questions over his shoulder. He remains seated unless otherwise granted permission by the court."

Ordering courtroom attorneys to stay seated is not common practice. In a lot of judges' courtrooms, lawyers—particularly defense attorneys—do a great deal of waltzing; a lot of lawyers have as a matter of very public record staked their careers on their ability to engage in fancier footwork by far than one-two-three.

Another time, when during a break in proceedings Mack Arnold disappears for five minutes, presumably to go to the men's room, Lykos tells him not to leave the room without her permission.

A former cop, a Republican who campaigns as a tough opponent of crime, Patricia Lykos can, from time to time, turn her strictness around so that it benefits a defendant. When Joe Magliolo calls Karla by her first name, the judge curtly reminds him that all people in her courtroom will be referred to by their last name, preceded by "Miss," "Mr.," or "Mrs." Thus, she raises the defendant's status.

I asked Pat Lykos if her reputation for toughness had anything to do with being a woman, having to come down especially hard to establish her authority over peacocky male attorneys.

"Honey," Pat Lykos sighed, "I worked my way through college in the police department. Would you like some coffee?"

The judge is touchy, but away from the bench she can be relaxed and homey.

"There is no place for theatrics in a courtroom," Patricia Lykos insists. "Leaning on the bar while a witness is testifying, making meaningful looks back over the shoulder to the jury? I won't allow it."

In her chambers the judge is dressed for the day—red suit, cream-colored blouse, a double strand of pearls; the only jarring note is her black leather aerobics shoes. Patricia Lykos's office is cramped, crowded, and awkwardly arranged. We are sitting in what is meant to be a hall outside her office. I'm on a low couch, she's in a chair. There's a coffee machine. People come and go.

She opens a small refrigerator, stands in the open door, pours milk from a four-ounce baby bottle.

"Kathleen's," she explains, holding up the bottle.

I accept the coffee and, knowing that the judge's courtroom is filled with people waiting for her to read the docket, offer to cut our visit short.

She waves me back down.

"Relax, honey," she says, taking a drag off her cigarette.

Patricia Lykos remembers Karla's trial quite vividly. Unlike Joe Magliolo, she thinks the weapon was not the only reason it got so much publicity.

"The violence. And because it was a woman. There aren't that many times when a woman is involved in a crime that violent. The state was asking for the death penalty. . . ."

She pauses, remembering.

"And there was what she said about sexual. . . . What was that expression she used?"

" 'Getting a nut.' "

"I'd never heard that before." She sips her coffee, takes a deep drag on her cigarette. "I thought I'd heard everything."

We are both quiet for a moment, contemplating Karla's epithet for orgasm.

I ask the judge if she remembers where at the defendant's table Karla sat.

"They usually put them facing the jury—you know, to appeal to their sympathy—but I'm not sure in Karla's case. You have to understand, my mother was dying during that trial, so there are some things I don't recall. But I remember exactly how she looked." With her index finger, Judge Lykos draws a cross between her breasts. "That white cross."

Describing Karla, the newspapers mentioned the jail-issue white plastic cross every day. When witnesses are asked to point her out in the courtroom they invariably refer to her as the one at the table in the pink sweater, blue dress, tan blouse . . . with the white cross around her neck.

When I ask Karla about her courtroom wardrobe, she rolls her eyes. "My granny bought my clothes. Them puffed sleeves. It was embarrassing. People knew about my life. I was up there on the stand telling them. I know my granny was trying to help, but still."

"Now you understand," Patricia Lykos explains, "I can't talk about the case." Karla has a court date coming up, at which time Judge Lykos will rule on Karla's recently filed petition for writ of habeas corpus.

The bailiff sticks his head in. Somebody else walks through. The judge puts out her cigarette.

I stand up and thank Pat Lykos for her time.

Before she enters the courtroom, the judge reaches behind her to get a pair of high-heeled shoes from a stack of boxes piled against the wall.

"I wondered if you wore Reeboks behind that big desk," I say.

"Oh, heavens no," she says, and she invites me to sit in the jury box while the docket is read. We shake hands and within seconds, Judge Lykos is out the door and everybody's rising.

On her high wooden desk Judge Lykos keeps one of those nontilt ceramic coffee cups, heavy and wide at the bottom, small at the top. At her machine, Kathleen Powers works with great diligence, blond hair bobbing, eyes focused on the middle distance as she taps out the unfolding story.

4. Lawyers

In the beginning, Karla had a private attorney, paid for by a friend of her friend Scott, the Green Beret.

"Gabe Nahas," another lawyer told me. "Don't say I said so, but Lord—he was on his last legs." In the winter of 1991, Gabe Nahas had his ticket lifted for incompetence.

Karla didn't like Gabe Nahas.

"But more than that, he didn't like me. He knew I was lying my butt off."

Larry Tucker and the grandmothers told Karla she was on her own as far as counsel went; anyway, the judge would appoint better lawyers than they could afford. Not just one lawyer but—because it was a capital case—two.

"They brought me over from County. Lykos asked did I want new representation, I said yes, and she went through all this about did I want her to appoint me an attorney and I said yes, and that was the first time I met Mack [Arnold] and Henry [Oncken]. Lykos said we could use the jury room to talk, so we went back there and I don't know, I sat down at that table and for the first time except to my chaplain, I told the truth, I mean everything. I don't know what they thought. I guess they might've been surprised."

Unless Patricia Lykos has changed a lot in the seven years since Karla's trial, it's doubtful Karla got away with simple yeses. Judge Lykos phrases her questions so that while yes may *do,* because yes is not the answer she's after she won't accept it.

"Now I am going to explain some things here," she will tell a defendant. "If you understand, say so. Do you understand?" She waits for an answer. If the defendant says "Yes," "I see," "I do," "Yes, ma'am," anything other than the required "I understand," Patricia Lykos cocks her head, tucks her chin, leans her ear in the defendant's direction, and waits to hear the right answer to the question. I saw her send one young woman and her court-appointed lawyer back to the drawing board because the young woman obviously did *not* understand the question, even though she gave the right answer to it, and her attorney was so ill acquainted with the case he could not provide much help. "I cannot pass judgment on this young woman when she so clearly does not comprehend what is going on," Judge Lykos declared.

Well aware that the Karla Faye Tucker case was going to attract a lot of attention, when Pat Lykos appointed attorneys to represent Karla, she went for two men she considered top-notch, with plenty of experience practicing criminal law. Usually on a capital case a judge will choose one attorney with a lot of trial experience. The other one—riding second—usually has less. But Judge Lykos wanted to be particularly careful with this case.

There are those who think her reasoning was flawed: both the attorneys Patricia Lykos appointed had spent most of their careers arguing for the state. They were known as prosecutors, not defense attorneys. Most attorneys think the distinction is as basic as blood type.

I asked a prosecutor high up in the D.A.'s office what he thought of Karla's representation. He shrugged and said, "They were prosecutors."

In October 1983, when Henry Oncken and Mack Arnold met Karla, she was still cocksure and hostile.

"I couldn't stand her," Oncken says. "The drugs were still in her. She didn't care about anything. I didn't want to take the case."

I asked Mack Arnold if he was surprised when Karla came clean about her participation in the murders. Mack Arnold looks wistful, says no, then adds, "You get to where nothing surprises you."

Mack Arnold is Irish and plays it up; during the course of a trial he will apologize to the judge for occasional outbursts, blaming Irishness. He also tends toward the traditionally dark Irish sense of humor: cynicism, fatalism, disguised as wit.

Henry Oncken is quiet, contained. The fatherly figure in the courtroom proceedings—tending fires, not much dirtying his hands in the actual fray—Henry takes care of Karla, rides second, advises the defendant, reassures her, does the backstage work.

A trial is pure theater. Like actors, lawyers have to figure out not so much what they *are* as how they come across: wise, fatherly, the spoiler, the crusader, or what.

A third player here—or fourth, counting Lykos, who as a vote getter also has to concentrate on appearance as much as if not more than reality—is the prosecutor, Joe Magliolo. Joe Mag is Italian, the only nondoctor in a family of five brothers and a doctor father. Quick on the trigger, Joe Mag is sharp, ambitious, intelligent, and in a hurry. Eats fast, moves fast. Worked as an assistant D.A. only four years before being appointed chief prosecutor, had been chief only three months when Karla's case came up. His first capital. No problem. Joe Mag was ready. Anyway, the state had all the ammunition.

Mack Arnold has a flair for the dramatic, a way with words, so it makes sense that Mack would handle the courtroom work, but as Henry was the one who, in time, would develop a relationship with Karla, some people wondered why Henry didn't conduct more of the trial, particularly when Karla was on the stand.

"Henry did not want to take this case," says Jackie Oncken. "But we needed the money. And after a while, he got to where he liked Karla so much . . . he would come home and say, 'You know, Jackie, there's another girl inside there. She's just now starting to come out.' And he told me how she took care of this little girl, I don't know, abandoned by some doper parents, and. . . . The day Karla got the death penalty he came home and sat in the dark in his chair and cried."

In 1981, after a stint in the D.A.'s office, Henry Oncken had been appointed by Republican governor Bill Clements to fill out the term of a judge who had died. When, in 1982, Oncken ran for reelection on the Republican ticket, he lost, tossed out by a Democratic sweep at the polls.

"I have been in private practice for only two years in my whole life," Henry Oncken states point-blank in 1989. "It was during that time that Judge Lykos called me to her bench"—he crooks his finger and wiggles it, like a witch baiting children into dark corners—"and said, 'I've got something for you.' Lord knows I didn't want to take it."

"Henry," Jackie states point blank, "is a born prosecutor."

That Karla's trial came before Danny's is luck of the draw, having to do with docket, schedule, the availability of attorneys. On a capital case, attorneys interview potential jurors individually and at length, and so the process of jury selection—voir dire—can and often does take longer than the actual trial. It took a month to choose Karla's jury of eight women and four men.

During voir dire, both sides were already thinking ahead, beyond guilt/innocence to the punishment phase of the trial. This is standard in capital cases. The prosecution tried to make sure no potential juror would go easy on Karla just because she was a woman. The defense was looking for men with daughters Karla's age. "Our thinking was, a man with a daughter her age would identify with Karla. He'd have a hard time giving her the death penalty."

"We were happy with the jury," says Henry Oncken. "We had strikes left over. We thought it was a blue-ribbon panel."

The trial lasted two weeks, from April 11 until April 25, 1984. The transcripts come to some two thousand pages, divided into thirty-six bound volumes.

The trial of Danny Garrett for the murder of Deborah Thornton would take place in A. D. Azios's court beginning in late July. Voir dire took from August 6 until October 8, when the actual trial began. The trial was not concluded, the death penalty doled out to Danny Garrett, until November 29, some four months later.

Danny Garrett's trial transcripts come to some ten thousand pages, divided into sixty-three volumes.

The reason Danny's trial took so much longer? Fancy footwork and rabbit trails instigated and performed by the attorney Danny's family hired to represent him, Ray Bass.

Ray Bass is a small man—he tells you so in the transcripts, about every five minutes; "Short," he will say of someone a witness has said is five feet two or three inches tall, "like me?"—a man born to defend, to shamelessly showboat. Attention sticks to Ray Bass like glitter to glue. As a performer, Ray Bass will juggle, turn cartwheels, put on a clown suit, show his fan kick. Whatever it takes.

Another attorney summed him up by saying, "Ray Bass is known for wearing a bowtie in court."

One of the first things you learn in law school is dress the part. People distrust a man in a bowtie. Ray Bass yuks it up.

Judge Azios, it is clear, permits attorneys a whole lot more room for twinkle-toed footwork than does Patricia Lykos. And in the end, Ray Bass's two-step didn't exactly bring down the house. His client still got the death penalty.

Against the Peace and Dignity of the State

April 11, 1984. In pretrial, the audiotape has been admitted, Douglas Garrett having been adjudged sane enough to testify. The state is ready. The defense says it is.

Joe Mag runs down the case he has been authorized to present by the state of Texas and the duly organized grand jury of Harris County, "that Karla Faye Tucker, hereafter styled the defendant, heretofore on or about June 13, 1983, did then and there unlawfully while in the course of committing and attempting to commit the burglary and robbery of Jerry Lynn Dean, hereafter styled the complainant, intentionally cause the death of the complainant by striking and stabbing the complainant with a mattock.

"Against"—a new paragraph—"the peace and dignity of the state."

Joe Mag offers a graphic opening statement in which he tells the jury what he expects evidence to show and calls his first witness.

1. The Story

At twenty till seven on the morning of June 13, 1983, twenty-six-year-old Gregory Scott Travers waited for his friend Jerry Lynn Dean to come pick him up in his El Camino. Gregory Travers lived in the Windtree Apartments, about a minute and a half from Jerry Dean. Both young men had jobs at Qube Security, installing burglar alarms. They were supposed to be at work at seven and so they ordinarily left at twenty till, but that morning Jerry didn't show up.

Gregory Travers waited until ten till and then went over to apartment 2313 to see if maybe his ride had overslept. He noticed that the

El Camino was nowhere in sight. When he got to the back door of Jerry Dean's apartment he found it unlocked. Gregory Travers knocked. When he knocked, the door came open a little, so he yelled inside the apartment. When there was no response he yelled again. The radio in the living room was on, loud, playing rock and roll music. He walked on in and . . .

You have to wonder how this sounds to the unsuspecting listener, one who does not know what has already taken place in apartment 2313; but then there is no unsuspecting listener, the jury has been told by Joe Magliolo what to expect, they know what lies ahead for Gregory Travers. Still and all, their sense of disbelief could be suspended by now, they may be in a high state of imagined apprehension, not despite of but *because* they know what lies ahead, as Gregory Travers relives the scene, leads us step by step through his friend's apartment. He is not fearful at this point exactly, not yet, but by now he is apprehensive—calling out so as not to invade his friend's privacy, hoping not to find anything amiss, reaching ahead of himself with his voice the way you do with your hand when you get up in the night and make your way through the bedroom without turning on the lights.

He goes first into the master bedroom, but nobody is there. This is the bedroom where four-year-old Jamie Kay, Shawn Jackson Dean's daughter, used to sleep when Jerry and Shawn were living together as a married couple and Jamie was with them. But nobody is in there.

The implication is that Gregory Travers knew the floor plan of apartment 2313—after all, he lived at Windtree—but not how Jerry Dean lived, letting Jamie Kay have the master bedroom, taking the smaller spare bedroom for himself and his wife when she lived there.

"Okay." Joe Magliolo is Mr. Interlocutor; our straight man. He eggs the narrator on. "And then what?"

And so . . .

Time clicks; it is almost seven by now, in summer, broad open daylight. As the apartments at Windtree have low ceilings and few windows, it would have been shadowy in the apartment, the light soft and grayish.

Gregory Travers comes out of the master bedroom, takes a step or two. Looking across the hall through the spare bedroom door, he "seen Jerry in the spare bedroom" and "he had a little blood over his head." Gregory Travers can't figure it out at first. And then he takes a closer look, and . . .

"And I seen the girl with a pickax in her heart."

The story is never just plot, the story is language and timing and very careful detail, rhythm and ordering and subtext and what words sound and feel like, the accumulated weight and fuzz words bring with them, like dust in a drawer.

In a trial the narrator of the story keeps changing, in voice, lingo, subtext. Joe Mag is not narrator but tour guide. He cannot control what people say, he can only prod, guide, take care what questions he asks. "I seen the girl with a pickax in her heart" is his payoff— than which no writer living or dead could do better.

Gregory Travers does the once-upon-a-time; gets the story the state wants to tell started; establishes the fact that two bodies, two dead people, existed, were found by him, in a certain place at a certain time, a guy and a girl, and the girl had a pickax in her heart. Which Gregory Travers knows because he was right there and he saw.

In her initial remarks to the jury, Patricia Lykos has said that in making a determination of what the facts of this case are, the jury may take into consideration the appearance, attitude, and behavior of a witness, as well as the interest of a witness in the outcome of the case, the relationship of a witness to one side or the other, the probability or improbability of a witness's statement—in other words, his or her basic credibility.

Gregory Travers's testimony rings shatteringly true; we believe him, trust him, he is not offering opinion but only description, and as he takes us through apartment 2313 in bare-bones prose, we come to share his sense of building apprehension.

Gregory Travers also establishes the theme and sets the tone of *State of Texas* v. *Karla Faye Tucker*. The theme is human viciousness, beyond what we think of as normal comprehension. The tone is pure horror.

To emphasize the point, Joe Mag will come back to the phrase "hacked to death" again and again.

Once Gregory Travers has seen the bodies, he goes home—"took out of the apartment"—to his place. Then he calls an ambulance and the police.

The story has been outlined: we have an overview. Joe Mag then takes Gregory Travers back to apartment 2313 for a more detailed narrative, this time with visual aids. First, he gets his witness to establish the fact that there had been a partially built Harley on a wooden stand in the living room of Jerry Lynn Dean's apartment and that on the morning of June 13, 1983, the Harley frame was gone. (This is an important fact for Joe Mag to establish if he is to get a death-penalty sentence for murder committed during the commission of a separate felony crime.)

Photographs are offered into evidence. (There was a lot of discussion in pretrial about the photographs: which ones could be admitted, which were unnecessarily inflammatory. Mack Arnold objected particularly strongly to a close-up shot of the blade of the pickax embedded in Deborah Thornton's T-shirt and chest.)

First come establishing shots: Apartment 2313 from the outside, from the parking lot. The back door of the apartment, the front door. Then interiors: living room, hallway. Gregory Travers says yes, that is the building; yes, the living room; yes, the stand where the Harley was when I was there last week. . . .

The spare bedroom is a mess: tools and boxes all over, aluminum stepladders, scaffolding. The bed is a thin mattress set away from the wall in the middle of the room. (An early newspaper story stated that police did not know whether or not Jerry Dean's apartment had been ransacked, as it was known to be in perpetual disarray.)

Joe Mag is taking the jury on this tour. Tracking, tracking. He is closing in now. The jury knows what is ahead—the bodies, the mutilated bodies. The jury also understands it is probably not ready for what it knows must come. Must be ready, cannot possibly be. Finally—pay dirt—he zeroes in on what Gregory Scott Travers saw when he arrived at the door of the spare bedroom: the dead man, Jerry Lynn Dean, from the foot of the bed, naked, on his back, half on the mattress and half off.

His head is thrown back and to one side—the side of him that is off the mattress, his right side. His long blond hair lies in streaks across his face. His left leg is straight, his right knee cocked. His penis rests quietly on his thigh. His left hand is curled in a soft fist at his hipbone. His right arm reaches out as if he were trying to hand somebody something, the hand very close to a cardboard box zealously wrapped in silver duct tape.

He might be asleep. Except for the blood streaks and what looks like cockroaches crawling on his chest, he could be dreaming. The cockroaches are pickax holes.

Deborah Thornton is on Jerry Lynn Dean's left, half on her side, curled slightly into herself. Her hair is limp across her face, one arm is across her chest, the other one flat on the bed next to some splotches of blood, palm up, fingers curled. She is wearing the T-shirt with the "Teller 2" logo on the front, a ring, and a gold chain around her neck. Someone has tucked the tail of her T-shirt between her legs so that her genitals are covered. (It is not clear who did this; no one remembers or is saying.)

A pickax handle is some four feet long; its iron head from tip to tip about two feet. The pointed end of the pickax is buried seven inches in the girl's chest, square through the "2" of "Teller 2." The rest of the instrument hovers over the girl's body, parallel to it, nailing her like a bug to a corkboard.

How innocent the dead look. Not as painted devils; more like children. In life they were not children, not innocent, but dead . . . it is as if they have been cleansed, purified. A jury is not supposed to allow itself to be inflamed, to be unduly influenced by tricks. These are not tricks. A jury is only human.

I did not see Peter dead until the funeral home had done its work. By then he had been turned into a show-biz version of his real self, powder, paint, stuffing. It is my one regret—that at the hospital, when the surgeon came out of the recovery room shaking his head, I did not insist on going in to see my dead son, and if the surgeon resisted scream, yell, throw a fit, whatever it took to be in on what and who the boy was or had become at that moment.

If someone had said "Do you want to see him?" I would have said yes. But no one asked, and as for me, I was not thinking, was light years gone from thinking, gone from self.

I study the photographs of the dead Jerry Dean and Deborah

Thornton, but there is nothing there. "They" are gone: from self, from thinking, from this black-and-white leftover husk in the HPD picture.

The last nightmare photograph taken in the spare bedroom is a close-up of the hole in Deborah Thornton's T-shirt and chest once the pickax was removed.

S. C. Pilgrim pulled the pickax out. S. C. Pilgrim says he performed this service because for one thing there was no way to transport the dead girl out with the thing sticking out of her—particularly, as he pointed out, with all the news media outside—and for another, as a crime-scene officer, one of his jobs was to recover all evidence and preserve latent prints.

Dirty job. Somebody had to do it.

Joe Mag brings on policemen, homicide, the medical examiner. Setting moves from the scene of the murders to the autopsy room, where violent and questionable deaths are investigated, explored, and pinpointed as to time, manner, and cause.

As deputy chief medical examiner, Aurelio Espinola screens all bodies brought to the Harris County morgue, then assigns autopsies to various assistants, taking the most difficult cases himself. Over the course of his career Aurelio Espinola estimates he has done no fewer than six thousand autopsies.

Having established Mr. Espinola's credentials, Joe Mag takes the deputy chief medical examiner on a tour of Jerry Lynn Dean's body, similar to the one he conducted of apartment 2313. He starts with an external description—height, weight, and general appearance, including lacerations, contusions, abrasions, scrapings, the twenty-eight stab and puncture wounds. Photographs taken at the lab are produced, the body of Jerry Lynn Dean in an autopsy tray with the cockroaches on his chest, neck clamped in a metal brace so that his head will not flop to one side. Deborah Thornton in her stainless tray.

Joe Mag asks the medical examiner for an internal description of the dead man's body—bone fractures, lacerations to various organs; liver, heart, temporal lobes; collected fluid and clotted blood—then moves to Deborah Ruth Thornton and takes us on the same tour.

When Joe Mag passes his witness, Mack Arnold immediately returns the discussion to the wounds made to the back of Jerry Lynn Dean's head, along the occipital ridge, where the skull meets the neck. Therein lies a dispute between the defense and the prosecution that will not be resolved.

Karla says after she sat in his lap, Jerry said, "Karla, we can work it out. I didn't file charges on Shawn. I didn't call her mother," then grabbed her arms. Karla struggled, Danny came between them, separated them, and she ended up on the floor. Danny, she says, then went *behind* the bed and began to hit Jerry over the head with a hammer. Karla Faye couldn't exactly see everything; except for the light coming through the cracked curtains it was dark; but she could make out outlines, like a shadow on the wall, and they were of Danny Garrett whamming Jerry Lynn Dean hard on the back of his head.

Once he had quit doing this, Danny Garrett left the room to go load motorcycle parts. That was when Jerry started making the gurgling sound—which the M.E. says makes sense, because when a person is hit hard enough on that particular place on the skull, hard enough actually to *unhinge* the head from the neck, blood and mucus are released, and run down into the lungs. The autopsy showed 600 cc of fluid and blood in Jerry Dean's left lung, 300 in his right.

It was after Danny left the room that Karla went—she doesn't know why—and turned on the overhead light. And Jerry was making the gurgling noise and Karla couldn't stand the noise, she wanted it to stop, she can't say why the noise was driving her crazy, but she couldn't leave the room, she was riveted, wired and looking for something to do, the noise not something she could stand, Jerry Dean was still after her, something beyond Jerry Lynn Dean was after her . . . and then she saw the pickax—"It was there, it was just there" —leaning against the wall and she went and got it and lifted it up and laid it into Jerry's back the same way Jerry had stabbed up her mother's pictures.

During this phase of a trial, a jury does not care about reasons; a jury's job is to focus on events, on the what happened and who did what to whom.

The question is who struck the death blow. The hit to the back of Jerry Lynn Dean's head was enough to put him away, but that blow did not immediately kill Jerry Dean, the gurgling is clear evidence of that—in addition to which, a number of blows to the back *and* front of Jerry Dean were inflicted while he was still alive.

But. If Jerry Lynn Dean was already as good as dead when Karla laid into him with the pickax to make him stop making the gurgling noise—"That sound," Karla would later testify, "all I wanted to do was stop him from making that noise"—how could she be guilty of murder?

Fine points. Beside the point in the broader human sense of what is tolerable and what is not. Our recoil is from the nature of the crime much more than from the actual moment of death. Had Karla or Danny shot Jerry Dean, little notice would have been taken; the killing would have been another argument between druggies and bikers, no way to predict which one will end up dead, and in the end, who besides their family and friends would have cared?

We recoil not from the murder but from the horror; what Karla calls the sick-mindedness it took to think of such a thing.

The jury, however personally horrified, must nonetheless keep its attention on fine points. The pertinent question for them is not who created the nightmare or why, but at what exact point the complainant actually expired, from which wound or wounds, inflicted by what person.

Jockeying on this point goes on throughout the trial and final arguments. Also there's the matter of the hammer, which Karla says she saw Danny using on Jerry, which Danny told other people he used and those people told still others, which hammer has never been found. Because the prosecution would like the jury to believe it was Karla Faye and not Danny Garrett who struck the blow on the back of Jerry Dean's head, Joe Mag and Aurelio Espinola let the possibility hang that there was no hammer and that Karla Faye was the one who hit Jerry Dean in the head, probably with the heel of the pickax handle. They don't come out and say this, don't have firm enough evidence that at 105 pounds Karla Faye could do all that without Jerry Dean as much as squirming; they just let the implication hang.

Joe Mag moves on to the breaking of the case.

J.C. Mosier gets up to tell how on the night of July 18, while in the homicide office, he "received a phone call from an old friend of mine who I have known for about eight years." The old friend turns out to have been Douglas Garrett, who, according to J.C.'s testimony, tells J.C. he needs to talk to him. The next night, J.C. testifies, he met with Douglas Garrett and Kari Burrell and they told him who the pickax killers were.

(In the police report, the initial caller is said to have been J.C.'s "personal C.I., who I have used many times"; talking to me, J.C. said that it was one of Danny's ex-wives who called. The ex-wife, he explained, had grown up in Oak Forest; J.C. knew her better than he did Danny or Douglas. It was *after* the ex-wife's call that J.C. talked to Douglas on the phone, then set up a meeting with him and Kari at the ex-wife's apartment. Or anyway, that's what he told me.)

J.C. describes wiring Douglas, waiting in the van, the scene of the arrest.

Mack Arnold goes hard at J.C. regarding the actions of Douglas Garrett. Hadn't Douglas helped Karla burn Jerry Dean's wallet? Didn't he throw stolen motorcycle parts in the Brazos River the very day before he called in? Shouldn't he have been arrested?

J.C. is an excellent witness; he stands firm. A good witness is never wishy-washy and does not doubt. J.C. reiterates: Douglas Garrett turned in his brother, wore the wire because one, he was afraid for his life and two, it was the right thing to do.

State calls Jimmy Leibrant. Joe Mag rushes in to establish in advance the fact that the state knows full well that Jimmy has served time in the pen for possession and makes speed for a living, also making very certain to drive home the point that Jimmy has been offered no deal with the state to reduce his sentence for his actions on the night of June 13, 1983, in exchange for this testimony.

After the intro, Jimmy begins to tell what went down that night, how he and Karla and later Danny had been eating pills, drinking Jack Daniel's and tequila and shooting speed, how they got totally wired—overamped—and Karla was agitated, Danny was agitated, and he, Jimmy, was to the point of yeah, okay, and they were all three looking for something to do, when Danny Garrett finally said, "I know what we can do." *Wasted but coherent* is how Jimmy Leibrant describes his condition. Leaving the house in Danny's Ranchero, Jimmy Leibrant says, he was under the impression they were going to Jerry Lynn Dean's apartment to run in on him because of a bad drug debt. His job as he saw it—or says he saw it—was to provide intimidation in case there was static.

When they got there, Jimmy Leibrant says Danny sent him on a reconnaissance errand and that by the time he got back things were far gone already and when he came in the back door, he had no idea what had gone down or was going down in the spare bedroom, but coming in the back door, actually *from* the back door, he heard a noise that "sounded like an aquarium pump that was broken."

Thus does Jimmy Leibrant, our new narrator, provide us with simile. He could have said a "loud" sound, a "raspy" sound, an "uneven" one. Instead, he engages the imagination: "Like," he says, and we have all heard the low hum of an aquarium pump and then we hear it broken, gasping, the air sucked, released, sucked, released. . . .

And so Jimmy went back to see what was happening and, standing in the spare-bedroom door with a box of stolen goods in his hands, Jimmy Leibrant says, he saw Karla Faye, one foot on the body, both hands on the handle of the ax, struggling to get the ax out of Jerry Dean's back. "Wriggling it," he says. Once she got the ax out, Jimmy Leibrant testifies, Karla lifted the ax over her head, turned, looked at Jimmy, "smiled, and hit the dude again."

That was when Jimmy Leibrant burned off, out into the night. (Joe Mag gets him to say maybe dawn was coming on, implying that Karla and Danny would have stolen more things from apartment 2313 if they hadn't been caught by the light.) Karla and Danny were plenty mad at him for tucking tail and running. The next afternoon, Jimmy says, the afternoon of June 13, they were all at 2205 McKean watching the news on TV and when they showed Jerry Dean's body being taken from his apartment in a body bag, Jimmy Leibrant says Karla said, "That's the motherfucker."

Jimmy Leibrant says. It's all we have. He is not a credible witness; in his final argument Joe Mag admits as much. The state insists that no deal was made with Jimmy Leibrant, but we know how things are done, that a trial is about winning and losing and that the state was a lot more interested in getting the death penalty for Karla Tucker and Danny Garrett than it was in putting Jimmy Leibrant away for any particular length of time. Anyway, Jimmy Leibrant's like the locked-up women in Rebecca Lewis's dream. He'll be back. Sooner or later, the state figures, it might have a shot at him as a habitual offender. The aim now is, win this one.

Jimmy Leibrant had been there. Saw, heard. First person. Nothing like it. Discredit half his testimony, the other half's enough. The state passes the witness.

"About that smile," Mack Arnold says. You didn't, he reminds Jimmy Leibrant, mention a smile the night you made your statement, yet now it's a thing you will never forget, when Karla turned to look at you, smiling, then hit the dude again?

Jimmy Leibrant shuffles his feet. And you know if you have read the whole story why Mack is pressing this point. Karla admits—will soon publicly confess—to having committed grisly, unthinkable acts with a pickax and yet she is firm on some points, among them that she did not *wriggle* the pickax out of Jerry Dean's back, nor did she look up at Jimmy Leibrant and *smile*.

Mack Arnold also presses Jimmy about what kind of deal he might have cut with the D.A. to reduce his sentence.

Jimmy Leibrant knows the answer to this question: no deal.

Meantime Karla is sitting, sitting, sitting, in her little-girl puffed sleeves and white plastic jail cross. I asked her how it was to sit there. Horrible, she said, not to be able to say anything; and Mack and Henry had instructed her not to make notes while the trial was going on: "I hate," Henry had said, "to see a defendant taking notes all the time." Henry had told her to try to look dignified and calm and so she was trying to look unmoved by the proceedings and when she did they said she was cold and when she looked out into the courtroom and smiled at Larry Tucker, the press reported that she had smiled at somebody else, and so she never looked out in the courtroom again.

Joe Mag calls Kari Tucker Burrell—now Garrett; she and Douglas having gotten married a few weeks before Karla's trial began.

Kari has a way with words. It's Kari who says Karla "picked" Jerry. Kari who uses the term—quoting Karla—"get a nut"; who says Karla told Jerry Lynn Dean, "Move and you're dead, mother-fucker." Kari who says they "bunted" Jerry Lynn Dean "upside the head with the shotgun" and that Karla "run the ax on home." To read Kari's testimony is to become acquainted with the language of a young woman who talks like a biker but switches over for the purposes of being credible to a respectable, middle-class audience and imitates television.

"It was a crime scene," she says.

"I cannot say because, you know, I don't know, ladies and gentle-men of the jury. . . ."

"Let me try to say what I'm trying to explain," she begins. ". . . And so forth and forth, you know, things like that."

Kari is like water. She wavers, wanders, strays from the point. Also, it's very clear, Kari never for one moment forgets in whose behalf she has come to testify.

Being a girl accustomed to short-term work, Kari can handle the job. For the duration of her testimony, Kari Garrett will be the prosecution's own girl. She will give the state and Joe Mag her at-tention and all her skill. For that length of time she will be there as totally as if she belonged to him.

And so she makes the story as vicious as possible. Karla had a flush, she says, after the murders. Karla wanted the motorcycle parts "for the simple fact to build her one." Karla said "the girl was a tough motherfucker to kill." And that they killed her "because she was there and of what had been said." As for Karla being wired that night, Kari says if there was any speed being eaten or shot, "I did not know nothing about it." To her "acknowledgment" there hadn't been any speed. Only a little pot. Some whiskey.

Kari knows about drugs; she knows what she is saying. The state is dead-aimed to prove that Karla Faye was not overamped that night: drugged maybe, but not wired. The state does not want the murders in any way mitigated by the presence of stimulants in Karla Tucker's system. Again and again Joe Mag presses the point. Drugs, yes. Speed? "Not," Kari says, "to my acknowledgment."

When Mack Arnold tries to get her to talk about the little girl Karla and her then-husband, Steve Griffith, took care of, Kari minimizes the years involved, down to, oh, maybe two. Actually, Karla mothered the child for almost five years.

When I told Karla that I thought maybe Kari's testimony didn't count for much because of the way she fluttered and shifted, Karla disagreed.

"Sister testifying against sister," she pointed out, and let it drop. "Kari pointed me out and said in this horrible tone, *That's her. That's the one.* Like, *Fry her, that's the one. That's her.* I cried so hard I thought I was going to be sick."

Weight. Photographs. The horror. Whatever questionable testimony follows, from however untrustworthy a narrator, the photographs stick. The innocent dead. The man with the cockroaches on his chest. The girl with a pickax in her heart.

HPD made a videotape of the murder scene, in color—one of the first crime-scene videos HPD had ever done. Joe Mag didn't use the video. It was gruesome, he says with relish. But he had enough without it. Sometimes you go too far, you turn a jury off. He had enough without it.

Most of the time when I am talking to Karla, I forget. She is who she is now to me, this warm, loving girl, my friend. The murders seem like some chapter in a worn old book.

It is Karla herself who reminds me: *What I did was horrible. Horrible.*

It is a fact of her life; the reason I know her.

2. The Tape

Joe Mag calls Douglas Garrett. The jury hears State 56, the tape. Joe Mag stops the machine from time to time to ask Douglas Garrett questions: "Who was that speaking?" or "What was going on there?"

Douglas Garrett is jumpy, emotionally frail; in a picture I have of him he looks distracted, fat, and a little pathetic. There's a funny fake smile on his lips and behind the glasses he seems slightly cross-eyed. Like Danny he's beefy. But while Danny's smooth—his skin has a cool, almost dampish quality—Douglas has a bumpy, unfocused look. Several people have told me Douglas beat up on Kari. It's easy to imagine. He's a powder keg.

State 56—the tape—does its work on the jury, right down to Douglas asking if Karla got sexual gratification killing Jerry and Karla's brash and husky answer, "Well, hell yes."

Douglas himself is questioned directly. He's unpredictable but not shallow. Eccentric, maybe broken down. But he's trying. To tell the truth. To figure it out. To get a glimpse into what really went down. It's happening *as* he testifies. "I tried not to listen to them," he says of Dan and Karla during the days immediately following the murders. "But they kept coming at me, telling me things, making it like I should approve of their actions. I could not find it within myself to do so."

Douglas Garrett says he believes in the devil and that the devil can take many forms and that whatever form it took on the morning of June 13, 1983—and maybe the devil was Ronnie Burrell—it was in Karla and Danny when they went over to Watonga Street; nothing else makes sense. Having seen the pictures of the man with the cockroaches on his chest and back and the girl with the pickax in her heart, sitting in the box face to face with a sweet-faced black-haired girl in puffed sleeves and white jail cross, the jury may have been inclined to agree. That's when Douglas says he thinks that Ronnie Burrell may be the devil. He doesn't know if drugs are, all he knows is, if Karla and Danny hadn't been influenced by the devil that night, they wouldn't have done what they did. Period.

On the stand, Douglas Garrett is not turning a trick for either side—nobody gains from his devil theory, really—he's digging, searching, trying to figure it out.

He goes on. Neither defense nor prosecution know what to do except let him. Danny and Karla were on a rib that night, he says. In all likelihood neither one of them would have committed such a crime if they hadn't been on a rib. And neither one of them was strong enough to bring the other one down off that rib.

Cautiously, Mack Arnold requests that Douglas Garrett explain to the ladies and gentlemen of the jury what a "rib" is.

Douglas flounders. "When you get on a rib you're not totally aware of . . . your perception is a little different. In other words, if you get angry your adrenaline flows, you're on a rib, you're liable to do something. A rib is like . . . jealousy is a rib, jealousy. Envy is a rib. Hatred is a rib. I believe the devil could make a person more conducive to a rib, easier to get on a rib, and weaker. So weak you couldn't get off of it."

He knows what he means but not how to tell it.

Karla says she understands why Douglas wore a wire and testified. "I love Douglas," she says. "He did what he thought was right."

As Douglas told the jury, "I can't think of anybody in the world that wants to sit where I'm sitting right now."

If he was a little weak in the knees, a bit frail, it made him more human; different from the killer couple.

"Douglas Garrett is a strange man," Mack Arnold says now. "One of those people you just don't know about. Sometimes I thought he was brilliant, other times he seemed plain lost—or worse." When asked if Douglas Garrett got a deal from HPD in exchange for wearing the wire, Mack says only, "Guaranteed."

Joe Mag brings Aurelio Espinola back, to make the point once again that Jerry Dean was still alive when Karla hit him. To run home the "hacked to death" point once again: twenty-eight blows to the body, some thirteen of them potential death wounds. On cross, Mack does a halfhearted soft shoe and it's done.

State rests.

Defense tries to bring in a witness to testify that she overheard Jimmy Leibrant making a deal with a D.A. Testimony not allowed.

Defense rests. No witnesses.

Henry Oncken: "It was horrible."

3. Final Arguments

Nothing new from the prosecution side. Mack Arnold made page one for his.

Mack got up and said he agreed with the prosecution and thought the jury ought to find his client guilty.

"The evidence is overwhelming that my client is guilty of capital murder," he said, "and I think it would be an injustice for you to arrive at any other verdict." And later on: "I don't think there's any doubt in my mind, in Henry Oncken's mind, or in Karla Faye Tucker's mind what the verdict is going to be." And he asked the jury to "arrive at the truth," because even though Danny Garrett may well have struck the first blow, Karla was "guilty, no matter which way it happened." And as for the drug issue, even "if she went there so wired she didn't know what she was doing, she's still guilty of capital murder."

Mack says to this day he gets flak about it. He pumps his shoulders in a black-Irish shrug. "I was trying to gain credibility with the jurors. We couldn't come up with a reversible error so we went with the idea."

Some say it was a workable ploy, giving up on guilt/innocence, looking toward the punishment phase, making an early pitch for his client's life.

Others say, you just don't do it, it's like throwing in the towel, that if you were going to plead innocent but not contest the evidence on guilt, you should have told the jury in advance. Sensing a change of tactics midstream, jurors feel duped.

Mack and Henry talked about the idea, of course; they talked it over with Karla. Mack was doing all the courtroom talking, he was the one with whom the jury had—they hoped—made a connection, and so he would be the one both to give the final argument and to take the heat afterwards. But it was a joint decision, between the two attorneys, after consulting their client.

Mack did not make a great pitch, however, and for such a long-shot tactic to work it had to be brilliant. Had to be one of those great speeches you know is leading you down the primrose path yet you trip willingly down it. In the argument, Mack said he didn't know why the prosecution was so dead-set against admitting that Danny Garrett might have struck the first blow. It seemed to him the prosecution was trying to convince the jury of Danny Garrett's total innocence, when he had already been indicted for capital murder. Mack also said he didn't know why the state had to go so far to prove Karla hadn't done speed that night.

He's whining, asking for too much. Also, it seems too real a position to take. It's as if at this late stage in the game, now that he's ended up agreeing with them, he's asking the prosecution to play fair, ease up, not go for blood, to play the game according to real-life rules—retroactively.

Mack still says it was the thing to do. He was trying to save his client's life. And that is what a capital case comes down to from the beginning, before voir dire. The defense is trying to save the defendant's life. To win—to justify trying the case as a capital—the prosecution has to convince the jury otherwise. Even if Karla were found guilty, a sentence of life in prison would be considered a victory for Mack and Henry. Mack says if the jury was going to trust him during the punishment phase of the trial and maybe vote to give Karla life, he had to do what he did.

At the time, he told newspaper reporters his decision would be proved right or wrong the next week. "If she gets a life sentence," he said, "I'll quit having to answer why I did it."

The jury did what Mack Arnold asked for; stayed out seventy minutes—longer than most people predicted—and came back in with a verdict of guilty.

Court recessed for the Easter holidays, to resume deliberations on Monday, April 23.

4. Punishment

In Texas, once a defendant is found guilty of capital murder, there are only two possible sentences, life imprisonment or death. The jury itself does not directly sentence the convicted murderer; the judge does. The jury's job is to vote on two special issues: (1) whether the conduct that caused the death of the victim was committed deliberately and with reasonable expectation that death would result and (2) whether there is probability that the defendant will commit criminal acts of violence that will constitute a continuing threat to society.

The issues are voted on separately. To vote yes, a juror should believe a special issue to be the case beyond a reasonable doubt. After the vote, the judge has no leeway as to sentencing. Yes on both special issues equals the death penalty. No on either or both results in life imprisonment.

In the state's first go-round of the punishment phase of Karla's trial, Joe Magliolo calls two witnesses, Kari Garrett and Douglas Garrett.

Both testify about Karla's violent nature, her fistfights with girls, with other women, with men, how she dotted Jerry Dean's eye and how good she was with her fists, how she worked out on the speed bag. They tell separately how afraid they were for their lives, taking turns sleeping, Douglas tucking a pistol in his robe pocket. Douglas says there was a lot of talk by Dan and Karla who to kill next, now that they had gotten away with the pickax murders, and that Danny had even approached him with a plan to kill Ronnie Burrell. Because Ronnie was already hot at Douglas for kicking his door in, Douglas could come to 2205 McKean one night when Danny was there, provoke Ronnie, then Dan could kill Ronnie in defense of his brother's life. That was, Douglas says, "you might say the last straw. I did not want to pick up a paper years from now and read about many graves being dug up."

State rests.

Mack Arnold brings on Karla's family, then a psychiatrist, Barbara Felkins, who, on direct, testifies to Karla Faye's ability to rehabilitate herself in a completely controlled environment—jail, in other words—and become a useful citizen, probably for the first time in her life. As long as Mack leads her, Barbara Felkins does fine. She tells of Karla's drug use; what it did to her as a girl.

Then Joe Mag has his go. Now, expert witnesses are basically bought and paid for. They testify for one side or the other of a case. But in Joe Mag's hands, Barbara Felkins's cool certainty turns to syrup. She oozes, she runs. After hearing her testimony on cross, you think maybe there is such a thing as being born bad. And that Karla was an example.

Mack: "A disaster. Before she got on the stand she was strong as horseradish. On cross, she folded. It was a disaster."

It's impossible to say whether if Barbara Felkins had kept her cool and remained strong as horseradish on the stand it would have made a difference in the outcome of Karla's trial. The defense had been allowed a total of four hundred dollars to spend on psychiatric evaluation of its client. Four hundred dollars. Mack Arnold asked for more; Lykos refused. In the world of psychiatry, four hundred dollars doesn't go far. The state, on the other hand, could spend as much as it needed to, and once the D.A. agreed to try Karla's case as a capital, he opened up his coffers to the prosecutors.

Miss Rebecca comes on, as well as several women who work at the county jail. Asking for mercy. Describing the change they have seen in Karla.

But the heart of the defense case lies in the testimony of the defendant herself, Karla Faye. She tells the jury the same story she told me, the same one she told when she later testified against Danny, the same one she told her attorneys. Her story never changes; she may elaborate, providing finer detail, but the story never changes and she never comes up against a blank wall the way people do when they are lying, a stony place beyond which they cannot keep imagining.

Mack says frankly they wanted to keep Karla up there as long as they could. Henry says their only chance was to humanize her, and the only way they could do that was to let her tell her story.

The drugs, tricks, her mother. Her and Danny's sick dreams about offing people in the night. The Allman Brothers, her marriage. The night of June 12, morning of June 13, 1983.

It is riveting stuff. Not even Joe Mag can shake Karla Faye's equanimity or make her change her story. She meets every challenge with conviction and honesty.

In the Houston newspapers, stories of the "Pickax Killer" move from the courts page to the front page of the city/state section, on up into the first section, and finally, as Karla's testimony gets splashier, to the front page.

When her own attorney asks Karla if she thinks she would have been a threat to society the way she was living before the murders, Joe Mag objects, thinking the question's self-serving. Lykos overrules.

Karla says yes. "The way I was going," she says, "I think I was." She says she does not deserve mercy for what she has done and that she doesn't know what could be done to her that would be bad enough to make up for it. When Joe Mag asks if that means she is asking for the death penalty, Karla—realizing how far she's gone—says she doesn't know.

Mack Arnold and Joe Magliolo give their final arguments. Mack asks for mercy. At the end of his summation, Joe Mag says, "Does Karla Faye Tucker deserve the death penalty? I'll let her answer that question for herself." And he punches the button that turns the cassette player on and Karla's brash, drug-husky voice fills the courtroom: "Well, hell yes."

The jury deliberated three hours, then came in with a unanimous yes to both special issues. In private conversations, several jurors told Joe Mag they hadn't wanted to give Karla the death penalty but couldn't find any way not to, under the law.

Karla went back to County. She would stay locked up there until the end of Danny's trial, in December 1984, when she was taken to Mountain View, where for a while she was the only woman in Texas on Death Row.

IV / Death Row

I have a life here. I'm not going to say that being in prison makes me happy, but . . . I can go to school and learn. Instead of being at a standstill, I'm moving ahead.

—KARLA FAYE TUCKER,
ON DEATH ROW IN GATESVILLE

I've had four or five cellies who were executed. It's depressing. It's . . . *depressing.*

—DANNY GARRETT,
ON DEATH ROW IN HUNTSVILLE

Sewing . . . concentrates the mind even more wonderfully than an anticipated execution.

—CHRISTOPHER BURNEY,
Solitary Confinement

Tribal Rites

The last time I saw Peter alive he was leaving the house to go take his friends home.

The next time I saw him, he was in his casket. We chose a metal one, black and silver for his favorite football team, the Raiders. Peter liked everything about the Raiders, their colors, the pirate, their roughness, their rowdy owner. They were still in Oakland then. He liked Oakland's bad rep. He'd gone to Houston with his friend Sugar Bear the Sunday before he died to see the Raiders play the Oilers. Oakland won. And I mean, how do you choose a coffin? *Peter would have picked it* was our thinking that day. You go through all that, think what he would have done, honor his likes, dislikes. It's something to do.

The night after Peter's death, his friends started coming to the house. Because they were mostly Mexican-American, raised in a death-centered culture, they knew what to do. They came up to us, made formal and very flowery remarks, sent bouquets, brought cards, and then sat, just sat. I let them go into Peter's room and look around, simply be there. They went through his photographs; kept coming.

Finally one of them, Eloy Barrera, came to me. Eloy was older than Peter and had always been the most articulate of his friends, but something had happened between them, I don't know what, and they had fallen out. And he said, "Can we see Peter? We want to see him."

Eloy's a handsome boy. Persuasive. He sat there waiting.

"We" meant his friends; his tribe. I had set the funeral services for four o'clock Thursday afternoon, so that the kids still in school could be there.

I was going to the funeral home to see Peter the next morning. Apparently he looked okay, not marked up or disfigured. Glenn didn't want to go; he wanted to remember Peter alive, and was afraid if he saw him the other way he'd forget. Colin was home from California by then; he didn't want to go either. I had to make sure . . . I don't know . . . I guess that it was really him. I was already regretful that I hadn't asked to see him in the hospital. Now I had to settle for the funeral-home version. My sister-in-law and an old friend from Houston had agreed to go with me. My friend said the dead didn't bother her, they weren't even there.

Eloy and I were sitting on the couch when he asked. A number of other kids were present, mostly girls; one sat beside me, a couple of others were on the floor at my feet. From an early age, Peter had numerous girlfriends. When he died he had two serious ones, Tina Gonzales and Cindy Rodriguez. Tina was present that night.

I took in their serious and sad young faces. *His life,* I thought, *was not with us. His life was with them, with Eloy, Bobby, Cindy, Tina.* I didn't understand Peter or know what he was after, but he was what he was. Sitting there looking at Eloy, I knew what I wanted to do. I wanted Peter's funeral to be for them, for his colleagues and girlfriends and running buddies, like the party he gave on Labor Day.

I told Eloy I was going to the funeral home to see Peter the next morning and if he looked okay, I would ask that the casket be left open, but if he didn't, then not. I wasn't going to violate their memory of Peter or subject his body to scrutiny if it simply didn't look like him. Eloy said if we did open it, would it be all right if they put some things in there with him? I said yes.

The funeral director was waiting to usher me in. They had laid Peter out in the small room where my mother had been. Where in a few years my father's body would lie. The funeral director went in ahead of us and opened the casket.

At the sight of him, I went down onto one knee. The two women pulled me up; we went closer. I had sent burial clothes: a new shirt Tina had helped him pick out, a conservative long-sleeved button-up shirt which was to indicate his new determination to get serious and finish school; a new belt. He'd taken to wearing a bandanna scarf around his neck, inside the shirt collar. They'd tied it correctly. There was fuzz over his top lip. Lately he'd decided to grow a moustache. It was him, all right. Him and not him.

When Lady Macbeth said the dead are painted devils and "as but pictures," she had it wrong. Lady Macbeth was talking about guilt and fear and not bodies, but she had it wrong anyway. The dead are not painted devils, they are only painted. They are not *as* pictures, they *are* pictures.

I stood there long enough to take in the tedious reality of what lay there; touched his hard cold face, then said, "He looks fine." And told the funeral director to leave the casket open.

If we were going to do that, he said, he would move Peter to the chapel, which was larger, because when a young person dies, he said, people—kids—show up. I said fine, fine, but I didn't get it. I didn't think that many would come.

I had forgotten about the romance of early death for the young. When I got there, the place was jammed. Cindy was standing beside the casket. Her mother was holding her up. Cindy was weeping, wailing, crooning; eventually her mother—for whose birthday I had signed a book, hours before Peter was hit—took her off to the bathroom, where Cindy gave in to a long shrill shriek. I wondered if she would ever be the same.

No sooner had that died down than I heard a scream from the back of the room.

"PEEEE-ter!"

Tina was at the door to the chapel, being held up by *her* mother. At the sight of Peter in his casket she collapsed like a sack of potatoes.

It was comforting for a time, to have them do all that. It was like a ceremony of sorrow I was staging but not, at that moment, participating in. I had to hold up for the kids. The kids took over the weeping and wailing, for a few hours.

I had put charms and mementos around his body—pictures of us as a family; a lock of his dog Maxine's hair; a rock from the river; the Foreigner, Rush, and Bad Company tapes he had played at his party; a copy of *Taxi Driver,* the only book I am certain he read through to the end; concert ticket stubs he had saved; a picture of Tina, a picture of Cindy.

Alex Navarro had put in the Bible Peter's grandmother had given him; I have no idea how it got into Alex Navarro's hands. Mostly the kids left notes written on small scraps of paper: "You'll live forever." "Rock 'n' roll forever." "I'll always love you, Peter."

They touched his face, his hands. I stood at the foot of his casket, receiving his friends like a mother of the bride. All those rock and rollers. I'd never seen any of them in anything but black concert T-shirts; here they were spiffed up in suits with their hair combed, coming up to me to say "I would like to offer my condolences on your loss." They knew what to do and it was magnificent, the solace of pure ritual.

His pallbearers were seven friends and one brother: Alex Navarro, Eloy Barrera, Jesse "Poppo" Machado, Arthur Contreras, Steve "Sugar Bear" Williams, Danny Longoria, Stephen Hurtado, Colin. Peter's all-time-best running buddy, Bobby Numbrano, was to have been a pallbearer. Bobby didn't make it to the funeral home in time. He had been seen in his car making the block again and again. He couldn't stand to come in.

When we got to the cemetery there were all these cars. I thought somebody else must have died as well, but no. Friends of ours had driven from Houston, Austin, San Antonio. People from town were there. And all those kids.

It was, as funerals go, as appropriate to his life and as minus clichés as I could make it. I'd arranged for a few of his friends to say something. Bobby showed up, tried to speak and couldn't. Sugar Bear—who is black and wears a diamond stud in one earlobe (a lot more unusual then than now)—said, "Peter was like a brother to me," and couldn't get much farther. Eloy Barrera was eloquent. Jim Pape, our lawyer, made a little talk, reminiscing about Peter. My brother played guitar and Glenn's sister sang "Amazing Grace" and "In the Sweet Bye and Bye" with a bluegrassy uptempo beat. We all sang the last verse. And it was fine. And the kids wailed to the heavens. Shrieked. Cried. Moaned. Held one another up.

I don't know how my friends did what they did, but they never let up taking care of us. The funeral was the easy part.

Dead is dead. I had to figure out a way to swallow that.

Death Row 1

The night Karla came back to the county jail after being sentenced, she found her cubbyhole in the twelve-cell tank empty. The day she got the death penalty, her things had been packed up and moved to the cells where the county puts incorrigibles and those who have been sentenced to die. This section of the county jail is called seg, short for segregation.

Rules governing the life of Death Row inmates vary from state to state, but all states separate those who have been condemned to die from general-population inmates. There are a number of stated reasons, one of which is that a prisoner who has been given the death penalty is assumed to be more dangerous than others. Also, segregation is a kind of punishment. But most of all, the rules are simply the rules. Rites surrounding executions are particularly formal and are strictly adhered to.

Death—even prospective death—demands ceremony.

Karla had had a nice life in the tank with her friends. She had her classes, her Bible studies, her work teaching others. In seg, she asked if there was any way she could go back where her friends were, where she felt needed; it wouldn't be that long before they took her to Death Row anyway. The officer said she'd see what she could do, and the next morning a psychologist came to evaluate Karla's attitude.

Karla Faye was allowed to move back to the tank that day, where she stayed until building repairs forced all the female inmates to move—at which time Karla was asked where she would like to live next. She said the trusty tank. She was allowed to go there. Karla wrote of that cell as being "like the grand sweet of the finest hotel!"

In County, Karla had access to a telephone every day and so she called people every day. Family came pretty often, once a week. She describes her life there as basically good, and after a time even better.

In November of 1984, a few people got down on her for snitching on Danny. It was something, some people thought, you just didn't do. But Karla had made new allegiances; her pact was with God now, not the tribe—jail, family, or biker—anymore. She did what she thought was right.

From behind the Plexiglas, Karla strains against the givens. Wanting to do more, more, and still more, she sends cards to my nieces, knits mufflers, crochets me a wildly colored sun visor, sends one to a friend of mine. Writes letters to kids with drug problems. "If you only knew," she says, "how much I want to help people. If you only knew what a gut-wrenching need I have to help people. . . ."

Karla testified in Danny Garrett's trial twice, once during guilt/innocence and again on punishment. On November 29, Daniel Ryan Garrett was sentenced to death by lethal injection. In this, Danny Garrett is a rarity: one of only about 6 percent of Death Row inmates in the country represented by privately engaged counsel.

After her testimony, Karla knew she'd be going to Gatesville, but nobody said when or who would come get her. She stayed in County in her "grand sweet" until the early morning hours of December 18, 1984, when between two and three A.M. she was roused from sleep. "Let's go," somebody said. Karla had no idea where. She knew she was going to be moved sometime; there had been no warning.

Let's go. Two detectives, men. Karla asked where, one of them said to the hospital; she didn't ask questions, just grabbed her smokes, comb, Bible and went. Going downstairs she was told the truth. She was, one of the dicks announced, on her way to the Big House.

(She giggles when she says "Big House." Nobody says "Big House" except in movies.)

At first the detectives were determined to be hard-nosed and tough. They knew this was the pickax killer; they'd show her. In response, the very canny Karla was all sweetness. When she insisted that she be allowed to go back to her cell and get her belongings—she knew she had the right—the dicks relented because they had to. It took two plastic garbage sacks to hold everything. The dicks told her she had to carry the bags herself, so she did, and was trying to drag the bags out with her hands cuffed behind her when the dicks finally relented and carried the bags to the car for her.

It is about two hundred miles from Houston to Gatesville. On the way, from the backseat Karla made conversation with the dicks until their attitude softened somewhat; then she dozed off. She awakened to hear one of the men in the front seat say, "I think she's waking up. We can turn the music back up a little."

When they asked if she was hungry and wanted to stop for breakfast, she naturally said yes to the prospect of real food on a real plate. She was wearing her own clothes. In the parking lot of an all-night cafe, the dicks told her they were going to trust her not to run off and would take the cuffs off if she promised not to let them down.

Karla: "I assured them I wouldn't and there I stood, *free!* It felt GREAT. I was in jeans, a powder blue long-sleeved sweater, my snakeskin boots. No cuffs, standing by a regular car with two nice-looking men in front of a restaurant. I hadn't felt so free, physically, in a very long time."

The three grabbed a booth. Karla ordered fried eggs over easy, bacon, hash browns, toast, orange juice—none of which she had tasted in nineteen months—and proceeded to pig flat *out*. She had always had a big appetite. That day she cleaned her plate; even ate some of what the *dicks* didn't want. The dicks said they got more pleasure out of watching her eat than they did on a lot of dates.

Afterwards Karla had to take a potty break. While one dick checked out the bathroom, another one paid the check. Karla used the bathroom, they left; she knew it wouldn't last. After eating all that fried food and being so hyped up about the move . . . if they'd given her some warning she'd have asked the infirmary for Lomotil, she only hoped she could make it to Gatesville without embarrassing herself. The dicks said they weren't going to recuff Karla until they got to Gatesville, and didn't. Meantime Karla had to make two more pit stops. The dicks were starting to wonder. Karla explained about her nervous stomach and the Lomotil.

In Gatesville, at diagnostic, where inmates are checked in, the dicks recuffed Karla, helped her with her plastic garbage bags, wished her good luck, and drove off.

That was the last Karla ever saw of them.

"I felt sad, because I felt two new friends were leaving."

For a while, Karla was the only woman on Death Row. An inmate named Pamela Perillo had been sentenced to die before Karla, but Pam was in Houston on bench warrant when Karla arrived in Gatesville. All alone there in the concrete square set off from the rest of the prison population of Mountain View, Karla got pretty down for a while. When Pam returned, she cheered up.

Death Row was in temporary quarters at that time. The women's prison had only recently been moved from Huntsville to Gatesville, and authorities hadn't yet set aside permanent space for female prisoners sentenced to die. When Karla Faye and Pam Perillo first came to Gatesville, they lived in quarters immediately adjacent to the psychiatric treatment center, separated from it only by bars. Karla and Pam could see and talk to the women over there. Many nights, water would seep through and flood the Death Row quarters, as a troubled patient in treatment ran water or made the toilet overflow. There was a *lot* of noise: banging doors and windows, screams. People breaking glass and setting fires and hanging themselves. People cutting themselves up—a *lot* of cutting themselves up. Screaming all the time.

Pam and Karla would call for help. The inmates in treatment, they would report, were at it again.

Karla and Pam didn't mind all the ruckus; it gave them something to do, they felt useful; it also meant they were close to other people. Daytimes, even though TDC rules specify that Death Row inmates are to have no contact with inmates in general population, Karla and Pam would talk through the chain link to the women in the psych unit, would listen to their troubles, try to boost their morale. Once they even saved a woman's life, by reporting a suicide attempt.

Nobody in a prison is not at every moment aware of Death Row. The presence of people warehoused like stored cheese until the day when they are taken off to be killed affects whoever comes near them or even knows of their presence.

I have seen inmates come by and wave to Karla inside her fences. I have heard a woman on the hoe squad being trucked to work say,

"Somebody on Death Row," passing Karla. There was a special quality to the woman's voice. Dread, respect. Beneath that, the tremble of something she can't help feeling, a sense of relief, the feeling we all have when we see somebody pulled over by a cop, for speeding, running a red light, anything. *I'm sorry it's him but, God forgive me, I'm glad it's not me.*

People on Death Row do not train for a future profession. They do not learn skills to help them readjust when they return to civilization. They are not there to learn skills or become educated or expect to return to civilization. They are there to wait to have their life taken from them.

In Texas, the women on Death Row spend six hours of every day making dolls—big, fluffy, stuffed girls and boys with dimpled knees and faces. The dolls are custom-ordered by prison officials according to sex, hair and eye and skin color, style of clothing. I have one, which someone within the legal system got for me. My doll has brown hair and brown eyes like me. She is wearing bright colors, as I do —bright plaid dress, lavender pinafore. The dolls are called Parole Pals. Parole Pals come with a certificate listing the terms of their parole. Karla calls them her babies, the way she used to her dogs.

The women on Death Row may, however, take high school and/ or college classes by correspondence. The state will pay for one course at a time; the inmate pays for any beyond that. After Karla got her high school diploma in prison, she began taking college classes— usually two at a time, one paid for by the state, the other by Granny B. or whoever sent the money.

The women read, sew, knit, crochet, write letters. Karla does aerobics, yoga, takes her fifteen-mile walks. I have subscribed to a number of magazines for her. She cuts out pictures of clothes she likes and sends them to me. She designs houses she'd like to live in, cutting out pictures and pasting them on paper. The women used to garden, but the yard is supposed to be used exclusively for recreational purposes and last year somebody decided that gardening wasn't recreational, so this past spring it wasn't allowed. After a time you get the picture: not only are the rules made for the sake of the rules, the rules are also changed periodically. You don't get your feet set, you don't whine or ask why. Reason is not an issue. Whining will make you crazy.

Because there are so few women confined to Death Row—in Texas or anywhere—the women in Gatesville enjoy a more open and socially rounded life than the men in Huntsville. When asked the difference between male and female prisoners, most prison officials say that while women whine and carp more than men—"drive you crazy," one officer told me, "yap-yap-yap"—they are also less violent. Fewer murders, knifings, escape attempts. No rape. And so authorities can afford to be a little lax with the women on Death Row, to let them have their lives and even to enhance them somewhat. Karla says she has never once been treated badly in Gatesville; that as long as she acts right she is treated with respect—like a human being, not an animal or a kid.

Weeknights, each woman on Death Row is racked down in an individual cell at 10:30; 1:30 A.M. on weekends. The cell is unlocked at 6:30 the next morning. Each cell—about eight feet by ten, with built-in bed, toilet, sink, some shelves—leads immediately into a common room the women call the day room, which they can see from their bunks. In the day room, the women eat, sew, watch television, live. The day room is decorated with their handiwork: crocheted flowers, crocheted tablecloths, patterned throws tossed over a park bench, crocheted everything they can think of to make the place look homey.

Adjacent to the day room is the women's work room, where they sit at a table making Parole Pals.

Each woman has her own radio. Three of them have typewriters. There is a television set, bookshelves. Books, magazines.

When they cook, they use a small electric appliance they call a stinger, a coil with a handle designed to heat a cup of water to make instant coffee or tea. They fill a bowl with water, put a stinger or two in the water, place a pan or bowl of food on top of the bowl and: instant double boiler.

Once a week the women make visits to the commissary for supplies and food. They don't actually go to the commissary, they check off items from a list; but it feels like going and so they call it that. Same with the library. The women order ice cream from the commissary, then, as they have no refrigerator, have to eat it immediately. Karla especially looks forward to the ice cream. They buy lipstick, shampoo, personal items, cigarettes for Pam—daily necessities, presents for one another for birthdays and at Christmas. The craft supplies they mostly order from suppliers.

When I asked Karla what she missed most on the outside she immediately replied, "My family." Then she thought a minute and added, "Next to my family, I miss food."

Besides state and prison officials, the only people allowed to visit the women inside their quarters on Death Row are official guests of TDC and those with a religious—Christian—message: outreach programs with a prison mission: speakers, singers, puppet shows, Christian witnesses.

When visitors do come, the women on Death Row sometimes serve their guests a meal. They also make a big to-do about food at holidays and birthdays, Halloween, Valentine's Day. They mark off the long term with these small but very formal celebrations.

The recipes from Death Row depend mainly on cream cheese. For main courses, canned chicken is big; also canned roast beef with gravy, and cream cheese. For desserts they depend on Wyler's Cool-off drink mix . . . and cream cheese. They use the noodles from Ramen Pride soup mix plus a can of roast beef with gravy to make TDC Beef Stroganoff, at the last minute spooning in cream cheese (six packages to one can of beef) thinned with a little vinegar as a substitute for sour cream. TDC Chicken Enchiladas (their favorite party dish) uses a can of chunk chicken, four small bags of crushed Fritos, a half-pint of milk, ten packages of cream cheese, one plain cheese squeeze, one jalapeño cheese squeeze, one package of flour tortillas, four small cans of chili, and a stick of butter. They also do beef burritos, using ten packages of cream cheese to one can of roast beef with gravy.

Dessert may be TDC Cheesecake—two packages crushed graham crackers, one and a half sticks melted margarine, eighteen packages of cream cheese, one-third squeeze jar of strawberry preserves—or maybe Julia's Dessert—six chopped-up granola bars, one package vanilla wafers, eight packages cream cheese, two cans of mandarin oranges, two single-serve packages Wyler's Cool-off, lemon flavor. Or it might be Karla's Delight: take one-half package Wyler's Cool-off, punch flavor, mix with four packages cream cheese, stir until smooth. Ice one chocolate Moon Pie, stack another Moon Pie on top, ice the whole thing. Stick multicolored plain M&M's on top for decoration and flavor.

"Eat up!" says Karla. "Boy, do I love this!"

One Halloween, they had a party. Karla, Pam, and Frances needlepointed masks—a mouse, a rabbit, a tiger, a cat—and Karla made formal invitations, asking the others to come to a scary Halloween party from two to five on October 31, R.S.V.P. She put the invitations in envelopes, gave them to an officer, asked the officer to deliver them. The officer left for a while, then returned saying she had mail for Pam and the other two but not Karla.

Mail? It was the wrong time of day for mail. They all knew about the party, of course. They also knew not to act like they did. If prison teaches you anything, it's how to answer the question.

Everybody RSVP'ed yes. Karla fixed TDC Chicken Enchiladas and Karla's Delight. Everybody had to devise a game. Pam drew a donkey, and they played pin-the-tail-on-the-donkey. Somebody else came up with the idea of seeing who could walk across the floor carrying the most rolls of toilet paper. The party went on all afternoon, and everybody was entirely *serious* about winning—rooting for themselves, giving the number-one signal like football players when they won. When you won a game, you reached back over your shoulder and took candy, blindfolded, from a bowl, the other women shouting at you not to get the candy they liked, to skip over to some other kind. They played like children, Karla says, and had a lot of fun.

"It was special," Karla says, "because of the situation. You appreciate things a lot more and differently when you're in here and know what it's like to miss those things."

Birthdays, they do trays of food: open-faced sandwiches—crusts *trimmed*—arranged in attractive patterns, chips for a decorative touch. They cut candy bars in thin slices so that they look partylike on the plate.

Pam's the best at knitting and crocheting. She makes a lot of gifts for the other women, and when the time comes for one of them to go to court, it's Pam who knits her dress.

Karla, Pam Perillo, and the other two women, Betty Lou Beets and Frances Newton, were all convicted of the same crime, capital murder. These are not pretty crimes. They are not murders of passion. Nobody gets sent to Death Row for shooting an attacker; and in the case of a woman—in death penalty trials, the double standard still applies—the crime has to be particularly lurid.

In 1980, Pam Perillo and two friends—a man and a woman— were hitchhiking around the Astrodome when two men stopped and offered them a lift. The men took the three friends back to their house, said they could spend the night, then went out for coffee and doughnuts. Finding guns, Pam and the other two decided to rob their hosts. When the men returned, Pam and her male pal held them up with their own guns, locked one man up and wrapped a rope around the other one's neck and—each pulling on one end of the rope—slowly strangled him to death. Then they let the other man out and strangled him.

The next month Pam turned herself in. In time, she and her friend were both convicted and sentenced to die. Pam Perillo has had two trials, both of which ended the same. After her second trial, Pam's attorney officially adopted her. The attorney and his wife are raising her young son. Pam Perillo is blond and lean. She has a tattoo she got during her wild life. The tattoo bothers Pam a lot. She has tried to persuade TDC medical to let her have it removed. They won't. Pam is always changing her hairstyle. It was Pam who taught Karla to knit, crochet, and do needlepoint.

At fifty-two, Betty Lou Beets is the oldest woman on Texas's Death Row. Betty's been married five times, to four husbands, has six children and several grandchildren. Buxom, graying, sexy, Betty wears her hair pumped up, paints her toenails, wears chunky jewelry and knotted scarves at her throat, could play the queen bee Miss Kitty in anybody's movie version of a Western dance-hall saloon. Betty's from East Texas—the only woman on Death Row not tried in Harris County. She was convicted of shooting her fifth husband in the back of the head, then burying him in a fake wishing well for the insurance.

She also has another murder indictment pending, in connection with the death of her fourth husband, whose body was found buried behind a shed in her yard shortly after the fifth's was discovered. That one had also been shot in the back of the head. Her third husband disappeared years ago and has not been heard from since. Betty says her son is responsible for the killings.

Frances Newton, twenty-four, is the youngest woman on Death Row, the only black one, and the most recent arrival. In pictures, Frances looks about twelve. She has the face of an adorable child, from whose warm eyes sweetness radiates in every direction. Frances has been convicted of shooting her dope-dealing husband after she found him in bed with his brother, a fifteen-year-old girl, and another woman. Frances would not have gotten much of a sentence for that, not in Texas, but after she shot her husband, her conviction claims that Frances Newton shot her children—a boy, seven, and a girl, twenty-one months—through the heart. A $100,000 life insurance policy taken out on her husband and baby daughter made the murders a capital offense.

Frances's conviction and sentence racked up another win for Joe Magliolo. Like Betty, Frances says she didn't kill anybody, a stance that, historically at any rate, draws those two women together and separates them a little from the two confessed punk killers.

Karla and Pam have confessed to their crimes; Betty and Frances claim innocence. On the outside, Karla and Pam led punk lives— sex, drugs, rock and roll—while Betty and Frances assumed at least a veneer of respectability.

Karla's and Pam's crimes are similar in that they are not the kind of murders women traditionally commit—of family members, lovers, husbands—and were not committed in the manner women tend to go for: gun, kitchen knife, poison. Also there is the immediacy of the violence committed: the embedded pickax, the slow strangulation.

Still, the four women are in the soup together and they have made a life for themselves down in it, the success of which depends more than anything else on a willing state of ego suspension, a common agreement to live in togetherness there. They don't know if they will get out of prison alive and if they do get out, when that will be. They can't be sure when they will have visits. The outside world is simply Out There, like a dream they once had. Their life is themselves, their community. If they have no community, they have no life. The community depends on rites and ceremonies, on the belief in and emphasis on small, short-term goals—knitting a sweater to wear for a court date, finishing a certain pair of socks by Christmas, finding surprising gifts for one another. When one of the women gets sulky or gives in to depression, the rest go crazy waiting for her to snap out of it so that they can all have their life back.

The success of their community also depends on each woman having within herself the sense of completion Rebecca Lewis described at her office in the Harris County Jail. Karla says there would be no community on Death Row, no happiness, no parties, no inner peace, without the women's mutual belief and faith in Jesus Christ.

When I say "religion," she corrects me: not religion, she insists, Christ.

"My main mission in life now," she says, "is to love. People out there." She makes a wide gesture, indicating the windows behind my head. "To love murderers, dope fiends, nonbelievers, everyone. Without Christ, I wouldn't be able to do that."

How so? I ask her, who is maybe the most loving person I have ever met.

She hesitates a few seconds, then comes up with it. "Love without having to get anything back. Without expecting to be loved in return. It isn't me doing the loving, really, it is the Christ in me. I am loving others with the love of Christ, and in doing so I hope to bring others to Christ."

I envy her faith, her certainty. In every letter, she says she prays for me. She "lifts [me] up in prayer."

When it comes to talking religion and Jesus, Karla can filibuster from now on. From the free side of the Plexiglas, when the subject comes up, I go blank, turn stone quiet, find a way to skirt the issue. Wisely, Karla does not press for a conversion. I expect her generosity in this area—allowing an opportunity to help bring an errant sinner to Christ slide right on by—weighs heavily on her conscience. I am grateful for her silence.

From outside the double fences, it's easy to sneer. When I tell people about Karla, they often say, "So I guess she's found Jesus now." And I always answer yes. She has. When she says she no longer believes in sex outside of marriage, I take that statement on faith. Born again is a hard concept for most of us to come to terms with. Most converts (to whatever) and fundamentalists cannot help ranting, and so they make certain that nonbelievers feel uneasy in their presence. Karla keeps her counsel, reaches out to me in the way she knows I can stand to hear, prays for me at night. Born again? Unquestionably. As the person she might have been the whole way through.

There are two showers in the Death Row quarters. Karla and Frances share one; Betty and Pam the other. They cut one another's hair. Inmates are not allowed to give one another perms in the dormitories; they have to be done at the prison beauty shop, and so occasionally a beautician will come to Death Row to do that for Pam, Betty, and Frances.

When Betty had to go for a court date in the winter of 1990, Pam knitted a dress for her. They all helped. All four women are the same height, five foot two or three. They all tried the dress on. Everybody else wanted one too, but in a different color. Pam said she'd knit everybody one. They all planned to wear them whenever they were called. Then they changed their minds.

Every time a date is set for Karla to go to Houston, she gets an outfit ready. Knits a sweater if it's winter. Crochets something lighter if it's warm. Then the court asks for an extension, the date is put off, and Karla starts planning what to knit next.

The women on Death Row have found a way to operate within the givens. They have a life. A TDC prison inspector told me, "The women on Death Row in Gatesville have the best life in the Texas prison system." Once when I said to Karla that I guessed if she ever got out of prison she'd never wear white again, she said, "That's prison thinking, the same as when people say 'I'll never drink from a Styrofoam cup again, I'll never eat with a plastic fork. . . .' I don't want to get into prison thinking. I *like* white."

In early 1991, the warden discovered a cat on Death Row. Then, while taking some visiting dignitaries on a tour of Mountain View, she found Death Row inmates idly chatting through the fence with general population inmates. The warden cracked down. Officers now handcuff Karla's wrists—behind her back—before transporting her from the visitors' center to the entrance of Death Row, some fifty feet away. When they do, Karla laughs, holds up her wrists as high as possible, and says, "You like my new jewelry?" When she is strip-searched, she says, she holds her arms up and croons, "My favorite part."

Adjust, readjust. Like those round-bottomed toy clowns you can knock down but not over.

You want to scoop up Death Row and set it on some island or on the moon, let them lead their communal life, make their cream-cheese-and-Moon Pie desserts, play their games, crochet flowers to wear in their hair.

A silly outsider's dream: they wouldn't go. What they miss is not freedom exactly, but their families. People. Food.

I asked Karla once if she were offered the chance to erase her death sentence in exchange for a sentence of life without parole, would she take it?

"You bet I would," she snapped. "I can make a life here. I *have* made a life." She stopped a minute, looked through the Plexiglas at the barred windows behind my head. "And besides"—her eyes sparkled—"you never know what might happen."

You bump up against the unthinkable thing, the very thing you say you could never, *never* tolerate, and—surprising, most of all, yourself—you adjust; you try to find a way.

Death Row 2

From a distance, TDC's Ellis I Unit in Huntsville does resemble the Alcatraz–Sing Sing version of prison we all carry around in our minds and imaginations. It's not built on granite, but it's brick, several-storied, and, behind the chain link and concertina wire, bleak and isolated.

Ellis I is located thirteen miles north of Huntsville, Texas, in pure East Texas countryside, surrounded by cool, tall pine trees so stiff they barely sway in the wind. Rolling terrain, rich dirt. Lakes abound, bass fishing is good. East Texas—the real East Texas, de-termined more by cultural mores than by the narrow strip of land constituting its geography—borders northern Louisiana. Racial at-titudes in the two areas are similar. East Texas is the only area of the state that is distinctly southern in its attitudes, and not south-western.

Pine trees are aloof and self-contained, like people who pull back when you talk to them. You drive a fair distance back down in the piney woods to get to Ellis I, then there it is.

I had written Danny Garrett, had had my books sent to him, had told him I was, with Karla's help, writing a book. Karla had written him as well. In a short letter thanking me for the books, Danny Garrett had said that because of his love for Karla and hers for me, he had decided to see me.

To set up the interview, I had to go through TDC's bureau of public information, the headquarters of which are in downtown Huntsville. The head of public information, Charley Brown, is an affable and handsome black man, who keeps on his desk a plastic statue of a black version of the "Peanuts" Charlie Brown.

Because an execution was scheduled for midnight of the day I arrived, December 6, 1989, Charley Brown was busy that day, fielding phone calls from the press.

The inmate, Carlos DeLuna, would be brought from Ellis I to Huntsville that morning, to be locked in a special cell in the basement of the building. DeLuna would be able to spend time with family and friends until six P.M. The Plexiglas, however, would still be there.

No physical contact, even in the inmate's last hours. "That's a no-no," says Brown, wagging his finger.

The room into which the inmate would be taken, strapped to a gurney, to receive a lethal dose of sodium thiopental was located in a building nearby. To indicate where the execution would take place, Charley Brown vaguely nodded toward the parking lot behind the building.

As he invited me to sit down, the phone rang. He listened for maybe half a minute, then said, "As far as I know it's still active. Call me later."

Charley Brown hung up, looked up, sighed, and heaved himself into his chair. "Means I'll be here twenty hours today," he said. "And get no credit." He shrugs, laughs. "Part of the job."

One of Charley Brown's duties as head of public information of TDC is to attend executions. So far, he has seen thirty. (Since 1976, when Texas reinstated the death penalty, the state has executed some forty-six men, more than any other state in the country. Florida has more Death Row inmates, but we get to them faster.)

Watching men strapped to a cot die from an overdose of a drug that slows their hearts until it stops is not, Charley Brown says, his cup of tea. He won't exactly say he's *against* the death penalty, but he will tell you one thing: if Charley Brown could make his own job description, he wouldn't include what he was going to have to do at midnight tonight as one of the requisites. But, he shrugs, he does what he has to; and since one of his responsibilities is to report to the press what happened—how the inmate responded, who the final visitors were, what the inmate ate for his last meal, who attended the execution, who the condemned man waved to, what his last words were, and how long it took him to die—well . . .

"The best way to tell it is to see it. The first few times I couldn't sleep at all. I sleep now, but . . ." Long pause, then Brown pulls himself together. "Well, Charley Brown has a family to support. It's part of my job."

Charley Brown doesn't think Texas is ready to execute a woman. He can't explain why but thinks it will be a while. Maybe he's hoping to hex the notion, thinking about having to watch.

Brown's assistant, David Nunnelee, comes in. "The Fifth turned him down," he says. That's the Fifth Circuit Court of Appeals rejecting Carlos DeLuna's last-ditch appeal.

When I tell David Nunnelee I am writing a book about Karla Faye Tucker, he nods, smiles, and says, "The sweetheart of Death Row."

It is Nunnelee who escorts me to Ellis I.

The grounds are meticulously kept. There are perfect pansies, lush monkey grass, flame-tipped ornamental cabbage. Prim boxwood clipped within an inch of its life into perfectly round mounds. Not one weed.

Inside, the reception room is light, airy, and alive with activity. The floors gleam like mirrors. Beyond the entranceway is an enclosed atrium in which are planted banana trees, dieffenbachia, lilies with broad green leaves, mother-in-law tongue—a veritable jungle of surprisingly lush and thick-fleshed plants.

They wave me in. No driver's-license check; David Nunnelee is my certification. Inmates with jobs—mop, broom, hoe in hand—stroll by, speak cordially. On the walls of the reception area are pictures of the warden, the governor, officers slain in the line of duty, some citizens—maybe the prison board. Beyond the atrium, there are three tiers of cells. The bars of the cells—they go both horizontal and vertical, making squares—are painted bright blue. The walls are made of red brick. With all that red and blue, not to mention the jungly atrium, the place is more colorful and a lot more, actually, cheerful than I would have expected.

Inmates leaning against bars looked down. One waved broadly. I returned his greeting.

Every man in the unit has been sentenced to die. That month, in all, there were 287. That night there would be 286, unless a miracle came to save Carlos DeLuna.

When you go there, you never lose sight of the fact that in prison lingo these men are dead men—"Dead man coming through," guards used to announce, escorting a Death Row inmate down the hall. But visiting there is not bad, not scary. There is nothing to be afraid of. The people smile, nod, tip their hats, speak. You can see and feel their great gratitude when you smile back. It is a life.

David Nunnelee calls me down the hall and into another room. The ceiling is low, the room quite dark. There are many more rows of visitors' counters than at Mountain View. Visitors are separated from inmates by glass-and-mesh walls that go to the ceiling. Counters are wooden, so are chairs. The mesh inside the glass is so closely woven you can't see through it. About eighteen inches above the counter, there is a narrow panel of clear glass with reinforcement wire inside it, below that a grille to talk through. The clear glass panel is the only place a visitor and inmate can see one another. To accomplish that, you have to either bend low or sit.

"Where's Garrett?" Nunnelee shouts.

There is a hulking figure on the other side of the glass where David and I are standing. I had felt his presence immediately and sensed it might be Danny but couldn't really see much, and . . . he looked so big.

"Here," he answered. Like roll call.

I try to see him, but through the glass-and-mesh screen he's a blur.

"I can't see a thing," I say.

"I recognized you right away from your picture," he says.

From the tone of his voice I think maybe he's glad to see me.

"Where do you want to sit?"

"I don't know." He's uncomfortable, would like me to take the lead. He can't or won't be too forthcoming. When the guard says "Sit anywhere," Danny says, "I don't especially want to be down there with them." He nods in the direction of some other inmates.

We go down the row a ways and sit. I offer to buy him a drink, he says he'll have a Cherry Coke if they have one, which they don't. I buy two Pepsis, place his in a small metal scoop at the end of the counter; the guard unlocks the scoop, rolls it in his direction, takes the Pepsi, opens it, hands it to Danny.

In the pictures Karla gave me, Danny looks blocky and short-necked, with handsome features but not much physical grace. Five years of prison have not improved his looks. He's beyond hefty now, says so himself. "I've let myself get fat in here," he says. He's fair-skinned normally. Now he's prison pallid.

I had had separate conversations with J.C. Mosier and Rusty Hardin the day before. They both said they thought I'd find Danny Garrett manipulative and cold. There was reason to think J.C. and Rusty might be right about Danny, but then they had their reasons. J.C. is a policeman. He had felt not only personally affronted and betrayed by what Danny had done but baffled as well. He still couldn't get it. Rusty prosecuted Danny, sent him to Death Row. A prosecutor sticks by a verdict in his favor.

Still, they had a point, which the transcripts of both trials do little to refute. And there was the other thing, what Karla calls her and Danny's sick-mindedness. Danny's lessons. Their sick dreams, running through ditches in the night dressed in black and wearing ski masks, carrying guns, jumping fences, seeing who was awake and who was asleep, who had left their lights on and how people lived.

Sick Dreams

There had been a photograph of the two of them posing in full camouflage regalia, toting an arsenal. Sometime after the murders, Karla asked Douglas to tear up the picture.

Danny had told Karla what it had been like in Nam when he was there, how it had been to kill gooks, told her he was in an elite assassination squad, so secret it wasn't in his service records. Karla had always gotten off on war movies, murder movies; now here was a man who had done wild, exciting things, things she thought happened only in movies.

They watched *Eye of the Needle* together at least four times. Donald Sutherland played a Nazi hit man. Danny explained to Karla how Sutherland made his kills, hitting places on the body where people died instantly, doing it swiftly, quietly, and—the main part—without emotion.

Danny was keeping his assassination skills honed, or so he told Karla, working for the Mob. Karla admired the Mafia, the way they made their own rules and were not sucked into the pansiness of a straight life in which other people told you what to do and when and where and how to do it. There was a man in Houston who owned clubs and bars, and who Danny claimed was head of the local Mob. Danny had worked in one of the clubs, then got into some trouble; now he said he did the man's undercover work.

"Hit man!" one attorney scoffed. "Anybody who wanted to be a macho guy in that world said he was a hit man. Houston's never even had a Mob."

Karla was turning tricks on a regular basis in those days; had been since she left Steve Griffith. She didn't really get into prostitution seriously until after Mama Carolyn died and she left her husband.

At the time when Danny met Karla, she had been at it for about two years. She turned some of her mother's old men. She took Kari's place one time in Midland, then hired on there. In the years since her mother died Karla had gotten tougher, harder, colder, more smart-mouthed and hostile. More drugs, less reason not to go wild. She went once a month to Midland to work her week, had another gig in Enid, plus she and Kari worked conventions in downtown Houston hotels. The Masons were one; you went there, a policeman at the door gave you a room key, you worked the crowd, the conventioneers paid one hundred dollars a pop. You could make a lot of money in one night.

Karla and Kari had meat clients, jewelry clients, clothes clients; a night watchman at Neiman-Marcus who opened the back door for you, you went in his office, turned him, he let you go in and pick out clothes up to a certain amount.

Like Mama Carolyn, those days—January 1983, when Danny met her—Karla was *operating*. On her own. Making money on the telephone. Living her own life.

So Danny had his work cut out for him, making himself special to the girl he knew right off he wanted, even though she gave him a rough time that day in their prescription doctor's office, calling him motherfucker and such, saying she'd had enough Garretts for one lifetime, referring to a different Garrett with whom Kari had been involved. Danny fell in love with Karla anyway; wanted her; charmed her; danced a slow dance with her that night at the Diamondback Saloon; brought her a zillion new prescriptions; paid her special attention; made it his business to make her want him until she was his.

Until Danny, Karla had had two orgasms in her life and they were accidents; in her business she was always having to fake feelings— that was the worst part, when a trick wanted you to tell him how great he was at making you feel something. It did not do to get *involved* with a trick or let yourself float down into your body when you were working, you had to keep your body separate from your self, sex was business, business was business; in the same way a clerk sold a gun not knowing whether the gun was for sport or murder or what, that was how Karla sold her snatch, as if it were pure product—which it was.

She liked leather coats, leather jackets, might have liked short leather skirts but didn't wear them; her bowlegs wouldn't let her wear short skirts.

Karla Faye was known as a girl who loved sex, craved it, had to have it; she was known as a literal sex *fiend*. Meantime, she went on, encouraging her reputation while not feeling much of anything. What she craved was not feeling—feeling wasn't in the cards—but action, power, the satisfaction of doing a job well, of doing what her mother had been so good at: operating on her own, by her own rules. At holding her own in any situation. Karla knew she was good at what she did, so she liked to do it. Liked to feel the man go crazy when she went down on him, then feel him give in, lose himself and every ounce of the power and control he ordinarily had at his fingertips. When she did that to a man, felt him go loose and woozy and shuddery, she knew that for an instant there she *had* him.

There was no way Karla Faye would let herself get that loose and woozy and shuddery herself. To get loose and woozy was to lose control, was to put yourself at the mercy of whatever was out there. Was to be there for the other person. And when you were there for the other person, it meant you were open to him, trusted him.

The night he slow-danced with her at the Diamondback Saloon, Danny Garrett took Karla to bed and wooed her there, got her to relax, took things slow, stroked her, loved her, kissed her, until her self finally eased down into her body and she let herself trust him, enough that she felt what Scott, Adele, and the gang in the apartment could not get her to feel for all the work and expertise they brought to the bedroom. Felt it and felt it. Rising levels of ecstasy, she says. It went on and on.

A few months later she got her divorce and then her birth name back.

In May, Danny had sex with Kari on the couch.

Danny was the first man Karla loved. "We were," she says, "except for the sick dreams a perfect match." Danny was not possessive like

Steve Griffith, they did not fight; he was perfect. Karla would never chip on Danny. Turning tricks was business, not cheating. She did not give up her jobs in Midland and Enid and at the downtown hotels for him, did not unplug the red telephone. She trusted him, but . . .

Danny Garrett had his work cut out for him. Considering the company she had kept—rock stars, roadies, Green Berets, a man with a fly tattooed on the head of his dick—convincing Karla Faye that in addition to giving her orgasms he was also the manly man of her dreams would not be a snap. Danny told Karla you could kill people for a lot of money. Danny said he would train Karla to be the first woman hit man in the Mafia. It was obvious now she wasn't going to be the first woman quarterback in the NFL, so now Danny was giving her the opportunity to be the first woman something else. Like a patient teacher giving lessons to a child, Danny began Karla's schooling. He was thirty-seven; she was twenty-three. He knew things she did not. He taught her how you went and watched people in the night without anybody seeing, when they came in and out, when they went to work and . . . different things.

Karla Faye had known a lot of manly men but none who'd gone so far. The "Kill Them All—Let God Sort Them Out" T-shirts fit her and Danny's train of thought exactly.

The McKean Street tribe was in on all of this. Some said they knew all along that the farthest place Danny went in the service was to the Philippines, where he worked as a medic. Others didn't know. Maybe he had been in Nam with the baby killers. They knew he was trying to get somebody to off his ex-wife Phyllis and bring back a couple of her fingers.

Ronnie Burrell says when Danny used to try to get him to kill Phyllis, he would finally get to the point of "Sure, Danny, whatever. Okay." After all, they'd usually been drinking when the talk-talk started, and Ronnie Burrell didn't get drunk too easy. So he still knew what was what.

It was part and parcel of the game, how a real man impressed a woman. Everybody knew that Danny was proud of Karla for being wild and strong with the ability to punch out a man and hurt him and that he liked the way she was on her own. Karla had a light about her. Those rare qualities.

On June 13, 1983, at apartment 2313, Karla Faye had come through. If she was trying to live up to the standards the man she was in love with was at, she had passed the test.

Rage had seen her through.

Death Row 3

I dreamed about Danny Garrett before I met him. In my dream he looked the way he does in a couple of snapshots Karla sent—pale, fair-haired, and square; short-necked and bullish-looking from the side, handsome from straight on. Karla says Danny's appeal derives more from what he is and how he carries himself than from the way he looks. Danny was a ladies' man, she says. In the dream I had, I was afraid of him.

I would not have recognized Danny Garrett at Ellis I. He is soft and thick now; his reddish-brown hair has some gray in it. Except for his dark, penetrating eyes, he's basically gone white-meat fuzzy. People confined to long prison terms tend not to age or change; it's as if once they are sealed off from real life, real-life processes simply cease. Danny's no exception; he could be thirty-five years old instead of forty-four—or possibly thirty-seven, his age at the time of the murders. His skin is smooth and unlined, his complexion fair and lightly freckled.

In the dim light I thought his eyes were brown-black . . . or maybe it was the contrast. His eyes are flat and without spark, but they focus hard and burn deeply, like black ball bearings set in clay. Karla corrected my mistake later on. Blue, she told me; his eyes are blue.

We stumble about, trying to make conversation. He asks what I'm writing and how Karla is. I give long answers. He nods, sips his Pepsi. Danny Garrett is a wary man. When I ask him the most offhand question he looks down at his hands for a long time before answering, as if considering the possible responses, trying to make sure he comes up with the right one. He would not have made a good witness for himself; he tries to be too shrewd and precise, is too obviously trying to figure what a question is really about, thinks too much, gives too little of himself. His reticent nature makes sense.

Danny Garrett was a bartender. Part of a bartender's job is to listen more than talk, to take in more than he gives out, to be there and absorb and listen.

He lights a cigarette and, waving the smoke away, asks if it is coming through the grille. I say no, it's okay, I'm fine.

The man is clearly wrecked, a shambles, a man in such an aura of pain and hopelessness I can barely stand to remember it. Even at the time I couldn't afford to think about it much. After I left, when I thought back and saw that sagging face, those dark, flat eyes, I wondered how I managed to stay.

Danny Garrett doesn't see his family. He has never given an interview. When he first got to Huntsville, his older brother, Joe, came to see him two or three times, but . . .

Danny shrugs his big shoulders. "It was pretty uncomfortable. We didn't have much to say. I knew what it cost him to come up here. He's a pharmacist, he has to pay somebody to work in his place, then drive up here and back, it's six, seven hundred miles. I told him not to bother."

As for letters, a few family members wrote in the beginning, but he didn't write back so they quit. "A cousin of mine. She kept it up for a long time, but when she never got an answer"—Danny smiles slightly—"she finally gave up."

In the punishment phase of Danny's trial, a number of Danny's relatives served as character witnesses. They talked about the Garrett family and how it had been traced back to the Revolution, made clear points about just what it was a Garrett would and would not do, let the courtroom know in no uncertain terms just how proud and upstanding a family the Garrett family had always been. Joe Garrett, the pharmacist, said he would never believe that his little brother would use a weapon like that on anybody. Us Garretts, he said, if we needed to settle something, we would use a gun. Garretts had always loved guns; guns were a part of the heritage of the great Southwest.

In prison, Danny has obviously written himself off as a Garrett and is asking others to do the same. His life, what life there is, is in Ellis I.

"I wasn't raised up," he says emphatically, "to be a killer."

Having noted the publication dates of the books I sent him, Danny is reading them in order. He makes intelligent comments on the one book he has finished—not an easy book to read—particularly about one scene which he says he read in the middle of the night and thought was so funny he laughed out loud. "Probably woke people up laughing," he says.

What he wants to know is how I come up with characters' names. I know he has something very specific in mind but have no idea what. I answer honestly, and tell him I am always on the lookout for a great name, I cannot possibly make up better ones than those that are real.

"What about the father in the book?"

I tell him the character is based on my own father and that most of the names I used were actually his. Big, Big Daddy.

"What about Chunk?"

"I made that one up."

He fools with his cigarette. When his hands are on the counter I can't see them. If I stood up and looked down through the clear glass panel I might be able to, but sitting there all I can see are his face, neck, and shoulders. His hands appear only when he takes a drag off his cigarette, sips his Pepsi, or makes a gesture.

"Reason I asked, I was called Chunk. In high school. Playing football."

He had been scrimmaging when he and another player hit head to head and the other guy's helmet cracked. That was when the coach started calling him Chunk.

He sucks on his cigarette. "Then," he says, "we moved."

Was he called Chunk in the new school?

"No. They called me Bevo there. Isn't that the name of—"

I nod.

"—the U.T. longhorn steer?"

When I ask Danny why they called him Bevo, he says he doesn't remember. There is something about either the question I asked or the answer he started to give that deflates his good mood and makes him gloomy again. The hopeless look returns, shoulders droop, he retreats into his shell.

TDC has the only work program for Death Row inmates in the country. The program began in July 1986, as an experiment which the staff and administrators were determined would work. Standard thinking about condemned prisoners is that since they are dead men already and dead men have nothing to lose, it is impossible for them to cooperate, or work in a group. They are supposed to be more violent than general population prisoners. And there is the other thing, that these are men society has presumably given up on, men beyond redemption, and so why give them a job, train them—why bother?

Until 1986, TDC devoted six wings of Ellis I to men who essentially stayed in their nine-by-eleven cells all day and all night long—twenty-three hours a day—with nothing to do except wait. In 1986, however, TDC offered certain Death Row inmates—those who hadn't been in trouble and weren't in seg—a chance to work in a garment factory. The work was strictly voluntary. They would not get paid. Danny has been on work detail since day one. He lives in a unit with sixty other men who are also in the program. He has a roommate.

"I was given a choice once I got on the work program: I could live by myself or have a cellie. I decided to go with a cellie. I could have changed since then. People get shifted around. But I don't know." He shrugs. "They're pretty good guys."

"Somebody to talk to," I suggest.

He doesn't answer.

Death Row inmates enrolled in the program work four hours a day, from twelve to four.

"I've worked all my life. There never was a time in my life I wasn't working. If you're not on the work program you stay in your cell about all the time. They give you twenty minutes a day in the yard, but . . ." He hesitates. "You have to be strip-searched going out and going in, and sometimes the guard is female. And . . ." He hesitates, looks off. "I don't know if you know what a thorough strip search is . . ." I nod yes. "Well"—he lowers his eyes—"it's embarrassing. Sometimes you stay in your bunk rather than go through that.

"Weekends," he goes on, "if you're not in the program you stay in your cell twenty-four hours a day, both days. You talk about hard time . . . *that*'s hard time. I don't know, some of those guys who won't work say they're not going to help pay for their own executions and in a way they're right, but our work section turns out more product than any on the unit—you can ask the bookkeeper, he's right down there, it's something like a million dollars a—I don't know but it's big. It's a garment factory. We make shirts, shorts, aprons, cook hats, you name it. And maybe I *am* helping to pay for my own execution, I don't know. But"—another shrug—"at least I'm doing something. I'm productive. Anything's better than just lying there."

The Death Row work program has been more successful than TDC ever imagined. In 1987, sales of its products to other state agencies totaled more than $1.25 million, more goods per inmate than any of the other TDC garment factories. There have been no serious violent incidents.

Danny describes his cell. Nine by eleven. Two beds. Nothing on the walls. "We're not supposed to hang a calendar. We're not even supposed to have boxes, but they let us. We keep our legal stuff in there. Mostly what I have is books."

Because he is on the work program, once every hour in the morning before he goes to work, Danny's cell is opened for three to five minutes.

"You can go out, walk around the day room, go to the bathroom, get a cup of coffee. If you don't go that time you know he'll be back in an hour."

I ask him if he knows Carlos DeLuna.

"I know him," he says.

I thought he might, but after all there are almost three hundred of them there, and I didn't know if he knew everybody.

"We're a pretty tight community."

He has had roommates who were executed.

"It's depressing," is all he will say. "It's depressing."

He says it again.

"It's depressing."

He smokes his cigarette down to the filter.

He asks about Karla, then looks up at me with those dark, piercing eyes. "If you can make me the heavy in this, do it. Save her." His eyes fill.

His attorney has given Danny instructions not to write to Karla, not to talk to the media. He shrugs. Is Ray Bass still his attorney? "Yes," he answers in his precise way. (It's as if there is always more to his response than he is owning up to, but it's impossible to guess what.) And then he says, "If he still . . ." He shrugs, gives a wry smile, and lets his sentence trail off. *Cares,* I think he was about to say.

Danny's death sentence has not yet been affirmed by the Texas Court of Criminal Appeals, which means that the first step in the many that will end in either his execution, the reduction of his sentence, release, or retrial has not been fully taken, even after seven years.

I tell him I have seen J.C. Mosier and that J.C. says tell him hello. Danny says, "J.C. is an honest cop. The only one I know." He corrects himself. "There may be others out there. But J.C.'s the only one I personally know of."

We talk about J.C. running for sheriff. Danny says he watched the news that night and thought J.C. had won, then woke up the next morning and found out he hadn't. J.C. is neighborhood, and Danny obviously takes some pleasure in his rise in prestige and position, but not much. He does not take pleasure in much of anything. Except maybe the work he does, making things. I am happy to have provided him a chuckle during that one night, reading my novel.

Danny has recently put his brother Douglas on his visitors' list for the first time. "I sent the list in. I haven't gotten it back. They"—he makes a gesture back over his shoulder—"have to approve it. I thought I'd have it back by now but I don't."

Until now, Danny had refused to let Douglas visit. The last time they spoke, Douglas had a reel-to-reel tape recorder in his boot.

We talk a lot about Karla; I tell him how she looks, what kind of life she has made for herself. I ask him if he in any way feels responsible for what she did that night; he looks down at his hands, thinks hard for a long time, in his very thoughtful, precise way says simply "No." Then waits for me to say something else. I say I thought he was the only one who could have stopped things. He says that is true, that he could have put the car keys in his pocket. "But you have to understand," he explains, "the best way to get Karla to do something back in those days was to tell her not to."

After they got together, he was hoping she would quit turning tricks. "You can't be in love and do that stuff," he says.

He thought she was getting ready to quit; she was talking about how much she didn't want to do it anymore.

So, I say, you thought that things were slowly changing.

He has a way of sulking like a balky cow when he's crossed or misunderstood. "It wasn't as slow as you'd think," he protests.

We talk about 2205 McKean. A nice house, I offer, but small for that many people.

"Not as small as it looks."

"No, but—"

"Small for four people. When Kari invited her ex-husband to move in . . ." He looks up at me to make sure I know who he's talking about, and I nod. "I didn't want him to come." Another pause. "I was outvoted." Pause. "Two to one."

Was Jimmy Leibrant a package deal with Ronnie Burrell?

He starts to say no, then reconsiders. "The way it turned out."

"That's what I meant."

"You could call it that."

His expression turns dark.

"This thing. . . . Karla went to Oklahoma, Enid I think, to work. She was there a couple of days. I missed her like crazy. I wished she wouldn't go. Then she went to Midland . . . you know about that?"

Yes.

"I called her while she was out there. I wasn't supposed to, that's something the man just can't do, call a woman when she's. . . . Anyway, I called her. She said she was unhappy and missing me and . . . you can't do that kind of thing when you're in love . . . and she might come on home and I said come now. I just wish she'd never gone on that trip."

Huge pause. There's something he's trying to get to, I'm trying to figure out what, he's looking up toward the thick black mesh wire above his head, head at a tilt, teeth clenched, mouth tight, and . . .

I wait maybe two full minutes, maybe more. It feels like an hour. Finally he brings his gaze back down, looks at me. His eyes are brimming.

"While she was on that trip, Kari and I . . . we got loaded and . . . we got together, Kari and me, and . . ." Shrug. "Everything changed. I don't think Karla ever really trusted me after that."

He can barely get the words out.

"I have only two regrets in my life. That, and . . . well, the other one is obvious."

I start to ask why he told Karla about the incident on the couch, but Danny keeps going.

"Now I knew better than to confess. Look . . . I wasn't fat when I was"—he gestures toward the door leading to the front gates—"on the street. I've been around. . . . I . . ." He's a modest man, but out there, before all this, he was not a nobody, he knew things. "Look . . ." He lights another cigarette. "I've been a bartender. As a bartender you hear stories, you know? Guys have told me about cheating on their wives, then confessing. It never works. I know that. I've been around. I know."

He gestures with his right hand in a half-circle, as if to indicate the places he's been, the people he's seen.

"I never understood why those guys confessed until it happened to me. And now I know. They couldn't stand to hold it in. They couldn't live with themselves. They did it because they loved the woman. And they couldn't hold it in. And . . ." Pause. "That's why I did it. And . . ."

It's as far as he can stand to go.

At the end of two hours, David Nunnelee comes and tells me I have five more minutes. I ask Danny if there's anything I can do for him; he says tell Karla he loves her, he'll always love her, and he repeats himself: "Anything you can do for Karla, do it.

"I don't want her to . . . I want her to live. I hate for her to be an old woman when she gets out. If she gets out."

He asks if I have a picture and I promise to bring one next time. (I could have this time; nobody even said I couldn't bring a purse.)

I tell Danny Garrett I will come back if he wants me to. He says he would like that. He might even look a little cheerful at the prospect. I say it could be a couple of months; he shrugs, not stating the obvious. I place my palm against the glass wall between us. Danny hesitates, then returns the gesture.

I say, "Take it easy," then wish I hadn't.

"Gotta do it." Danny's tone is flat but not bitter.

Several months later, I received a note from Danny Garrett saying he had decided not to see me again. It had nothing to do with me, he said. He liked me. He had just made that decision. He wished me luck.

In a way, I was relieved.

When I told Karla what Danny said about not being able to hold in his confession because of being in love with her, she didn't blink.

"I think," she said, "he could have found a way."

Susie

I was in the office of Danny Garrett's prosecutor, Rusty Hardin, one day in the fall of 1990, shooting the breeze. Rusty was asking about Karla. When he talks about her, his eyes soften. Somebody had told Rusty about Peter's death. He winced at the thought, then asked a very simple question.

"Do you think maybe Karla is your substitute daughter?"

I don't know why I hadn't thought of it, it seems so obvious. Maybe it was timing; the fact that Rusty had fit the possibility right next to Peter's death. At any rate, at that moment it seemed a new idea.

I gave him a nothing answer. Then came home and thought about it.

I don't think she's a substitute anything. I think Karla's more like the Susie my mother and I created and waited for, the sister/daughter I never had.

Karla says I remind her of her mother sometimes, some expressions I use, the music I like, my forthrightness, and there is something about the spirit she senses. "Your hands," she once said. "You have small hands like Mother." My hands are not small at all; I laid one hand against the Plexiglas to show her. Karla placed hers against mine, through the plastic. "I thought they were small," she said.

We are locked together, she and I, in this odd union of forgiveness, guilt, and a rock-bottom faith in impulse and mystery.

We bring each other news, stories. Life.

Funny stuff.

Karla's Dreams

In Karla's first dream about me, we were living in the same neighborhood, but her house was on a working-class street while mine was in the better part—only a few blocks away—where the upper-middle-class people lived. I called her on the telephone, saying I was sick, asking if she had anything. Karla said yes and came right over. At my fancy house, a party was going on; Karla was wearing only a tank-top and shorts and felt out of place, then she found me and gave me the pills. Kari and a child had come with her. I had told her we were going swimming and she was welcome to come, but that we might be doing some skinny-dipping. Karla said no thanks and took the child's hand and went out into the yard.

A storm came up, bending tree limbs to the ground. Karla told the child and Kari to hold tight to a thick tree trunk. They all did, and soon I came back and the storm passed.

The child and Kari left. Karla and I went into the kitchen, where Glenn was. "Did you ask her?" he said. And I started to ask Karla for something, but I was embarrassed. At that point, my brother came into the kitchen to stop things. "No," he instructed. "She's too young!"

And Karla thought, *Oh, no, not them too.* Because she knew then what we were going to ask: to have sex with her, the two of us and her. And she had thought we were different, were looking after her, knew that she wanted to be a daughter, not a sex partner.

In the second dream, I was in one of her childhood houses, like a mother, and nothing much happened, but Karla felt safe.

In the third, Carolyn Moore was with Karla and me, and Karla was introducing me and her mother was welcoming me.

Karla says she felt safe and happy.

V / Until Whatever

I would like it to be known, we are not just
these horrible *things* in here, we're normal people. We may have done a terrible thing, but
we're humans. We change. It happens. I don't
mind dying for what I've done, but I would
like that to be known.

—KARLA FAYE TUCKER, 1990

I like her and I hope she doesn't die.

—RUSTY HARDIN, 1986

Labor Day

We lived in the country, our driveway a winding tree-lined one-lane road a third of a mile long, at the other end of which is a four-lane asphalt highway. Turn west on Highway 80 and you're headed for I-35 and San Marcos; turn east and you get to Luling, then Interstate 10. 80's a busy road. Big trucks use it, dodging the weigh stations. From our bedroom window we could see traffic going by beyond the field at our front door. When the windows were open we heard the rush of late-night trucks and cars. Many nights waiting up for Peter I have stood at those windows waiting for his car lights to turn in.

Labor Day, Glenn and I talked a while, read a while. I expect when it got to be past eleven-thirty we made remarks about the fact that the next day was Peter's first day at school and he wasn't home yet. We didn't know Cindy's telephone number. Her father was dead, her mother remarried, the phone listed in her stepfather's name. I didn't know where she lived. Peter kept us in the dark about his friends, many of whom had no telephone.

Eventually we went to sleep for a while. At two I woke up. The instant my eyes opened, Glenn said, "Is he home?"

I dodged the truth. "I don't think so."

Glenn threw off the covers and shot up out of bed.

That trouble grinds you down goes without saying. You're up, you're down, your mind gets mushy, you can't think straight. Then it gets worse. After a while trouble gets boring. You hear yourself saying the same thing in the same voice over and over again. You rant, rail, rave, whine, and when you are done, you start all over again. You become—are—a cliché, even (maybe most of all) to yourself.

In the middle of the night, you never know whether to be mad or scared. You keep hoping there is nothing to be afraid of. You are too mad to be afraid, too scared to be too mad. Sometimes we took turns. Glenn would be afraid and I would be mad, then we'd switch.

Downstairs, Glenn took Peter's plate out of the oven. While we watched football, Peter had eaten his dinner. This seemed somehow comforting. Glenn hacked the steak bone apart and gave it to the dogs.

We folded clothes. We said the regular things.

"He was sober. I wouldn't have let him go, but he was sober."

"You have no idea what Cindy's number is?"

"I am not going to go look for him again. I've done it too many times. I never find him."

"I guess I'll go look for him."

"Is that him? Did you hear something?"

We put the folded clothes in baskets, went back to bed, and soon somehow—I have never decided if "mercifully" fits here or not—went to sleep.

If we hadn't been asleep we'd have heard the dogs bark. The dogs always bark when there is news on the highway, especially our white shepherd, Maxine, who was Peter's dog. If we had heard the dogs and had looked to see in which direction they were barking, we would have seen, on Highway 80 not an eighth of a mile from our driveway, the emergency vehicle, the highway patrol, the lights, the cars. They were all there, easily within range of our vision. There is a window on either side of the bed we sleep in, about two steps from our pillows. The windows overlook the field, Highway 80. Had we wakened, stepped from bed, looked out . . .

It was all right there. Cars, lights, the highway patrol. The Emergency Medical Services ambulance carefully zippering its unconscious patient in a blood-pressure-stabilizing bag and heading for Austin. . . .

It was a hot night, the central air was on, the windows shut. I still wonder why we didn't hear sirens; I always hear sirens. I don't know.

The rain had stopped. The night was still, close and muggy. Clouds hung low, covering the moon. Mosquitoes swarmed.

From time to time during that hour or so, I woke up. I watched the ceiling for his car lights, listened for his radio, his voice as he spoke to Maxine. The front door, refrigerator door, his bedroom door.

Waited. Slept. Wakened. Slept.

It was close to five when I thought I heard a light tap-tapping at the front door.

"Was that . . . ?"

"Yes."

"I'll go. . . ."

I tell this—to Karla, to whoever will listen—like a fictional story, down to the minutest detail. When I write a novel I usually know where I am headed, what the ending will be. This time the ending is, the boy dies.

While Glenn threw on some clothes, I went into the bathroom, stepped into the tub, stood on the rim to look out the high bathroom window.

"Is it the police?"

I didn't want to say. "I think so." My heart went nuts. All I could think was: more trouble.

Glenn went down. By the time I got dressed and made it to the front door, he was telling the patrolman at the door, "We waited up, then finally went to bed. . . ."

Peter was hurt, maybe mugged, they didn't know; he had been taken to Brackenridge Hospital in Austin. Mike Holmes, the highway patrolman, had had to figure out which house was ours as we had a rural-route address.

"Oh, my God." I remember saying exactly that. I remember wondering why Glenn was taking time to make conversation. We dressed, I picked up the book I was reading (which I did not finish and never went back to) and, knowing how cold Texas air conditioning can get, took an extra shirt for warmth, picked up a red bandanna printed with black cowboys and Indians for a handkerchief.

On the road, I pumped Glenn for information he didn't have. All he knew was that Peter was in bad shape but Mike Holmes said if any hospital could take care of him it was Brackenridge, which is the trauma center for central Texas.

It is twenty-nine miles from our house to Austin. We turned west on 80. By the time we went north on I-35, we had passed Peter's car on Highway 80, where it sat on the south side of the road just this side of the Blanco River, a blowout on the left rear tire. We didn't see the car, weren't looking for it.

I was familiar with the Brackenridge surgical and ICU waiting room, having spent many hours there the year before, waiting out the amputation of one and then the other of my father's legs. Desperation hangs over that room heavier than the cigarette smoke, which the zapping, crackling filters do little to dissipate. People sleep on tacky, uncomfortable couches, waiting out the hours between twenty-minute visits to intensive care units. Stretchers bearing post-op patients come and go. The pay telephone rings. Somebody answers, makes an announcement. "The family of ———. Is anybody from the family of ——— here?"

I went to the information window. There was a small piece of white paper tacked to the frame of the window, on which was written, "Peter. Kidney." At that point I did not know if anyone even knew his name.

In an emergency you have to have a speech.

"My son, Peter Lowry, was brought in by EMS this morning. He may not have had identification. He was hurt near San Marcos, we don't know how."

The nurse paged through papers on her clipboard.

"He's still in surgery," she reported, and she looked up at me. "He has two broken legs."

I asked if she knew how it happened.

If she knew she was not saying.

Broken legs? Good Lord, we could handle broken legs. The patrolman had said that mugging was a possibility and he thought there were head injuries. Broken legs did not sound right, but I bought it. I went back to the smoky waiting room, made my report, Glenn said nothing. We settled in for the wait.

He read newspapers; I opened my book and stared at the words.

From broken legs a person recovered, a person went on. I imagined what we'd do next, wheelchair, crutches, a tutor. . . . I even, God forgive me, entertained the thought that since this had not turned out to be a life- or mind-threatening event, maybe it would turn his life around. Maybe, I said to myself, Peter will see the light now, take this opportunity to get his life together. At least now, I thought, we will know where he is. I can't believe I thought that, but I did.

We waited. Seven, seven-thirty.

At about eight a man with casts on both legs was wheeled out of surgery. A woman walked beside the man, bending to whisper in his ear.

I said nothing. Glenn said nothing.

At eight-something, I went back to the window, made my speech to another nurse, told her that Peter had two broken legs and I was wondering if it wasn't time for him to be out of surgery.

The nurse checked her clipboard. "Peter?" she asked, as if she knew him. "Oh . . ." She hesitated. "It's not broken legs. He's . . . still in surgery."

Could she say what his injuries were?

"I really can't," she said. "The surgeon will be out to talk to you when he's finished."

I went over to Glenn, who by then was standing leaning against a wall.

"It's not broken legs," I said.

"I didn't think so."

I stood beside him and, leaning against the wall, we waited. We had spent more than three hours thinking our son had broken legs, and now that we knew that wasn't so, we simply took it.

Mike Holmes showed up. He handed me a plastic Baggie containing Peter's belongings: his black nylon wallet and surfer shorts, his car keys with the silver ZZ Top key ring, his Oakland Raiders cap, his aviator-style sunglasses—one lens was out.

Mike Holmes asked what we had learned so far, I told him, and then he said, "Do you remember what kind of shirt Peter was wearing?"

It was one of his favorites, a black concert shirt with "Cheap Trick Cheap Trick Cheap Trick" written in slashy white script across the front. Peter had ripped the shirt up the way he and his friends liked, torn out the sleeves, shortened it so that it did not cover his navel. He'd been swimming, I explained to the patrolman; he was in river clothes. The river that runs by our house also runs through downtown San Marcos and is widely used by canoes, swimmers, and tubers. People understand about river clothes. In the summertime in San Marcos, half-naked young people roam the town like ants.

When I told him the shirt was black, Mike Holmes shook his head.

"It was a black night last night," he reminded us. "Not a sign of the moon. The T-shirt's been lost."

"They probably thought it was a rag."

Mike Holmes nodded, frowning.

It was at this moment that we first heard the possibility of a hit-and-run.

"We've located Peter's car," Mike Holmes said. "He had a blowout just beyond the bridge over the Blanco. There are skid marks where he hit the concrete divider. We don't know if he fell asleep, swerved to miss a dog or what. The road was wet. But he must have been thinking straight because he did the right thing—secured his car, crossed over to the left side of the road to walk the rest of the way home. But it's too bad about the shirt. If it was a hit-and-run, the shirt would have provided clues what hit him. Color of the vehicle, height, material."

In a crisis, you latch on to mantras. "They probably thought it was a rag."

Mike Holmes nodded, then did what he knew how to, to cut our losses. "I want you to know," he assured us, "he wasn't out there long. Three cars stopped right after it happened. Somebody flagged down a car, they called 911. EMS was there in two minutes. Somebody stayed with him the whole time. He didn't lie there."

I said well, that was good, and hoped I believed it.

At about nine-thirty, the surgeon who had been in the operating room for almost five hours working on Peter finally came up and introduced himself. He led us to a consultation room. Mike Holmes asked for permission to go with us.

The story is winding up, the end set up, Peter dies will be what it gets to. . . .

A kidney, we were told, had been removed, also his gall bladder and spleen. Whatever hit him hit him with such force, it had severed his kidney from the arteries and veins that fed it. In surgery, all they did was lift the organ out. All the blood in his body had flowed through the severed vessels into his midsection. His blood pressure was zero; it was a mystery how he had lived long enough even to get to Brackenridge. Whatever hit him hit him high, four feet from the ground, at the point beneath his rib cage on his right side, so the thinking was, it might have been a truck, a big one. There were no injuries to his legs; one rib was the only broken bone. He had hit the base of his skull hard on the pavement when he came down, but they had not yet done a CAT scan, they were too busy trying to replace his blood and save his life.

Glenn asked what the surgeon thought Peter's chances were.

It was the kind of question a surgeon could answer. "I would say 30 percent."

At that—I couldn't believe I was doing it *as* I was doing it—I went to the far wall of the consultation room, leaned my head against it, beat my fists on the wall, moaning like a cow over a lost calf.

The surgeon said Peter hadn't been drinking, if that was any comfort; that when you open the chest cavity of a person who's had a lot to drink there is a whiskey-ish smell, which he didn't have. When he had wrapped the situation up, the surgeon offered his office to sit in and wait.

"Feel free to make telephone calls," he said.

It was freezing in the surgeon's office, even wearing the extra shirt. I remember shivering.

Glenn reached for the telephone.

"We failed him."

Glenn set the telephone down.

"Whether he lives or dies."

"Either way."

At last we agreed on something.

We made some calls. Within half an hour the surgeon came in. Peter's chances were down to about 5 percent, he said. He asked if we'd like to see him. "I know if it was my son . . ."

We rushed down what seemed like miles of hallway, the surgeon constantly urging us on.

The boy is dying now, maybe already . . .

As we turned the last corner, the surgeon was paged, which came not as a surprise but as the expected thing. Everything was right ahead and I knew it all before I got to it, all I had to do was step onto the information, like stones in a garden path.

We made the final corner. The surgeon asked us to wait. He opened a door and went in. In seconds he was back out again, shaking his head.

So trite. Beating fists against the wall. The head shake in place of the words. The dumbest kind of TV.

The boy is dead now.

Feeling as if I'd been punched, I went down onto one knee. Down there on the cold Brackenridge floor, I felt my son taken from me as surely as if I were still pregnant and a hand had punched through skin and womb to snatch him.

Glenn lifted me up. I walked down the hall with the red cowboys-and-Indians-print bandanna over my face.

Leaving Brackenridge, we passed the surgeon in the hall. He was in his street clothes. Glenn thanked him for doing what he could to save Peter's life. The surgeon could not speak.

On the way home we saw Peter's car just past the Blanco River bridge on Highway 80. Saw the skid marks. Mike Holmes told us we would be able to see where Peter was hit by the orange marks in the road.

Beyond Peter's car, we slowed down, looked for the highway patrol marks, went on. And on.

When we were within sight of home, we saw the orange outlines in the asphalt; his body, his hat, cigarette package, sunglasses, keys.

At our drive, some fifty yards beyond the orange outline, we turned in.

By definition, irony is bloodless, heartless. Anytime we went to town, we would drive past the place where Peter was hit. There was no other way to get to town; when we came home we would see the skid marks. Anytime we looked out the window we would see the place, on the other side of the field, to the north, where the orange outline was.

The night was black, the road slick. There were no skid marks. It might have been a house trailer, swinging to the right, that hit him. Could have been something protruding from the bed of a truck. The driver may not have known. For all his lawless shenanigans, Peter was a graceful boy, a good athlete. He knew how to handle himself. It was hard to imagine him not getting out of the way in time, if he'd been able to see what was coming.

Because of the missing Cheap Trick shirt there was no way for the police to gather clues as to what kind of truck or trailer, what color, made of what kind of material.

Mystery, I was to learn, was the final answer. Mystery and not knowing.

Forgiveness, Mercy

Hearing that story, except for a couple of gentle questions, Karla is quiet.

When I am finished, the Mountain View visiting room feels muffled in a thousand layers of wet cotton, the silence is so stiflingly oppressive.

It is March 9, 1989, our first visit, the first time I went to see Karla, the day before the filly was born, when for three and a half hours we sat on either side of the Plexiglas telling each other our horror stories.

Everything happened that day; we told each other everything. Whatever has been added since has been mere refinement, correction, clarification.

After studying my face for a very long time, Karla finally asks a question. "Did you ever find out who hit him?"

I tell her no. I tell her a psychic I went to said the driver was a woman, drunk, pulling a trailer, and that for a whole week I believed the psychic and was comforted. And that the week of solace made the session with her worth double her fee, at least.

"Now I want to ask you something." She hesitates. She isn't altogether sure she should say what's on her mind.

"How would you feel," she says after a bit, "if they found the driver of the truck that killed Peter and there was a trial and they brought the driver up and said, 'Oh, but he's changed, he's a new person now. See how good he is?' How would you feel?"

Just before I started telling the story of Peter's life and death, we had been talking about Karla's decision not to give interviews. She did not, she said, want to reap benefits from the crime she had committed, at the expense of Deborah Thornton's son, who had to read about his mother's horrific murder every time the story cropped up again. "I've done enough to him," she said.

"*My* victims." She always refers to Jerry Dean and Deborah Thornton as "*my* victims."

"I don't know," I finally manage to say, questions of mercy and forgiveness flying through my mind. "I hope I would be generous. I'd like to think I'd be kind. But . . ."

The least I could do was tell the truth.

". . . I have to tell you, I don't know."

"That's why I don't give interviews. It doesn't matter what I'm like now, I've done enough."

She leans away.

Appeal

Karla's death sentence was affirmed at the state level by the Texas Court of Criminal Appeals. The U.S. Supreme Court refused to consider overturning the state's decison.

The thrust of the writs Karla's appellate attorney—George McCall Secrest, whom everybody calls Mac—is now filing goes in two directions. One has to do with her jury charge, the other with Jimmy Leibrant.

Over the years, the U.S. Supreme Court has repeatedly ruled that in the sentencing phase of a capital case, a "fundamental respect for humanity" demands that a defendant be given every shot at making a convincing argument that he or she not be put to death. In case after case the justices reiterate that when it comes to inflicting a sentence of death, a judge or jury—whoever does the sentencing— must not be precluded from considering as a mitigating factor "any and all aspects of the defendant's life and character, as well as special circumstances of the crime itself." Because consideration of such evidence is a "constitutionally indispensable part of the process of inflicting the penalty of death," the sentencer must be allowed to consider "the unique individuality of every criminal defendant" in order to "reflect a reasoned *moral* response to the defendant's background, character and crime."

The quotes come from Mac Secrest's latest brief, filed in January 1992, the first section of which deals with the effectiveness of the legal representation Karla received. According to Mac, Karla's defense was pretty good—pretty good is acceptable, he says; we are not promised Clarence Darrow—but, as he told me over breakfast at the 59 Diner in Houston, when it came to the jury charge, Mack Arnold and Henry Oncken dropped the ball.

Joe Magliolo says he decided to let Karla's attorneys write the charge any way they wanted, he was that confident of the outcome whatever they wrote. Before sending the jury out to consider the evidence given during the punishment phase of Karla's trial, Judge Patricia Lykos explained that in Texas it is possible to consider drugs and/or alcohol as mitigating factors in determining proper punishment for a defendant once she's been found guilty, but not as an explanation of, or an excuse for, or in defense of the crime itself.

They could, then, consider drugs as a mitigating factor in Karla's sentence. But then, they couldn't . . . unless they decided that the drugs had brought her to a state of temporary insanity. The jury's sole responsibility was to vote yes or no on the two special issues. For starters, mitigating yes or no is a tough one. Surely if the only alternative is no, a mitigated yes still comes out yes. And then there's the thornier question: why did Karla have to be found temporarily insane for the jury to consider drugs a possible factor?

Mac's 1992 Amended Petition for Writ of Habeas Corpus claims that Karla's constitutional rights were violated on the grounds of ineffective counsel—a blanket charge many appellate attorneys use to get to the finer points of an appeal. In his petition, he cites a great many federal rulings regarding the need to consider mitigating factors when assessing sentence in a capital offense. The 76-page-long petition is (to an amateur reader of legal briefs, at any rate) brilliantly assembled and written. It's even readable. In the end, what the petition comes down to is essentially what Mac told me at the 59 Diner. Mac Secrest has had long conversations with Mack and Henry concerning all of this. Karla agrees with what Mac is doing, but she worries that Mack and Henry will have their feelings hurt.

The second charge in Mac's appeal on Karla's behalf has to do with Jimmy Leibrant and the fact that the jury was not allowed to hear testimony regarding a deal he might have made with the state in exchange for testifying at Karla's trial.

Mac Secrest believes that Karla's constitutional rights have been violated. He is asking for an evidentiary hearing at the state level, at which—if granted—he would be allowed to present evidence supporting his claim that Karla Faye deserves a new trial. The state, of course, will argue against any such claim. Joe Magliolo will not participate. He has moved on from his prosecutor's job into the U.S. Attorney's Office as a narcotics prosecutor. The state will be represented by Lester Blizzard, a lawyer from the Writ of Habeas Corpus Division of the D.A.'s Appellate Division—a specialist, in other words. Mac says he's honest and fair.

Mac is a good, ethical lawyer—an opinion shared by defense attorneys and prosecutors alike—who loves appellate work. He is optimistic about Karla's case and looks forward to arguing it. At stake and in question are death-penalty issues that federal justices have demanded that the state of Texas address. Mac would love to be the first to take on those issues. If he does win a new trial for Karla, the state will have to decide whether or not to retry her on a capital charge. In the face of new rulings regarding mitigating factors, not to mention her excellent record in jail and the support of all those law-and-order folks who say she has rehabilitated herself and don't want to see her die, the D.A. might decide it wouldn't be worth doing. Instead, he might be willing to make a deal for a life sentence.

When Clarence Darrow asked for mercy for Nathan Leopold and Richard Loeb, he asked the judge to consider their age and not to kill the two young men but to put them away for long enough that their bodies and their minds would have changed on them.

On April 29, 1992, Patricia Lykos held a hearing to consider Mac Secrest's writ. The judge had two choices. She could go along with Mac's request and order an evidentiary hearing so that Mac could formally present evidence and testimony in her courtroom backing his claim. If she went with the state, the appeal would be kicked to Austin, to the Texas Court of Criminal Appeals.

The April 29 hearing took place in a jury room, with only Judge Lykos, a court reporter, Mac, and Lester Blizzard attending. Mac didn't argue his appeal. He let the written statement speak for itself. The hearing was brief. The judge chose to go with the state's recommmendation. She denied Mac's request for an evidentiary hearing and ordered Karla bench-warranted to Houston in thirty days. On May 29, 1992, in her courtroom, Patricia Lykos was scheduled to set an execution date for Karla Faye.

Mac Secrest was in no way surprised at Judge Lykos's decision. "I'd have bet my mother's soul on it," he says. While chilling, an execution date is, in reality, as Mac says, simply the next procedural thing that has to happen. The Texas Court of Criminal Appeals has not yet seen his writ. He expects to get an immediate stay, especially since he has been careful not to paper the courts with writs. "That's what makes them nervous," he says, "getting one writ after the other. This is Karla's first."

The time frame is up for grabs. The Texas Court of Criminal Appeals could take two weeks to decide whether or not to order Judge Lykos to hold an evidentiary hearing in her courtroom. They could sit on Karla's appeal for two years. Three. If they do order the evidentiary hearing, the eventual results will be sent to the appeals court. It is they who will decide if Karla deserves a new trial, not Patricia Lykos.

Karla is figuring out what to wear when she goes to Houston. She is trying to finish up her geography course fast. She could be put in lock-down in the Harris County Jail as soon as she gets a date, but more than likely, considering the overcrowding at the county jail and the special treatment required by a Death-Row inmate, she'll be sent back to Gatesville. Meantime she is plenty busy, doing her lessons, firing questions off to Mac, writing letters, taking her walks, drawing back into herself and her union with God, where she has found her own kind of solace and truth.

Graveside

In the beginning, I went to Peter's grave a lot. His Mexican friends had brought bright plastic flowers and stuck them in bunches in the dirt. The live flowers I brought kept dying on me; anyway, I liked the look of the fake ones. The trick was to have a whole lot of them, and so I went to the local Ben Franklin and bought hundreds. Not silk, nothing that looked real or even pretty; the fakest, ugliest version of the real thing I could find.

Plastic-flamingo pink. Rain-slicker yellow. DQ red. Dumpster blue.

I stuck the plastic flowers in his grave, arranging them in waves of color. It was fall by then. The landscape had gone dull. Even the pecan trees were bare. The mimosa shading the gravesite, decorating it with pink, fuzzy powder puffs during his burial ceremony, was down to bones. The only real flowers in the cemetery were straggly chrysanthemums.

I stood back and admired my work. Grass had not yet grown on his grave; red-brown rocky dirt was still lumped up like a fat man's belly. With the fake flowers in place, the dirt no longer showed. The grave looked like a combination cheap dime-store scarf and Lava Lite, exactly the effect I was after.

Now grow, I said to the flowers. And turned around and left.

I stopped going after a while. For months after Peter's death, I had kept myself occupied by reading every book dealing with the death of children I could come up with. None was too poorly written, too ill conceived or self-indulgent to capture my attention. I read them all. Many of the books dealt with, among other issues, the problems of brothers and sisters of a dead sibling. Children hate to go to the cemetery, the books said. Children know immediately what it takes grown-ups much longer to figure out, that nothing happens in the cemetery, nobody appears, you don't feel anything. A cemetery is trees and statues. Nobody is there.

We got Peter a beautiful black marble stone. It says simply, LOVED. MISSED. His friends used to go out after cemetery hours and smoke and drink around his grave. They left tokens of themselves: half-filled packages of cigarettes (the other half obviously for Peter), cigarette lighters, roach clips, notes, letters, small whiskey bottles, concert tickets.

"Rock and roll forever," the notes mostly said.

One time somebody left an empty Coors beer bottle, the bottom of it pushed down in the dirt so that it would stay upright. Dead flowers hung from the mouth of the bottle. Some stones had been arranged in a circle around it. There was a note under one of the stones: "All we are is dust in the wind."

Bobby still comes by. Cindy sometimes calls. Cindy got pregnant within three months of Peter's death. She did not marry the father of the child but had the child and kept it, then a couple of years later married someone else. Last I heard, they lived in Kyle, thirteen miles north of San Marcos. Within six months of Peter's death, Tina's father was killed in a car accident, also on Highway 80; a year or so later a new boyfriend of hers was killed in another car accident.

I have mostly lost track of Peter's friends. Sugar Bear had given Peter a leather football jacket and I tried to give it back, but he said he didn't want it, it belonged to Peter. Colin took the jacket for himself, then went to visit my brother in Utah. My brother's house burned down the night Colin arrived. Everything went, including the jacket, and a lot of Peter's things Colin had taken for himself, and the piano my father had bought my mother to replace the Baldwin they lost to the bank back in Greenville all those years ago.

Peter's dog, Maxine, got so bad in the hips she couldn't stand. We had to have her put down.

Christmas the year of Peter's death, during an argument with his girlfriend in California, Colin stepped out of a moving car, bashed his head on the concrete, suffered a concussion. We all went back into family therapy.

Trouble comes in bunches. Then it lightens up.

Recently I was at a sandwich shop getting lunch. The girl fixing my meal said she thought she knew me, didn't I have a son or daughter who went to San Marcos High, I said well, yes, a son, but. . . . I wasn't sure how old the girl was; in a college town everybody looks eighteen. . . . It was a long time ago, six or seven years.

"You're Peter's mom," she said. And she turned to the boy who worked with her and told him what had happened and then went on to say what a horrible thing his death had been for everybody in school and how sad they all were and that, well, it had been just devastating and did I know they had dedicated a football game and the high school yearbook to him. I had not known. But yes, I agreed, the girl was right, it had been, and was, extremely hard. But I had gotten past being in the business of making myself and others sad, and so in parting I managed to make a halfway-upbeat comment, paid for my sandwich, and left.

After the funeral was over and I got into the humdrum every-dayness of swallowing a new reality, I fought being resentful of every young person alive. Whenever I saw a car full of them, I'd hated the way they laughed and had fun, hated the life they had, hated grad-uation ceremonies, weddings, any rite of passage Peter had not lived long enough to get to. This is not pretty but it was real. If there was only so much room in the boat, why did Peter have to be the one to get elbowed out?

I got over that too. Now when somebody remembers him, especially somebody I didn't know even knew him, I feel grateful.

If he's not in that grave, he's got to be somewhere.

Mountain View

Usually when our visit is over, the guards take Karla out some back passageway. After we say our good-byes through the Plexiglas I don't see her anymore, but—going through the front room where the drink machines are, from behind the door marked Employees Only in English and Spanish—I hear her, as the guards do their strip search, laughing, jabbering like a child. The officers laugh with her. I go outside and wait and . . . that's it. I wave out my car window, in case she's at the Death Row window watching me.

A couple times they did it differently. I don't really think all these shifts in routine are planned. A new guard comes on, she does things in a new way, that's all.

One day the two officers brought Karla out the front door just behind where I was waiting for the white TDC station wagon, under the sycamore tree at the double chain-link and concertina-wire gates. It was a windy day. My hair was blowing wildly. It was winter and, as dusk descended, the air was growing cold. Karla told me I should put my jacket on and cover my head. This was before the crackdown, and so her hands were free. As the officers unlocked a gate, she told me good-bye again, blew a kiss with both hands, and waved hard. I waved; blew her a kiss with both hands.

For some reason, instead of shutting her up in her quarters the way they usually do, the officers let Karla stay in her yard that day. Between the brick wall separating the visitors' center yard from the one on Death Row and the chain-link fencing, there is a gap of maybe an inch or so. Karla stuck her face in the gap, yelled "Bye" again, blew me more kisses. As I walked to my car parked in the parking lot of the house with the churchy roof, she was still yelling, still blowing kisses.

Driving down the asphalt road toward the front gatehouse, I rolled down my window. I can see Death Row until I turn the corner beyond the gatehouse. Karla was still out in the yard, waving both arms so hard her body pumped up and down, blowing such strong double-fisted kisses into the wind they made her jump in the air.

The last I saw of her, when I turned down the road where one sign, facing the other direction, warns you that your car can be searched and another says Slow—Children, she was still at it.

In time, murderers usually learn if not to depersonalize their victims, then at least to disconnect from them, to think of the victim as somehow *out there,* in their own world and time. It is an act of pure emotional and psychic survival, which obtains whether or not the attacker has admitted having committed the crime. In his prison memoir, *99 Years Plus Life,* Nathan Leopold says it took seven years in prison before the enormity of what he had done hit him and remorse set in.

Karla never removes herself from blame or responsibility and never does not put herself square in the middle of this grisly picture. While she does not talk about the murders anymore, she never does not acknowledge what she has done or give that act its full measure of significance and horror. When she refers to Jerry Dean and Deborah Thornton as "my victims," Karla is doing something very deliberate; she is reminding not so much the listener as herself, once again, just what is what here: what went down that hot June night in 1983 and who did precisely what to whom.

I have told Karla if it comes down to that, I will be with her at her execution. She has not asked me to, will not ask that of anybody, not even the officer of her choice, though she has that right.

"The only way I won't be there," I have told her, "is if you specifically request me not to. And you have to promise not to do that for my sake."

She said she wouldn't.

Larry Tucker has retired and moved to Arkansas. He comes to Gatesville three times a year. Granny T. usually comes with him.

Kari finally left Douglas. According to Karla, Douglas beat her up one time too many. Kari got a divorce, got pregnant by a new boyfriend, got married. The baby was—naturally—a girl. Karla knits and crochets endlessly for her new niece. As for Kathi, Karla says, she "has her spells. She keeps in touch then she doesn't, then she does."

Larry Tucker sold the bay house.

Granny B.'s getting too old to make the trip from Houston to Mountain View on her own, but she does it anyway from time to time.

Debi Bullard wants to go see Karla, keeps planning to, then somehow keeps putting it off.

Same with Shawn.

Jackie and Henry Oncken make their regular trips to Gatesville. Jackie writes Karla often. Karla makes us sweaters and sun visors and afghans and crocheted everything. Through a Christian anti-drug program, she writes letters to kids. They write her back. She gets a lot of mail. She is supposed to make an antidrug talk to be videotaped and distributed to public junior high and high schools.

They changed the soft-drink machines at Mountain View, from R.C. Cola to Cokes.

Karla is not lonely, does not feel abandoned or set aside; her life is exactly where she is: in Mountain View, on Death Row, with the other women. In May 1991, Betty Lou Beets's conviction was over-turned on a technicality. If the decision holds up, Betty will go back home to Athens, Texas. She'll probably be tried again—if not for the murder of her fifth husband then for her fourth—but the D.A. may decide not to pursue the case as a capital.

I go to see Karla whenever I can and will until, I don't know . . . whatever.

Snapshots

On the same wall with Karla's family album, I have tacked up Xeroxes of two of the photos Joe Magliolo offered into evidence at Karla's trial.

One is of Jerry Lynn Dean half on, half off the mattress with the cockroaches on his chest.

The other is of Deborah Ruth Thornton with a pickax in her heart.

It is important to keep things in perspective, to hold on to the fact of just how sad a story this is; to remember why this winning, loving girl-woman Karla Faye is where she is today. After all, if I sometimes tend to forget, Karla never does. Karla keeps the dead bodies of Jerry Dean and Deborah Thornton alive in her mind all the time.

I have thought often of that question Karla asked at the end of my first visit to Mountain View—*How would you feel if they found the driver of the truck that killed Peter and there was a trial and they brought the driver up and said, "Oh, but he's changed, he's a new person now. See how good he is?" How would you feel?* Forgiveness is at issue, mercy, the right of one human being to hold another accountable, and to judge. *How would you feel?*

It doesn't happen, I think; we don't have the right to forgive *or* avenge. To one another, we offer aspirins. There's little else to give.

My life is over. I felt that when Peter died; I still do. It's amazing how much happiness you can find within completely unacceptable givens. People used to say, "I don't know what I'd do if my child died. I don't think I'd make it." They still sometimes say that. And I think to myself, *What in God's name does "make it" mean—you kill yourself, you go crazy?* Crazy's an option I rejected, suicide seemed unfair to the people who'd been good to me; anyway, to quote Peter, suicide is not my way.

Life does reserve its quirky options, its talent for surprise. I thought happy was not in the cards for me, ever again. This has turned out not to be true. Yet I still have the feeling that there is a line in my life separating the alive part from the part that is over. You go on or you don't.

I asked Karla one time what she'd done over the course of some holiday.

She shrugged and smiled. "Eat, sleep, sleep, eat."

As she says about Death Row: "I can make a life here. I have made a life. And if I'm executed, well, I know this, I can handle it."

For her May 29 court appearance, Karla has asked her grandmother to get her some new underthings. I am going to buy her some shoes to wear. A bench warrant gives an inmate a chance to get new ones, not prison issue, which she can then wear back to prison. For her aerobics and her walks, Karla has requested Nike Airs. Colorful, if possible.

You bump up against the final, most unacceptable thing, you see what you can come up with.

A NOTE ON THE TYPE

This book was set in Granjon, a type named in compliment to Robert Granjon, type cutter and printer, active in Antwerp, Lyons, Rome, and Paris from 1523–1590. The face was designed by George W. Jones, who based his drawings on a type used by Claude Garamond (c. 1480–1561).

Composed by PennSet, Inc. Printed and bound by
Arcata Graphics, Martinsburg, West Virginia.